Criminal Justice
Recent Scholarship

Edited by
Marilyn McShane and Frank P. Williams III

A Series from LFB Scholarly

Self-Reporting and the Diagnostic Screening of Substance Abusing Prisoners

William R. Crawley

LFB Scholarly Publishing LLC
El Paso 2009

Library of Congress Cataloging-in-Publication Data

Crawley, William R.
Self-reporting and the diagnostic screening of substance abusing prisoners / William R. Crawley.
p. cm. -- (Criminal justice : recent scholarship)
Includes bibliographical references and index.
ISBN 978-1-59332-302-8 (hardcover: alk. paper)
1. Prisoners--Substance use--United States--Prevention. 2. Substance abuse--United States--Prevention. 3. Substance abuse--Treatment--United States--Methodology. I. Title.

HV8836.5.C73 2009
365'.66729--dc22

2009032449

ISBN 978-1-59332-302-8

Printed on acid-free 250-year-life paper.

Manufactured in the United States of America.

TABLE OF CONTENTS

CHAPTER I – THE SELF REPORT PARADOX IN CRIMINAL JUSTICE 1

Statement of the Problem........ 2

Background........ 5

Purpose of the Study........ 10

Research Design and Methodology Overview 10

Definition of Research Terms........ 14

Significance of the Study........ 15

Organization of this Book........ 16

CHAPTER II – EVOLUTION OF SELF-REPORT METHODOLOGY........ 19

Chapter Organization........ 21

Methods of Knowing........ 23

Historical Value of the Self-Report Methodology........ 24

CHAPTER III – SELF REPORT SCREENING AND ISSUES OF VALIDITY 53

Concerns and Threats to Validity Regarding the Use of the Self-Report Methodology via Diagnostic Screening Instrumentation........ 53

Summary........ 70

CHAPTER IV – EXAMINING THE VALIDITY OF SELF-REPORT SCREENING IN PRISONS 75

Data Collections 80

Data Analyses 100

CHAPTER V – RESEARCH QUESTIONS AND RESULTS........ 113

Goodness of Fit Tests 116

Criterion Validity and Efficacy 123

Construct Validity........ 131

Individual-Level, Drug-Related, and Developmental Influences on Criterion Validity........ 144

CHAPTER VI – ADVANCING THE SELF-REPORT METHODOLOGY........ 199

Considering the Validity and Efficacy of the Self-Report Screening Methodology........ 200

Summary........ 211

Limitations of the Research 212
Strengths of the Research 214
Policy Implications 216
Implications for Further Research 217
Conclusion 219

APPENDICES 221

REFERENCES 249

INDEX 267

ACKNOWLEDGEMENTS

To name everyone who helped make this book possible would likely not be feasible. Some took time to read the entire manuscript, while others made small but significant contributions or suggestions. To this end, I am deeply grateful to those individuals who lent their time to answer interview questions and/or read and comment on relevant sections of the manuscript.

My thanks go to the various law enforcement personnel (correctional administrators and staff, police officers and detectives, federal and state prosecutors, treatment providers), university researchers, and jail and prison inmates who have extended themselves to me in confidence over years of research to contribute to my ongoing education and understanding of the "drug-crime nexus."

I would be remise if I did not offer special thanks to Lisa Dopke, as her early, often, and very detailed feedback served to convert the original proposal for this book and helped shape the final result in very essential ways, affecting everything from its structure to the accuracy of information delivered. This would have been a very different, and probably less worthwhile, book without her penetrating insights.

To my family, friends, colleagues, students, and everyone who supported me in this creative process – thank you.

To my wife Amy – "you and me."

PREFACE

In the wake of an exploding incarceration rate, U.S. correctional facilities have struggled, armed with relatively diminishing resources, to address issues of "need for treatment." To address this contemporary mandate it has been necessary to develop and implement mechanisms to triage incoming inmates. To this end, a variety of self-report-based screening methodologies have begun to be extensively employed throughout the criminal justice system as tools to collect diagnostic information in place of clinicians. Although various self-report screening instruments have indeed experienced scientific support as applied within the general population, there exists a need for empirically-based support for this methodology as utilized within criminal justice populations. It was therefore the goal of this research to examine the effectiveness of the self-report screening methodology in generating valid data regarding drug and alcohol disorders within institutionalized criminal justice venues.

In addressing these gaps in the research, a cross-sectional research design was used where data were collected on a randomly drawn sample of 424 recently incarcerated prisoners throughout the year 2001. The current research employs a "meta-method" examination to assess issues of validity between self-report screen findings and forensic clinical psychological findings. Moreover, the study also affords secondary data to make statistical comparisons between multiple diagnostic screening instruments generated via self-report methodology, forensic clinical psychological assessments, a variety of other indexes of substance misuse, and variables gathered across inmate cases. Results indicated strong support for the aggregate criterion validity and construct validity of this methodology. Additionally, while some cautions regarding a bias for "overclassification" were realized, this methodology also produced relatively valuable findings regarding efficacy. Finally, the examination of individual and collective case variables developed some basic insights into relationships associated with levels of criterion validity.

Findings will serve to improve the understanding and advancement of policies and practices related to self-report based screening protocols designed to triage "need for treatment" in criminal justice institutionalized populations. Findings may also provide practical evidence-based assistance to researchers, mental health practitioners, and criminal justice institutions involved in the designing, interpretation, and/or deployment of these instruments.

CHAPTER 1

The Self-Report Paradox in Criminal Justice

Drugs of abuse and the problems that stem from their use are among society's most incessant legal (Broner, Borum, Whitmire, & Gawley, 2002; Mateyoke-Scrivner, Webster, Hiller, Staton, & Leukefeld, 2003; Panzer, Broner, McQuistion, 2001; Regier et al., 1984; Sandra, 2004; Tonry and Wilson, 1990), medical (Substance Abuse and Mental Health Services Administration [SAMHSA] 2004, 1995, 1996) and social concerns (National Institute of Alcohol Abuse and Alcoholism [NIAAA], 1987, 1994; SAMHSA, 2004, 1996). Clinically valid instruments for use in drug abuse and dependency screening are becoming increasingly essential to clinicians and other public agency workers (Inciardi, 2000). While various screening methodologies have become extensively employed by medical institutions throughout the United States as tools to collect diagnostic information in place of clinicians in recent years (Atkinson, Zibin, & Chuang, 1997; Reynolds, 1993), recently the American criminal justice system has begun to use self-report-based screening methodologies (Andrews & Bonta, 1994; Winters & Zenilman, 2000). This innovation has come about as criminal justice agencies have begun to focus more on the benefits of treatment for offender populations rather than the traditional strict use of incarceration (Broner et al., 2002). While the incorporation of treatment into the U.S. criminal justice system has been examined previously, the full interface between criminal justice organizations and the medical community in their delivery of "drug abuse treatment" has only recently been more fully explored in terms of "harm reduction" policies and practices (Caulkins, 2000; White & Gorman, 2000).

Behind the modern attempt to interface the missions of these two traditionally unique institutional perspectives is a common goal: to produce the most effective outcome for individual offenders with the most efficient allocation of government resources. This goal has been additionally informed and supported with a growing and ever-evolving body of research examining the prevalence of drug use, abuse, and dependency in the United States, both in general population (Kessler et al, 1994; NIAAA, 1987, 1994; SAMHSA, 2004, 1996) and within special populations (e.g., criminal justice settings, post-release prisoners) (Baumer, 1998; Ball, Schaffer, & Nurco, 1983; Belenko, 2006; Berman, Bergman, Palmstierna, Schlyter, 2005; Chaiken, 1986; Fishbein & Reuland, 1994; Kouri, Pope, Powell, & Oliva, 1997; Peters & Kearns, 1992; Peters, Greenbaum, Edens, Carter, & Ortiz, 1998; Peters & Hills, 1999; Tonry & Wilson, 1990; Welsh 2007). While the utilization of the medical and research community's knowledge regarding drug abuse issues progresses, it is necessary to carefully consider the instruments and methodologies used to screen for drug abuse and dependency, especially as applicable within special populations (e.g., individuals incarcerated in criminal justice institutions). *It is therefore the goal of this research to examine the effectiveness of the self-report screening methodology in generating valid data regarding drug and alcohol disorders within institutionalized criminal justice venues.*

STATEMENT OF THE PROBLEM

In the process of investigating the self-report-based screening practices regularly used across criminal justice populations (e.g., incoming jail arrestees, adjudicated prison inmates, probationers/parolees), it is apparent that although screening instruments grounded in the self-report methodology have been regularly used in a multitude of research settings and across a substantial number of cases expressing a range of individual variations, this methodology has nevertheless not been tested and validated by means of empirically based research. Rather, while various self-report-based screening instruments have been developed over the years, often based on criteria grounded in the American Psychiatric Association's (1994) Diagnostic and Statistical Manual of

Mental Disorders, 4th Edition (DSM-IV), and additionally informed by the input of "experts" (Winters & Zenilman, 2000), nevertheless the self-report methodology used has not specifically undergone scientific testing to assess its general validity and/or efficacy. This limitation might be more readily understood if further considered from several points of view.

First, previous research evaluations have usually consisted of individual self-report screening instruments and have therefore typically been limited to the testing of only one screening protocol (Lazowski, Miller, Boye, & Miller, 1998), rather than more readily assessing the underlying methodology itself. Even when multiple screens have been evaluated within the same research setting, subsequent analysis typically has involved comparing screen findings to one another (Knight, Sherritt, Harris, Gates, & Chang, 2003; Peters, Greenbaum, Steinberg, Carter, Ortiz, Fry and Valle, 2000). In such cases, the objective of understanding the value of the self-report methodology itself may be less than informative as individual and/or unique screening protocols may produce "white noise" (via spurious variables) in the data. Therefore, the testing of individual screening instruments has not been able to readily evaluate the aggregate validity of self-report-based screen findings.

Next, when self-report screening validity has been examined in the literature, such studies have typically employed relatively "weak" criterion measures, normally other DSM-IV-based self-report instruments (Peters et al., 2000). Such practices have been considered problematic in providing constructive insight into issues of validity. Researchers have therefore, with some dissent (Grove, Zald, Lebow, Snitz & Nelson, 2000; Meehl, 1954, 1965), regularly promoted the importance of clinical judgments to serve as the most appropriate external criteria (Gastfriend, Najavits, & Reif, 1994; Knight, Sherritt, Shrier, Harris, & Chang, 2002; Miller & Lazowski, 1999). This practice allows for findings produced by means of the self-report screening methodology to be compared directly to clinical findings that were informed by not only self-report information, but also had the benefit of accessing face-to-face interactions and non-verbal information as part of diagnostic decisions.

Another limitation evidenced by the literature includes an inadequate understanding of individual and case-level influences on the self-report screening methodology. Much literature examining self-report data collections has tended to focus on analysis of aggregate-level data in order to gain insights into issues of validity (Braithwaite, 1981; Elliott, Huizinga, & Morse, 1987; Gove, Hughes, & Geerken, 1985; Hindelang, Hirschi, & Weis, 1981; Thornberry & Farnworth, 1982). While such information is quite valuable in and of itself, it must be acknowledged that such analyses are not capable of providing insights with respect to the accuracy of an individual's response. This limitation is a result of aggregated data potentially reflecting compensating errors that balance out (Wentland & Smith, 1993). Therefore, it is essential to the understanding of various screening dynamics that individual-level analyses be conducted in compliment to aggregate-level analyses to more fully understand potential threats to validity.

Yet another limitation realized with respect to the evaluation of the validity of the self-report-based screening methodology has been its limited understanding across different settings and populations. As might be expected, the screening process, as used in criminal justice populations itself, has received relatively little attention in the research literature compared to its actual utility in such settings. On those rare occasions when a screening instrument has been tested within this intended population for issues of validity, the findings have been again simply limited to the specific instrument under examination, rather than producing more generalizable findings which could potentially produce valuable insights for the development of future screening instruments based on the self-report methodology, or lead to greater insights into the dynamics of addiction as it manifests itself in unique criminal justice populations.

Finally, while individual screening protocols have been examined for issues of validity, it is seldom the case that institutional decisions are based on a sole instrument's findings. Rather, there seems to be a widespread institutional practice of utilizing and consulting multiple screening instruments in order to arrive at a more "informed" decision regarding the allocation of resources (e.g., Nebraska Department of Corrections - Nebraska, Pottawattamie County Jail - Iowa, Michigan Office of Community Corrections - Michigan).

In the wake of an exploding incarceration rate throughout the 1980s and 90s, U.S. correctional facilities have struggled, armed with relatively diminishing resources, to address issues of "need for treatment" in their respective populations. In order to address this contemporary mandate it has been necessary to develop and employ mechanisms to triage incoming inmates. Therefore, the practice of utilizing self-report-based screening instruments to establish the probability of "need for treatment" in criminal justice settings has increased in frequency of use to the point of becoming routine as the constraints on institutional treatment resources has become progressively limited along with the integration of the Public Health and Harm Reduction models into America's criminal justice system. Although various self-report screening instruments based on diagnostic criteria have indeed experienced scientific support as applied within the general population, there exists a vacuum and need for empirically based support for this enhanced self-report screening methodology as used within criminal justice populations. With these insights recognized, a compelling paradox has emerged. Specifically, *why has the practice of triaging institutionalized criminal justice populations utilizing the self-report-based screening methodology exponentially increased in the absence of ample empirically grounded support for the validity of this practice?*

BACKGROUND

The issues of central concern in this study and resulting research questions came about as a consequence of the researcher's involvement in various research efforts where drug use prevalence and corollary "need for treatment" issues were examined (Crawley and Wakefield, 2002; Crawley, 2003; National Institute of Justice's Arrestee Drug Abuse Monitoring Program, 1998, 1999, 2000, 2001, 2001a, 2001b, 2002, 2002a). Specifically, these research efforts each involved the utilization of diagnostically based screening instrumentation data collected by means of self-report methodology. While it has become a commonplace practice in many institutional venues (e.g., detention centers, jails, prisons) to assess individuals for probability of "need for treatment" using a self-report-based screening methodology, there nevertheless exists an absence of evidence-based-policy research to support such practices.

The central tenant of social science research lies in its ability to analyze, assess, and predict human behavior and its consequences. To realize this mission, social science has employed numerous methodologies and sources of data in efforts to understand human behavior. However researchers have held that data is often corrupted as it is filtered and interpreted through various research processes (e.g., official data, observational data). Therefore, as a result of the self-report methodology's capacity to collect first-hand data, it is perhaps the best data collection technique for minimizing many threats to validity (Sellin, 1931). It has been held that this, in combination with the self-report methodology's ability to access information from "hard to reach" populations, is why it has become the most frequently used method in criminological research (Hagan, 1993).

While the self-report methodology was used as early as the late 1800s as part of various psychological undertakings (Atkinson, Zibin, & Chuang, 1997), it was not until the mid-twentieth century that the use and importance of self-report data became apparent in the greater social sciences (Cantor & Lynch, 2000; Junger-Tas & Marshall, 1999; Sudman, Bradburn, & Schwarz, 1996; Thornberry & Krohn, 2000). Not surprisingly, early utilization of the self-report methodology brought with it tremendous doubt as to its utility – whether interviewees would indeed consent and agree to provide self-report information about personal issues, and moreover, if they did, would such information be accurate or valuable in content. This was especially troublesome in the collection of self-report information regarding issues of deviance and criminality (Junger-Tas and Marshall, 1999; Klein, 1989; Thornberry & Krohn, 2000). Moreover, despite the growing use of the self-report methodology, research has demonstrated that even minor variations in question wording or format can strongly influence self-report responses (Sudman, Bradburn, & Schwarz, 1996). Conversely, additional research has also indicated that "carefully collected" self-report data are as accurate, and in many cases may sometimes be more accurate, than information obtained by means of objective alternative measures (Babor, Steinberg, Anton, & Del Boca, 2000; Del Boca & Noll, 2000). In general, as the utilization of self-report methodology continued to advance in the social sciences, it became clear that the role of the environment in which self-report information was gathered may have often influenced the validity of data.

With the incorporation of self-report methodology into criminological research efforts, early studies (Porterfield, 1943, 1946; Short & Nye, 1958; Wallerstein & Wyle, 1947) were capable of unveiling potentially critical shortcomings in the use of official data to estimate crime rates. Subsequent research regularly found that information collected by means of official data severely underestimated criminal behaviors more readily captured by means of the self-report methodology. As part of this progressive development, a variety of motivational factors played a role in advancing the use of self-report methodology, including: a need to conduct meaningful cross-national analyses of criminal data (Bayley, 1985; Klein, 1984; Klein, 1989; Lynch & Grove, 1986), a desire to address criminal justice-oriented questions with data otherwise restricted to public researchers (Klein, 1989), a call to facilitate political oversight (Klein, 1989), and a need to provide a means by which to deal with the growing awareness of the limitations of official data (Braithwaite, 1981; Elliott, Huizinga, & Morse, 1987; Gove, Hughes, & Geerken, 1985; Thornberry & Farnworth, 1982).

Following the gains realized through the use of self-report methodology in addressing general criminal justice related subject matter, the benefits of its application to understanding drug use within this unique population was next realized. A multitude of examinations of self-report drug use data derived from institutionalized criminal justice populations have, over the years, consistently evidenced distinct findings relative to data derived from the general population, strongly suggestive of population dynamics as an influence on self-report drug use findings (Regier et. al., 1984, 1990). As has proven previously to be the case regarding the use of the self-report methodology in the general social sciences and again in the criminological literature, research involving drug use employing this data collection technique has also found that individual and case level differences across respondents as well as the environment in which self-report data was collected may potentially influence the validity of research findings.

The evolution of self-report methodology being employed in research on drug use as it relates to crime and criminality was next considered within the criminal justice venue with respect to screening arrestees and inmates for "need for treatment." Thus, it is here, with the assessment of an individual's "need for treatment," that the self-report screening methodology provides a unique perspective and information about substance use and abuse in criminal justice populations. It is important to note that screening protocols are not intended to produce diagnosis, rather, they are charged with "flagging" individuals who need further assessment (Winters & Zenilman, 2000). In addition to providing diagnostic information on an individual respondent, the aggregate examination of screening instrument results might also provide estimates of prevalence rates for a particular population.

While self-report information derived via diagnostic screening instruments certainly seek to gather and estimate the "objective facts" with the greatest amount of sensitivity, specificity, and accuracy achievable, such endeavors surely suffer from limitations akin to (and probably greater than) verbally self-reported information, as there is no opportunity to qualify respondent answers by means of this later methodology (Meehl, 1965)[1]. Because self-report involves an individual providing personal information, analysis, or evaluation of phenomena as it is understood by and affects the respondent, and as all individuals are unique social animals drawing on a personal history and sets of experiences, those experiences will be influenced by, but not limited to, various personal attributes (Groves, 1989; Locander, Sudman, & Bradburn, 1976). Research has found that the perceptions and understandings generated by means of self-report are certainly influenced by these conditions and others (Wentland & Smith, 1993). This realization creates a central concern for collecting and utilizing self-report data, namely the validity of such information. Specifically, "a prerequisite for effective treatment planning is the ability to conduct a valid assessment of the patient's illness and needs" (Gastfriend, Najavits, & Reif, 1994). With this in mind, it is imperative that a further understanding of validity issues regarding the self-report methodology as applied via diagnostic screening instrumentation be developed. The current need for such evidence-based-policies and

---

[1] In consideration of the difference/fluctuations across "hit-rates" between clinicians and formalized ("mechanical," "statistical") procedures examining multiple populations, Meehl (1965) held that "we have no good means, either from theoretical considerations or estimators calculable from the data, of deciding whether there is a difference between the efficiency of the statistical method and the judges…" (p. 28).

increasing use of self-report with diagnostic screening in criminal justice populations renders this research both timely and relevant.

With each new application and venue in which it has been collected, a variety of insights and limitations have been identified across the literature pertaining to the use of self-report information. However, as self-report-based information has begun to be used in a very critical mode – to screen individuals housed in institutional criminal justice settings for "need for treatment" – it is essential that a more in-depth understanding of potential threats to validity be developed. Beyond the more general concerns regarding the validity of self-report screening data, numerous issues relate, either directly or indirectly, to the use of this methodology as it is employed in the evaluation of need for substance abuse treatment for individuals housed in the criminal justice system and must be explored. Many of these issues are likely tied to individual and/or case level influences, while others may be more related to the restrictive setting itself. Potentially influential issues and corresponding variables identified in the literature include: 1) Evaluation Setting and Psychometric Qualities, 2) Competency and Development, 3) Social Desirability, and 4) Self-Disclosure.

All users of self-report screening data obtained from criminal justice institutionalized populations must be aware of the upper boundaries to the validity and accuracy of such information. Researchers have acknowledged that data derived by means of self-report methodology are certainly available for critique as a result of "known contaminations" to self-report screening measures (Spector, 1994). However, many of these same authors have quickly pointed out that the fallibility of the self-report methodology is not in itself a cogent critique. Rather, it is important that possible threats to the validity of information grounded in self-report methodology be fully explored in order to arrive at a more accurate understanding of the screening data produced. To this end, understanding the degree to which various influences may pose threats to validity is essential in developing, interpreting, and deploying self-report-based instrumentation.

PURPOSE OF THE STUDY

The purpose of the current research study is to assess the self-report screening methodology in its ability to produce valid data regarding drug and alcohol disorders within institutionalized criminal justice venues – specifically, incoming prison populations. To date, little research has directly addressed the general validity of the self-report screening methodology in these special populations. This study uses various data drawn from prison populations in order to accomplish such goals. Questions addressed in this research include 1) Do screening instrument findings derived via self-report methodologies generate high levels of confidence when compared to forensic clinical psychological assessments, and 2) Does the value of the self-report screening methodology vary based on case attributes? Having informed the above research questions, this study will serve to improve the understanding and advancement of policies and practices related to self-report-based screening protocols designed to triage[2] "need for treatment" in criminal justice institutionalized populations.

RESEARCH DESIGN AND METHODOLOGY OVERVIEW

Following the inception and effective use of screening instruments as a means to triage cases in the medical and psychiatric communities, their use has become progressively more widespread within the criminal justice system. However, notwithstanding the growing subscription in use of self-report screening instruments, there still remain questions regarding the validity of this methodology, especially as applied within criminal justice venues. Therefore, in order to address these gaps in the research, the current study employs a "meta-method" examination to assess issues of validity between self-report screen findings and an optimal independent external criterion – forensic clinical psychological findings. Moreover, the current study also affords secondary data to make quantified statistical comparisons between multiple diagnostic screening instruments generated via self-report methodology (i.e., the Simple Screening Instrument – SSI, the Substance Abuse Subtle

---

[2] Triage is derived from the French *trier,* meaning "to sort." Surgical triage developed from the need to prioritize the care of injured soldiers in battlefield settings. Here it also imparts a meaning to sort individuals with respect to prioritize access to various institutional mental health care resources.

Screening Inventory – SASSI-3, the 31 Question Substance Abuse Treatment Oriented Program Instrument – 31 Question SATOP), forensic clinical psychological assessments, a variety of other indexes of substance misuse (e.g., age of first drug use, frequency of recent drug use, primary route of drug administration), and variables gathered across prison inmate cases (e.g., demographics, intellectual functioning).

The culmination of three self-report-based screening instruments, logistically available, serendipitously designed for different audiences, and used within the Nebraska state prison system to provide insights into and inform institutional decisions, are central to this study's methodology. Using a cross-sectional research design data were collected on a randomly drawn sample of 424 recently incarcerated prisoners from the state of Nebraska (The Department of Corrections' Diagnostic Evaluation Center) throughout the year 2001. Because data was collected on multiple screening instruments across all cases reviewed, the author was able to generate a number of data sets, each capable of providing some insight into the validity of the screening instrument outcomes collected via self-report methodology.

In this study's analysis, collected data is examined as a means to assess the validity of the self-report screening methodology and possible case variable influences that may impact screening efficacy. To achieve this, initially, analytical comparisons to an external 'standard' (Thornberry & Krohn, 2000) or criterion (i.e., full forensic psychological assessments) were conducted to establish the cumulative validity (criterion validity, construct validity, and efficacy) of screening instruments utilizing the self-report methodology as a means to generate diagnostic screening measures for substance disorders within the criminal justice system. Here, concordance tables were additionally used to examine criterion validity for accuracy and four distinct epidemiological criteria – 1) sensitivity, 2) specificity, 3) positive predictive power (PPP), and 4) negative predicative power (NPP).

Next, individual inmate cases were scored by the number of positive (i.e., high probability of "need for treatment") self-report screening instrument outcomes. This study next examines theoretical relationships (construct validity) between cumulative screening outcome scores and various indexes of substance misuse (e.g., previous substance abuse treatment, under the influence at the time of current offense, current offense type).

Finally, individual cases were weighted and scored through an examination of screens found to be convergent with psychological assessments. Subsequently, cases were categorized using multiple classification methodologies (i.e., different potential regression models) and assessed via power analysis to determine statistical power available for analyses. Finally, individual and case level variables (i.e., drug use history, treatment history) were examined across the different case classifications via discriminate (also referred to as discrimination) analysis to identify potentially significant influences upon convergent findings produced by screening instruments using self-report methodologies and full forensic psychological assessments.

Scope of the Research

This study includes recently incarcerated inmates entering the State of Nebraska's Department of Correction (DOC) Diagnostic Evaluation Center (DEC) during the year 2001. The number of inmate subjects which data were collected on was 424 (27.9%). The study focuses on exploring the validity and efficacy of self-report as a methodological modality by which to arrive at diagnostic screen findings for "need for treatment." Analysis was conducted following the collection of all institutional data required for research purposes. No longitudinal follow-up information related to individual inmate assignments within the DOC is included in the current study.

Assumptions

A central assumption to recognize in the current research involves the external criterion to be used throughout this study. In order to proceed with this research effort, it was assumed that the standard (the criterion) to be employed herein – diagnostic clinical interviews with licensed and experienced forensic psychologists – to assess the self-report methodology was indeed accurate itself. It is important to note that while criminological research on issues of drug-use have often employed pharmacological data as external criterion to independently assess self-reported information (Richter & Johnson, 2001), such a practice was not appropriate in the current study. According to the

American Psychiatric Association's DSM-IV diagnostic criteria, drug use does not automatically constitute abuse or dependence on a drug (American Psychiatric Association, 1994). As a result, general prevalence levels established via official records and/or pharmacological data are often inappropriately cited. This is simply because these types of data are not able to assess "need for treatment," rather they are limited to simply establishing recent drug use.

Therefore, the most practical and valuable means for establishing the validity of individual and cumulative screening instrument data collected by means of self-report methodology is to generate comparisons between findings from screening instrument outcomes and the corresponding clinical psychological assessments for these same inmate cases. Psychologists operated under the generally accepted criteria of the DSM-IV of the American Psychiatric Association (1994). In addition, because of the professionalism, care, and diligence exercised by the psychologists producing each inmate's psychological review, combined with the careful scrutiny of each record on the part of the Principal Investigator (PI), the use of clinically based assessments in this study was considered acceptable as a reasonable amount of confidence has been established in their accuracy. This procedure for assessing the clinical value of screening inventories has previously been used throughout the literature as a criterion measure to identify participants with substance abuse and dependence disorders (Bohn, Babor, & Kranzler, 1995; Gastfriend, Najavits, & Reif, 1994; Lazowski et al., 1998; Millon et al., 1997; Torrens et al., 2004).

Delimitations

In addition to the assumption regarding external criteria, it is also noteworthy to acknowledge that while this study sought to generate research findings representative of the respondent population drawn upon for the purposes of data collection – adult male inmates adjudicated in the state of Nebraska – generalizability beyond this population must be done with caution. Specifically, while analyses of the current research sample was found to be representative of the population from which it was drawn (across designated census variables), it is nevertheless limited in its ability to fully estimate the value of the self-report screening methodology as it might be administered throughout other criminal justice system venues (e.g., parole, probation, court settings, community corrections). Furthermore, because of the cross-sectional nature of this study, the findings are also limited to the time period from which the data were collected (the year 2001). Finally, this study is bound by its use of secondary data collections and analysis. Specifically, as is traditionally the case when pre-existing data is employed, there existed an innate inability to select potential research variables beyond those available in the case files.

DEFINITION OF RESEARCH TERMS

In order to facilitate a review of the literature and an examination of the current study's subject matter it is necessary to use a variety of scientific terms. Therefore, it will be beneficial to provide definitions for terms of central interest to this research effort.

Self-Report Data: The direct response of an individual to some form of stimuli (Sundberg, 1977) or simply information provided by an individual in reference to themselves.

Diagnostic Screening: A range of evaluation procedures and techniques, with the note that the screening process is discernibly different from comprehensive assessment procedures. Screening is a preliminary assessment or evaluation that attempts to measure whether key or critical features of the target problem are present in an individual (Knight, Hiller, Simpson, & Broome, 1998; Knight, Wechsler, Kuo, Seibring, Weitzman, & Schuckit, 2002), where a comprehensive assessment is more holistically oriented in nature (Broner et al., 2002; Winters & Zenilman, 2000).

Validity: A measure is valid to the extent that it measures the concept that it sets out to measure and nothing more (Campbell & Stanley, 1963; Carmines & Zeller, 1979). "Validity concerns the crucial relationship between the theoretical concept you are attempting to measure and what you actually measure" (Thornberry & Krohn, 2000, p. 50).

Criterion Validity: "The relationship between test scores and some known external criterion that adequately indicates the quantity being measured" (Huizinga & Elliott, 1986, p. 308) (also referred to as convergent or concurrent validity).

Construct Validity: "The extent to which the measure being validated is related in theoretically expected ways to other concepts or constructs" (Thornberry & Krohn, 2000, p. 51).

Prevalence: The number of cases that demonstrate a specific attribute ("need for treatment") in a given population divided by the total population assessed for the attribute.

Accuracy: The number of cases (both "need for treatment" and "no need for treatment") that demonstrate correct classifications by both the clinical psychological findings and the self-report screening methodology divided by the total sample population.

Epidemiological Criteria: The four categories into which diagnostic screening results may be classified: two types of positive results (true positives and false positives) and two types of negative results (true negative and false negatives) (Winters & Zenilman, 2000).

Predictive Power: An epidemiological concept that incorporates measurements of sensitivity and specificity in order to determine a screen's positive and negative predictive values.

Evidence-Based Policy: the development, implementation, and evaluation of effective programs and policies through application of principles of scientific reasoning, including systematic uses of data and information systems, and appropriate use of theory (e.g., behavior and social science) and program planning models (Brownson, Baker, Leet, & Gillespie, 2003, Walker, 2006).

SIGNIFICANCE OF THE STUDY

To date, the research literature has identified a variety of insights and limitations with respect to the use of self-report-based information. These developments have resulted through the progressive use of this methodology across different populations and in unique settings. However, as self-report-based information has begun to be used in a very critical mode – to screen individuals housed in institutional criminal justice settings for need for treatment – it is essential that a more in-depth understanding of potential threats to validity be developed. It is therefore anticipated that the current research effort will prove significant in that it produces an examination of a specific and unique sub-population which is beginning to heavily employ the use of the self-report screening methodology for variables of potential influence on self-report-based diagnostic screen outcomes. Moreover, as a result of aggregating a battery of self-report screen findings for criterion comparison, this research provides insight into the value of the self-report screening methodology overall. Finally, research findings may provide practical evidence-based assistance to researchers, mental health practitioners, and criminal justice institutions involved in the designing, interpretation, and/or deployment of self-report-based screening instruments.

ORGANIZATION OF THIS BOOK

This chapter outlined the major steps taken by the researcher throughout the course of this study. In setting forth these steps, the researcher reviewed the following topics: 1) the statement of the problem, arriving at the paradoxical underpinnings motivating the current research effort, 2) background to the current study to include a brief consideration of the historical evolution of the self-report methodology, along with a progressive understanding of potential threats to validity, 3) purpose of the study, to include the main research questions to be explored, 4) research design and methodological overview, including a consideration of the scope, assumptions, and delimitations to the current research undertaking, 5) definition of key research terms, and 6) the significance of this study.

Following the initial introduction and discussion of this research endeavor, the remaining chapters will serve to present an academic examination of the validity of the self-report methodology as used within an institutionalized criminal justice population. Here, chapter two includes a historical review of the self-report methodology as it has developed and progressed over time and across a variety of research disciplines, while chapter three provides insight into how the self-report methodology has evolved to become central to the diagnostic screening process, as well as its potential insights and limitations – specifically issues and concerns related to threats to validity. The subsequent section of this book, chapter four, communicates the research steps, methodological choices, and study rationales. This chapter concludes with a discussion of the various research analyses to be employed herein. Chapter five, the data analysis portion of this study, presents and interprets research findings from the current study. Finally, in chapter six, a discussion of research findings is generated examining issues of the validity and effectiveness of the self-report-based screening methodology as applied within institutional criminal justice populations.

CHAPTER 2

Evolution of Self-Report Methodology

The current topic under study in this book and the subsequent research questions were a direct result of the author's years of involvement in the United States Department of Justice (DOJ), with the National Institute of Justice's (NIJ) Arrestee Drug Abuse Monitoring Program (ADAM). While serving as the Coordinating Investigator for this intelligence gathering program, self-report information was collected and used from criminal justice institutionalized populations. This self-report-based information included basic demographics (i.e., age, race, education, employment, marital status), prior experience with the criminal justice system (i.e., arrest and incarceration information), history of prior substance use and abuse (i.e., type of drug used, age at first use), history of mental health treatment (to include substance abuse treatment), drug market activity (i.e., cash/non-cash transaction types and amounts, primary and secondary drugs of choice, location and frequency of purchases, relationship and method of contact to drug sources), and drug use dynamics (i.e., frequency and intensity of use, primary route of administration). However, the information this program gathered that predominantly inspired the current research effort involved diagnostic screening data collected via the self-report methodology to assess the probability of need for drug and alcohol treatment.

Upon investigating the self-report dependent screen, clustered within the larger ADAM data collection instrument (ADAM, 2000), it became apparent that although this screening tool was being used in a multitude of research sites (approximately 35 to 38 sites), across a considerable number of cases (approximately 60,000 cases annually), it had yet to be tested and validated by empirically based research. Rather, as is all to common, this self-report-based screening methodology, like many others of its kind (e.g., Substance Abuse Subtle Screening Instrument [SASSI-3], 31-Question Substance Abuse Treatment Oriented Program Screen [31-Q SATOP]), had been generated based on expert insights and criteria rooted in the American Psychiatric Association's (1994) Diagnostic and Statistical Manual of Mental Disorders, 4th Edition (DSM-IV), but had not specifically undergone scientific testing within the population in which it was to be applied. Specifically, it seemed problematic to this investigator that in light of the recent emergence and advancement of "evidence-based-policymaking" practices in the fields of both health-care[3] and criminology[4], that the collection and utilization of such sensitive and

---

[3] Walker (2006) stated that "evidence-based policy originated in England with the Cochrane Collaboration, which examined the effectiveness of health care policies" and has since spread to inform health care policy in the United States (e.g., the Vanderbilt University Center for Evidence-Based Medicine and the Center for Evidence-Based Practice of the State University of New York; a program in evidence-based mental health; the Evidence-Based Medicine Resource Center; a program in evidence-based pediatrics at the University of Michigan; and the Coalition for Evidence-Based Policy supported by the U.S. Department of Education) (p. 8).

[4] Examples promoting the principles of evidenced-based-policy to crime control have included the Home Office (England's equivalent to the U.S. Department of Justice) report "Working out What to Do: Evidence-Based Crime Reduction" (Tilley & Laycock, 2002) and the Justice Department Coalition for Evidence-Based Policy report titled "Bringing Evidence-Driven Progress to Crime and Substance-Abuse Policy: A Recommended Federal Strategy." In the later of these examples, recommendations included "that the federal agencies develop a concise, uniform, user-friendly set of principles on what constitutes 'rigorous evidence' of an intervention's effectiveness." Walker (2006) reported that "one result of this effort was a National Forum on Evidence-Based Crime and Substance Abuse Policy" (p. 8).

costly data would require protocols based on solid foundations of evidence drawn from "best practices" (Walker, 2006).[5]

Moreover, this practice of employing self-report-based screening instruments to establish the probability of "need for treatment" in criminal justice venues had increased in frequency of use and become more commonplace with the increases of constraints on institutional treatment resources and the advancing integration of the medical/public health/harm reduction models into America's criminal justice system in the late 1980s and 90s. Although various self-report screening instruments based on diagnostic criteria have indeed experienced scientific support as applied within the general population, there exists an obvious vacuum and specific need for empirically grounded support for self-report screening methodologies as used within criminal justice populations. With these insights recognized, a compelling paradox emerged. *Why has the practice of triaging institutionalized criminal justice populations utilizing the self-report-based screening methodology exponentially increased in the absence of ample empirically grounded support for the validity of this practice?*

CHAPTER ORGANIZATION

To date, the research literature has identified various insights and limitations associated with the use of the self-report methodology, as they have been used and developed over time in each new application and venue. However, as the self-report methodology has begun to be employed in a very critical manner – to assess and provide insight into issues of mental health, to allocate treatment programming resources, to provide documentation on individuals, to inform institutional policy, etc. – in a unique population (e.g., jail and prison inmates, parole/probation, court settings), it is imperative that the validity of self-report methodology as applied via diagnostic screening

[5] The "evidence-based-policy" movement suggested herein involves very specific standards. Walker (2006, p. 10) stated that these included, 1) a demand for empirical evidence of the effectiveness of a policy, 2) setting a very high requirement of experimental or quasi-experimental research design in which subjects are randomly assigned to treatment and control groups – to include assessments of the quality of the research design of studies, 3) the requirement of replication, and 4) the use of systematic reviews of studies (e.g., meta-analyses).

instrumentation be examined. Because current diagnostic screening promotes new applications of self-report in criminal justice populations, this research is both timely and relevant.

This book explores the validity of the self-report methodology as used via diagnostic screening instrumentation within criminal justice institutionalized venues, assessing the validity and efficacy of self-report-based screen findings as they relate to the current standard of clinical psychological assessments. Moreover, this investigation reviews case-level variables, identified in the literature and available for examination, that may influence the validity of diagnostic screen findings grounded in the self-report methodology.

In order to explore various issues of validity (i.e., criterion and construct validity) as they relate to self-report-based screening, it is first necessary to briefly consider the value of the self-report methodology in various research venues. This examination includes a brief historical review of the use and characteristics of self-report methodology as it has evolved to its recent use in diagnostic screening instrumentation within the field of criminal justice. The questions addressed by this review are 1) How and why has the self-report method been used as a means of gaining information in the social sciences, and 2) What are the benefits and concerns regarding self-report methodology?

The review identifies the necessity of considering the self-report methodology as it has been specifically employed in the gathering of diagnostic screening data to include 1) What are the central concerns of employing this methodology with respect to issues of validity, and 2) What has research brought to light in terms of assessment information and potential threats to validity with respect to utilizing the self-report methodology? While such a review will certainly necessitate some cross-disciplinary examination of the literature (e.g., criminology, sociology, psychology, treatment, medical), this effort is in no way intended to be exhaustive in its content. Rather, relevant literature will be used to highlight points of intersection between various fields of study as they inform the central research focus – the validity of screening data derived by means of the self-report methodology. In part, the intent of this chapter is to provide a relevant background for the understanding of self-report methodology as used via diagnostic screening instrumentation in criminal justice populations.

As this review of the self-report methodology progresses, from early use within the social sciences toward the more contemporary venues in which the current research interest rests, potentially influential variables affecting response accuracy will be considered. Finally, in order to provide a greater sense of organization within this review, potential variables of influence will be discussed across four major "issue sections" prevalent in the literature with respect to the validity of self-report data – 1) evaluation setting and psychometric qualities, 2) competency and development, 3) social desirability, and 4) self-disclosure. While this review will inventory a variety of variables worthy of consideration, the primary focus herein will be on those variables theoretically understood to influence self-report methodology which are also available for direct analysis as part of the current research effort. The current review of the literature anticipates presenting a progressive understanding of this topic and consequently arrives at the focus of this study: to explore the validity, efficacy, and influences on self-report methodologies used via diagnostic screening instrumentation in criminal justice institutionalized populations.

METHODS OF KNOWING

The central tenet of social science research is its ability to analyze, assess, and predict human behavior and its consequences. To realize this mission, social science has employed numerous methodologies and sources of data in efforts to understand human behavior. Information collected via behavioral observation, significant other, expert judge, unobtrusive measures, archival information, and official data have long served as means for gaining insight into human behaviors and interactions. However, social scientists have come to understand that investigators and institutional biases often directly impact the value of research data. How a social phenomenon is defined and corresponding information collected certainly drives how it might subsequently be measured and interpreted – we experience it as we define it. When such discretionary decisions are left up to a bureaucracy, there is no doubt that data may become somewhat compromised by institutional agendas and/or available resources. Moreover, even when institutionalized biases are removed, as is to some extent the case with field data collection efforts, observational data is still filtered through the lens of the researchers themselves and thereby subject to biases sometimes resulting in less than valuable information. It has been held that "the value of a crime rate for index purposes decreases as the distance from the crime itself in terms of procedure increases" (Sellin, 1931, p. 337). For each additive layer of interpretation that data passes through, the opportunity for corruption of the information is exponentially increased. As such, as a result of the self-report methodology's capacity to collect first-hand data, it is perhaps the best data collection technique for minimizing many threats to validity.

HISTORICAL VALUE OF THE SELF-REPORT METHODOLOGY

Research has varied in what constitutes the description of a measure as a *self-report methodology*. Some have employed a broad description where self-report simply involved the direct response of an individual to some form of stimuli (Sundberg, 1977). Others have held self-report methodology to include "all manner of assessment that utilizes a direct response by the subject, within a natural or controlled setting, with or without stimuli (structured or unstructured)" (Reynolds, 1993). Within the scope of the current research effort, subscription to a more conventional conceptualization of self-report methodology as requiring an individual to respond to a set of structured verbal or written statements or questions will be maintained. More specifically, self-report data is simply information provided by an individual in reference to themselves.

However, for any scientific measure to be valuable, to include self-reported data, it must first be *valid*. A measure is valid to the extent that it measures the concept that it sets out to measure and nothing more (Campbell and Stanley, 1963; Carmines & Zeller, 1979). "Validity concerns the crucial relationship between the theoretical concept you are attempting to measure and what you actually measure" (Thornberry & Krohn, 2000, p. 50). Consequently, as the *accuracy* or *truth* of self-report information is of central concern to the current research effort, it is therefore necessary that these terms also be clarified. To this end, the terms accuracy and truth are not intended to denote intentionality. Rather it is recognized that subjects may sometimes unintentionally self-report inaccurate or untruthful information but indeed believe themselves to be reporting honestly. There are of course several scenarios in which this discrepancy may occur. For example, respondents suffering from erroneous recall (Belli, 1998; Conrad,

Brown & Cashman, 1998; Spanier, 1976), jumbled memories (Barbor, Stephens, & Marlatt, 1987; Cahalan, 1968), or simply not fully understanding the questions posed to them (Wentland & Smith, 1993; Groves, 1989) would fall easily into this category of inaccurate response without intended deception. On the other hand, certainly the intentional delivery of inaccurate or untruthful responses is quite possible, especially when the sensitivity of subject matter is escalated (Del Boca & Noll, 2000). In addition, issues such as social desirability (Crowne & Marlowe, 1964; Crowne, 1979; Howard, 1994; Klein, 1989; Orne, 1962; Victorin, Haag-Gronlund, & Skerfving, 1998), willingness to self-disclose (Reynolds, 1993), denial of a problem (Del Boca & Noll, 2000), and fear of punishment (Junger-Tas & Marshall, 1999; Klein, 1989), may also provide motives for intentionally self-reporting inaccurate information – thereby decreasing the validity of such self-reported information.

While the self-report methodology was used as early as the late 1800s as part of various psychological undertakings (Atkinson, Zibin, & Chuang, 1997),[6] it was not until the mid-twentieth century that the use and importance of self-report data became apparent in the greater social sciences (Cantor & Lynch, 2000; Junger-Tas & Marshall, 1999; Sudman, Bradburn, & Schwarz, 1996; Thornberry & Krohn, 2000). Not surprisingly, early utilization of the self-report methodology brought with it tremendous doubt as to its utility (Vold, 1958)[7] – whether

---

[6] It is known that psychologists such as Wilhelm Wundt (1832-1920), who established the first psychological laboratory (Leipzig, Germany), and his student Edward Titchner (1867-1927), who brought their research to the United States, used self-report methodology as early as 1879 to collect "systematic introspection" data as a scientific means of measuring experience. However, it is worth noting that this early use of the self-report methodology was done without any support of objective measures and consequently was heavily criticized as suffering from a lack of validity (American Psychological Association, 1999).

[7] In a review of methodological contributions to the field of criminology made by James F. Short, Jr., Meier (1988) stated that "there was some initial skepticism about the [self-report] method" advanced by Short and Nye's survey of youth. He further cited a prominent researcher of the era, Vold (1958, p. 267), to have complained that "...some authors have published statistical findings on the frequency and distribution of *unreported crimes* and of *non-criminal criminals*!" In addition, he reported Vold to have suggested that this

interviewees would indeed consent and agree to provide self-report information about personal issues, and moreover, if they did, would such information be accurate or valuable in content. This was especially troublesome in the collection of self-report information regarding issues of deviance and criminality (Junger-Tas and Marshall, 1999; Klein, 1989; Thornberry & Krohn, 2000).

However, the initial utilization of self-report data not only provided a previously unconsidered new perspective directly from the actors under examination, research early on established, moreover, that interviewees were agreeable to providing self-report information, even when questioned about issues of delinquency and criminal behavior, they did so at an unexpected frequency (Porterfield, 1943; Thornberry & Krohn, 2000; Meier, 1988; Wallerstein & Wyle, 1947). While the utilization of self-report methodology originally involved measures of attitudes and beliefs, attention to further areas of interest developed in time (Junger-Tas & Marshall, 1999; Sudman, Bradburn, & Schwarz, 1996). If an individual's perception is their reality, then this new source of data now provided researchers with direct access to such realities.

However, despite the growing use of the self-report methodology, researchers have continued to raise questions about the value of data obtained by means of self-report (Del Boca & Noll, 2000; Schwarz, 1999; Spector, 1994). To this end, research has demonstrated that even minor variations in question wording or format can strongly influence self-report responses (Sudman, Bradburn, & Schwarz, 1996). Conversely, additional research has also indicated that "carefully collected" self-report data are as accurate, and in many cases may sometimes be more accurate, than information obtained by means of objective alternative measures (Babor, Steinberg, Anton, & Del Boca, 2000; Del Boca & Noll, 2000). Therefore, it may be argued that:

> The self-report method is no longer novel and significant progress has been made in assessing its methodological strengths and weaknesses...The self-report method has been used on a large variety of populations, sample, subgroups, and designs (longitudinal and cross-sectional), in a variety of

---

work was "mild and harmless nonsense...although, something might come of it."

> contexts, in a number of different countries. Because of this wealth of experience, we have developed a much better understanding of the conditions under which the self-report method appears to "work" (and when it does not) (Junger-Tas & Marshall, 1999, p. 298).

With these considerations from the literature, because self-report involves an individual providing personal information, analysis, or evaluation of phenomena as it is understood by and affects the respondent, and as all individuals are unique social animals drawing on a personal history and sets of experiences, those experiences will be influenced by, but not limited to, various personal attributes (e.g., age, race, cognitive processing ability, perceived sensitivity of the subject matter) (Groves, 1989; Locander, Sudman, & Bradburn, 1976). Research has found that the perceptions and understandings generated by means of self-report are certainly influenced by these conditions and others (Wentland & Smith, 1993). This realization creates a central concern for collecting and utilizing self-report data, namely the validity of such information. With this in mind, it seems imperative that whenever self-report data is employed, it must also be assessed for issues of general validity as well as identifying respondent and/or case level variables potentially affecting such validity (Wentland & Smith, 1993).

Use of the Self-Report Methodology in the General Social Sciences

As the historical utilization of the self-report methodology progressed in its application to the general population, data collected by such means began to be understood as a valuable tool in terms of both accuracy of findings and accessibility to information not identified by other traditional data collection methods. Early on in its development, information gathered by means of the self-report methodology in the general population provided unique insights into human behaviors, beliefs, and attitudes (Sudman, Bradburn, & Schwarz, 1996)[8]. These

---

[8] One celebrated example early on in the historical use of the self-report method was known as the "Kinsey Report" (1948; 1953). Meier (1988) held that "Kinsey's contribution was not only substantive by informing us about all manner of things concerning sexual behavior in the United States, his was also a methodological contribution. He was dealing with some of the most, if not *the*

innovative sources of data assisted in developing predictive theoretical models in the social sciences, and producing more informed public policies and practices. In general, this methodology of collecting social science data provided a pioneering means to address questions that had previously not been accessible to the researcher.

The influx of self-report methodology into social scientific data collections brought with it advantages previously unrealized with respect to data collection protocols. Such advantages included the relative ease in administering questionnaires to large samples, the ability to administer surveys simultaneously in several different locations, and easily quantifiable and therefore analyzable responses; and it offered the researcher the ability to question respondents across different areas of interests (Richter & Johnson, 2001). In addition, self-report instruments were also relatively inexpensive to create and administer and they could be administered by means of numerous protocols and across various venues, including face-to-face interview, telephone, mail, email, or the Internet (Patrick et al., 1994). In the era following an influx of ethical considerations and oversights of social science research involving human subjects (since the 1970s), self-report-based instrumentation has permitted respondents to select to pass over items that they did not desire to answer, thereby protecting a respondent's choice as to what information they wished to reveal to the researcher. Finally, the use of data obtained via self-report methods, in combination with data arrived by means of "traditional methods" (e.g., official data), has in many cases been able to provide rationales for higher levels of confidence in findings by demonstrating convergence across data sources (triangulation), as well as insights into limitations and values of "other methodologies" when such data presented divergent conclusions.

However, along with this innovative and distinct methodology came significant concerns regarding the validity of data produced for

---

most, sensitive areas of human existence. Yet, Kinsey and his associates were able to obtain data that no one thought possible up to that time. Kinsey's respondents, both men and women, told him about orgasms, homosexual encounters, meetings with prostitutes, frequency of intercourse, masturbation, adulterous affairs, and favorite sexual techniques. The idea that people would disclose such private or confidential information, under the proper circumstances, was a radical one to many scholars at the time" (pp. 231-232).

the social sciences by self-report methodology. At the heart of this concern were issues that researchers had not previously dealt with directly, namely, the potential influences of environment, context, case, and individual level variables. Researchers considering the potential threats to validity exacerbated by self-report methodology have reported extensively on the many ways in which research settings can influence the responses of study participants (Schwarz, 1996; 1999). In different instances respondents may use the context in which they are queried and providing self-reported information to form a frame of reference for estimating their responses, possibly resulting in data that is less than valid and/or difficult to compare across research studies on the same subject matter but conducted in different environments. For example, researchers have held that "by their nature, self-report measures allow respondents to strategically alter their true responses to suit their particular self-presentation motives" (Richter & Johnson, 2001, p. 2). It is understandable that in many circumstances, respondents aspire to present themselves in a socially desirable (or undesirable) light and, as a result, may modify their true responses in an effort to achieve some anticipated outcome (Orne, 1962; Victorin, Haag-Gronlund, & Skerfving, 1998). To this end, research has suggested that often respondent attributes, such as gender, ethnicity, and prior experiences may differentially influence their accuracy in self-reporting (Johnson & Glassman, 1999).

In general, as the utilization of self-report methodology continued to advance in the social sciences, it became clear that the role of the environment in which self-report information was gathered may have often influenced the validity of data. Furthermore, empirical evidence regarding the influence of individual and case level variables upon the accuracy of data obtained by means of self-report methodology also become apparent. Because public policy is certainly influenced, if not often driven, by responses to public opinion polls collected by means of the self-report methodology, it is therefore critical to understand potential threats to the validity of such data. This is especially important when considering the high costs associated with implementing programs or developing policies based on erroneous data (Wentland & Smith, 1993). These concerns remain for the contemporary researcher when employing self-report methodologies as part of a study design.

Self-Report and Deviant Behavior – Crime

> It has been held that although nearly everyone has committed crimes, only a few were picked up and officially processed.
>
> (Junger-Tas & Marshall, 1999, p. 292)

As was previously discussed, while the utilization of the self-report methodology increased with investigations related to the general social sciences, other disciplines quickly began to employ this technique for gathering data. The field of Criminology was no exception, as early studies recognized the opportunity afforded by the use of the self-report methodology, namely, accessing previously unavailable sources of data – "hidden or shadow populations," the "dark figure of crime" (Gibbons, 1979; Meier, 1988). Beginning in the middle of the twentieth century, self-report methodologies began to emerge in criminological research as it was found useful in dealing with an extensive array of criminal and deviant behaviors, covering varying segments of time, and often able to be coupled to peer associates or other contextual matters including official arrest and court actions (Klein, 1989). Early studies, conducted in the 1940s (Porterfield, 1943, 1946; Wallerstein & Wyle, 1947), employing self-report methodology as the primary data collection strategy, unveiled potentially critical shortcomings in the use of official data to estimate crime rates. Here, researchers regularly found that information collected by means of official data severely underestimated criminal behaviors (both felony and misdemeanor crimes) more readily captured by means of the self-report methodology.[9]

While initial research involving the use of self-report methodology was relatively unsophisticated by contemporary standards, progress

---

[9] Comparing official rates of delinquency (across 55 different offenses) by means of court records to self-reported rates of delinquency (from a college student population), Porterfield (1943) found that the non-adjudicated population in his research had committed the same crimes for which the adjudicated population had been sentenced – however, at less frequency. Shortly thereafter, in 1947, Wallerstein and Wyle employed self-report methodology to collect information from adult populations regarding crimes they had committed prior to the age of 16. Nearly all respondents self-reported having committed at least one illegal act.

toward the use of self-report studies employing more systematic and methodical frameworks began to appear in the 1950s (Erickson & Empey, 1963; Junger-Tas & Marshall, 1999) with Short and Nye's research of an adolescent school population (Short, 1957; Short & Nye, 1958).[10] These authors have been noted as the first criminologists to have paid extensive attention to methodological issues impacting the validity of their collected data, and consequently stimulating interest in the use of the self-report methodology (Meier, 1988; Thornberry & Krohn, 2000). Over the course of the next decade, criminologists following Short and Nye's work further enhanced use of the self-report methodology by advancing the significance and attention given to issues of validity (Clark & Tifft, 1966; Dentler & Monroe, 1961; Gold, 1966; Hirschi, 1969). Subsequently, the self-report methodology played a key role throughout the 1960s (Dentler & Monroe, 1961; Elliott, 1966; Erickson & Empey, 1963; Hirschi, 1969; Matthews, 1968; Polk, 1969; Reiss & Rhodes, 1964; Stanfield, 1966; Voss, 1964) and 1970s (Akers, Krohn, Lanza-Kaduce, & Radoscevich, 1979; Anderson, Chiricos, & Waldo, 1977; Elliott and Voss, 1974; Jensen, 1973; Jensen, Erickson, & Gibbs, 1978; Kaplan, 1972; Silberman, 1976; Waldo & Chiricos, 1972) in exploring and testing etiological theories of crime and delinquency.

As part of this progressive development, a variety of motivational factors played a role in advancing the use of self-report methodology, including: a need to conduct meaningful cross-national analyses of criminal data, a desire to address criminal justice-oriented questions with data otherwise restricted to public researchers, a call to facilitate political oversight, and a need to provide a means by which to deal with the growing awareness of the limitations of official data.

---

[10] Short and Nye's (1958) research employing self-report methodology via survey generated "revolutionized ideas about the feasibility of using survey procedures" (Hindelang, Hirschi, & Weis, 1981, p. 23) as it challenged previously held ideas on the relationship between socio-economic-status (SES) and delinquency rates. Specifically, their research held that among different SES groups, relatively few differences in delinquent behavior were statistically significant. "The Short and Nye research firmly established self-reports as a method of measuring delinquency, and at the same time it produced findings apparently directly demonstrating that official statistics on criminality contain important, consistent biases" (p. 23).

The first of these, a growing need for effective cross-national analyses, was an important factor in promoting the employment of self-report methodology. On this subject, researchers held that the use of official statistics inevitably conveyed innate problems reflective of nation-specific histories, values, penal codes, and institutional needs, and were additionally compounded in direct proportion to the number of nations involved (Bayley, 1985). It was found that the use of self-report methodology allowed for the production of crime data more readily available for uniform comparisons, with fewer data coding inconsistencies regularly produced by major national, regional, and local statutory differences (Klein, 1984; Klein, 1989; Lynch & Grove, 1986).

The utilization of self-report found value as it was recognized that various data were not readily available to the public for analysis, such as information under the protection of civil rights in the United States, which might be overcome (within the limits of Human Subjects protection) by means of the self-report methodology. Specifically, the utilization of the self-report methodology frequently permitted access to data typically restricted in police and court records.

Next, researchers have held that the promotion of self-report methodology was further driven by a political need to ameliorate government oversight.

> The U.S., more perhaps than any other nation, has devoted a great deal of attention and resources to the empirical evaluation of crime prevention and control programs. Such programs run by, or accountable to, the justice system agencies most properly should be evaluated using data not controlled by those agencies...Self-report data permit the maintenance of an independent approach to assessment (Klein, 1989, p. 3).

Finally, as previously mentioned, another part of the background to the development of self-report studies of offending behavior stemmed from a growing awareness of the limitations and ensuing dissatisfaction with official crime statistics. For example, when working with aggregate national-level data, such as the Federal Bureau of Investigation's (FBI) Uniform Crime Reports (UCR), there were inherent errors and gaps of information produced by local records that could not be overcome, whereas the utilization of a self-report methodology would have more readily avoided such problems (Klein, 1989).

A prime historical example of the benefit of self-report methodology in such an effort was realized in Elliott and Ageton's (1980) study, which employed an instrument developed for the National Youth Survey. Here the use of a single, uniform self-report instrument was developed and deployed to in turn generate highly valuable national-level data absent many of the limitations present when using instruments engineered to collect official data but which lacked the ability to capture significant local differences in criminal classifications. However, this study found that the data collected via self-report indicated relatively clear differences by class and race, more so than previous research had identified, bringing to light potential threats to the validity of such findings. This emerging issue was next directly examined by Braithwaite (1981) who found that official crime statistics did indicate a strong negative relationship with class, and that self-report studies revealed a similar but much weaker pattern. In this same study Braithwaite (1981) also held that "lower-class" respondents were less likely to report that they had been in trouble previously and also tended to score higher on scales measuring deception in self-report measures.

Compared to self-report, official sources of criminological data tend to greatly underestimate the prevalence and incidence of criminal behavior. Specifically, research has held that official data sources significantly underestimate participation in felony crime; exaggerate disparity by age, gender, race, and social class (Gove, Hughes, & Geerken, 1985; Thornberry & Farnworth, 1982); and have a tendency to overstate the effectiveness of prevention and control programs (Elliott, Huizinga, & Morse, 1987; Klein, 1986). In two large-scale extensive studies on the value of the self-report methodology as employed in criminal justice-related research, it was held that self-report advantages over official data included a greater sensitivity to the wide-ranging continuum of criminal behavior. More adept flexibility of use across research venues, more sensitivity to offense details, and greater overall levels of validity were attributed to self-report methodology as compared to the use of officially derived data (Hirschi,

Hindelang, and Weis, 1980; Hindelang, Hirschi, & Weis, 1981). It should be noted that these findings were later critiqued for not including sufficient representation across the international research literature, and rather grounded their conclusions in a limited application of self-report methodological findings (Klein, 1989).

In contrast to the previously noted divergence between self-report and official findings, an examination of the research literature has also evidenced a variety of criminological subject matter where aggregated findings obtained by means of self-report methodology realized high levels of concordance when compared to official measures of the same domains, to include: convictions (Blackmore, 1974; Farrington, 1977), status offenses (Rojek, 1983), and delinquency (Hardt & Petersen-Hardt; 1977; Hathaway, Monachesi & Young, 1960; Hindelang, Hirschi, & Weis, 1981). Similar research examining issues of validity at the individual level of analysis has demonstrated significantly different validity coefficients associated with seriousness of offense and respondents' race and gender. For example, Elliott and Voss (1974) examined the concordance between self-reports of crime and official records and found that more serious offenses were more likely to be under-reported. Furthermore, in studies conducted by Hindelang, Hirschi, & Weis (1981) and Huizinga and Elliott (1986), it was found that validity coefficients between self-report and official data were at best moderate for African-American males, whereas all other race-gender combinations presented reasonably high correlations. A more recent study, using comparative information derived from juvenile school populations for purposes of assessing concurrent validity, found no such discrepancy by race or gender (Farrington, Loeber, Stouthamer-Loeber, Van Kammen, & Schmidt, 1996).

Researchers (Gove, Hughes, & Geerken, 1985, Hindelang, Hirschi, and Weis, 1979) have held that major attempts to interpret the evident disparity between official rates and self-reported crime rates have revealed some key conclusions. First, self-report-based instruments regularly had the ability to access a domain of "non-serious" criminal behavior virtually outside the domain of official data. Second, they presented reliable and valid indicators of the domain of behavior they typically measured. Third, the self-report method demonstrated the ability to deal with behaviors in the domain of official data. However, conclusions also held that self-report has traditionally been inadequate to extrapolate clear conclusions regarding correlates of offending behavior as compared to the correlates evidenced by official data.

With this the case, it would seem that, in general, "self-report instruments have proven their capacity to surmount at least some of the problems associated with official data sources and avoid some biases often noted in official statistics" (Klein, 1989, p. 3). Therefore, as a partial reaction to the limitations historically evidenced by traditional data collection methodologies, especially officially derived information, data collection using self-report began to be drawn on heavily in the criminological literature throughout the 1960s and thereafter (Thornberry, 1989), both in the U.S. and in Europe (Junger-Tas & Marshall, 1999; Klein, 1989).

It is important to note that self-report research on criminal behavior differs significantly from self-reports in other arenas in several respects. Klein (1989) held that "self-report crime is admitted crime, derived from interview and questionnaire responses obtained from adults and juveniles (regardless of whether or not they have been arrested) concerning their own illegal behaviors" (p. 1). As such, "it tries to measure behavior that is punishable by law, usually hidden, socially unacceptable, and morally condemned" (Junger-Tas & Marshall, 1999, p. 291). The difference in subject matter, combined with the difference in respondents (drawn from a criminal justice population rather than the general population) poses several challenges when assessing the validity of data obtained by self-report (Meehl, 1965). Researchers have held that:

> Empirical evidence suggests that crime [like other social phenomena, to include drug use and abuse] does not have a clear unidimensional structure that would facilitate the sampling of a few items from a theoretically large pool to represent adequately the entire domain…[suggesting that]…an adequate self-report scale [for crime] will be relatively lengthy. A large number of individual items are required to represent the entire domain of [criminal] behavior, to represent each of its subdomains, and to ensure that each subdomain…is itself adequately represented (Thornberry & Krohn, 2000, p. 41-42).

Thus, while the use of self-report methodology within criminal justice populations continues to present the same challenges as those typical within the general social science population, it presents unique challenges and considerations as well. Taking this research as a whole, it becomes apparent that the role of the environment in which self-report information is gathered may often, directly and/or indirectly, influence the accuracy and value of the collected data. Further inquiry demonstrates that individual and case level variables may also play a role in influencing the accuracy of data obtained by means of self-report methodology.

In spite of the challenges and potential threats to validity, criminological researchers (Thornberry & Krohn, 2000) have held that the psychometric quality of the self-report methodology has increased considerably since its inception, and while further refinement and understanding of response accuracy remains essential, self-report data nevertheless appear acceptably valid for research purposes. Many criminologists have argued the far-reaching value of self-report methodology in its ability to protect against errors and false study conclusions that would have otherwise resulted should researchers have been limited to official crime data (Klein, 1989). It has been held that following the origination of the self-report methodology in the middle of the twentieth century and its progressive development thereafter, it has become the most frequently used method in criminological research (Hagan, 1993).

Self-Report Methodology and Drug Using Populations

> Other than the general concerns with self-report measures…numerous additional questions have been raised about the…validity of self-report measures of substance use.
>
> (Richter and Johnson, 2001, p. 4)

The evolution of the use of self-report methods to study drug use was rooted in two primary developments of the time. First, the influx and spread of crack-cocaine throughout many U.S. cities in the mid-1980s created a myriad of challenges for the criminal justice system in its "War on Drugs" (Inciardi, 1979; 1995), and for the presidential administrations of the era (i.e., Presidents Reagan, Bush, and Clinton,

Bush) that made drug use and abuse key priorities. Second, criminal justice scholars began to re-examine the relationship between drug use and criminality. Over the fifty years leading up to this point, the relationship between drugs and crime had been studied extensively and had consistently revealed high crime rates among drug abusers and high drug-use rates among offenders (Fishbein & Reuland, 1994; Mateyoke-Scrivner et. Al., 2003; Tonry & Wilson, 1990). Researchers (Ball, Schaffer, & Nurco, 1983; Chaiken, 1986) had found that drug use was likely to increase involvement in criminal activity, and that drug-related offenses had been directly related to the rapid increase and influx of the number of inmates into jails and prisons in recent years (Bureau of Justice Statistics, 1995; Kubiak, Boyd, Slayden, & Young, 2005).

It is worthy to note that as the study of the prevalence, frequency, and duration of drug use progressed throughout the 1980s and 1990s, self-report was considered *the* major data source in research on drug use and misuse issues (Del Boca & Noll, 2000; Richter & Johnson, 2001). Much like the historical use of self-report methodology in the general social sciences, researchers in the field of criminal justice were able to produce significant and innovative findings related to drug-using behaviors not previously available for empirical examination.

A multitude of examinations of self-report drug use data derived from institutionalized criminal justice populations have, over the years, consistently produced quite distinct findings relative to data derived from the general population, strongly suggestive of population dynamics as an influence on self-report drug use findings (Regier et. al., 1984, 1990). In addition to an examination across general versus criminal justice populations, as a result of large-scale research efforts it was realized that the prevalence of drug use has typically differed based on the setting under examination (e.g., Drug Abuse Warning Network [DAWN] - SAMHSA 2004, 2003, Monitoring the Future [MTF] - National Institutes of Health [NIH] 2004, National Household Survey on Drug Abuse [NHSDA] - Substance Abuse and Mental Health Services Administration [SAMHSA] 2004, National Longitudinal Survey of Youth [NLSY] - Bureau of Labor Statistics, 2004, Youth Risk Behavior Survey [YRBS] - Center for Adolescent Health 2004). For example, research has often revealed differences in drug use prevalence across environmental settings even within the criminal justice system (e.g., prison versus jail prevalence levels) (Peters & Kearns, 1992; Peters, Greenbaum, Edens, Carter, & Ortiz, 1998). However, unlike many other areas of criminological research where data from different sources have been compared (UCR versus NCVS) to assess issues of validity, research on drug use is unique in that there has often existed the availability of a true external criterion for comparison to self-report information – pharmacological data (Richter & Johnson, 2001). Here pharmacological data (e.g., urinalysis, toxicology reports, saliva swabs) have often been used to independently assess recent use of various substances, and to subsequently compare findings to self-reported information provided by respondents.

Often, such examinations have evidenced differential rates of self-reporting (accuracy) associated with individual or case level attributes. An ideal example of research having evidenced such findings existed within the DOJ NIJ's ADAM (1998, 1999, 2000, 2001, 2001a, 2001b, 2002, 2002a) program, which sampled incoming arrestees in major cities (over 100,000 in population) throughout the U.S. As part of an arrestee's voluntary participation in this data gathering process, he or she provided self-report information on drug using behaviors (e.g., timeframes of use, type of drug, frequency) along with a urine specimen for pharmacological testing.[11] Thereafter, these two sources of information were compared at the individual and aggregate levels of analysis in order to estimate the value of self-reported data – to establish levels of confidence in both data readily available for comparison and peripheral information with no external criterion for comparison. As part of such efforts, data from the ADAM program was able to establish that respondent accuracy was often directly associated with the type of drug under consideration (NIJ, 2000, 2001; U.S. Department of Justice, 1990).[12] Such research has produced a variety of

[11] Pharmacological samples underwent testing for ten distinct drugs: marijuana, cocaine, amphetamines, opium, methadone, barbiturates, benzodiazepines, methaqualone, propoxyphene, and PCP.

[12] An analysis of 1990 ADAM data collected in the city of New York revealed high concordance levels between self-report and pharmacological findings for marijuana use (28% self-reported having used versus 30% testing positive for recent marijuana use). Again, this finding was similar in the city of Philadelphia during this same timeframe (28% self-reported having used marijuana versus 32% testing positive for recent use). In contrast to these high levels of convergence, data collected in the city of Houston during the same

findings, ranging from high levels of concordance between self-report and pharmacological findings to high levels of divergence across data sources. In general, differences in the validity of findings have been linked to variables such as setting, race, seriousness of offense, and drug type (Elliott and Voss, 1974; Huizinga and Elliott, 1986; Thornberry & Krohn, 2000).[13]

As has previously proven to be the case regarding the use of the self-report methodology in the general social sciences, and again in the criminological literature, research involving drug use employing this data collection technique has also found that individual and case level differences across respondents (e.g., race, seriousness of offense, drug type) as well as the environment in which self-report data was collected may potentially influence the validity of research findings (Tyon, 1988). Unlike the previous subjects under consideration, the study of drug use, and especially drug abuse, brings with it additional limitations. Specifically, research has regularly found prevalence estimates of alcohol and other drug use among adult arrestees and adjudicated inmates to be consistently high – typically falling between 60 and 75% (National Institute of Justice, 1998, 1999, 2000, 2001, 2001a, 2001b, 2002, 2002a). Moreover, the documentation of such high rates of substance abuse and dependence disorders have been established in the majority of inmates in correctional populations in the United States and other countries (Kouri, Pope, Powell, & Oliva, 1997; Peters et al., 1998). It is important to note that, according to the

---

time period evidenced a vast discrepancy between data provided via self-report (15%) and that produced by means of pharmacological analyses (43%) regarding marijuana use.

[13] When discussing data collected and comparatively analyzed as part of the DOJ NIJ's ADAM/DUF (Drug Use Forecasting) program, Thornberry & Krohn (2000) stated "The data collected in DUF differ considerably from those collected in typical self-report surveys. The sample is limited to people just arrested, who then are asked to provide self-incriminating evidence to a research team while in a central booking station. How this setting affects the results is not entirely clear. On the one hand, individuals are likely to be reluctant to provide additional self-incriminating evidence after having just been arrested. On the other hand, if one has just been arrested for a serious crime…admitting to recent drug use may not be considered a big deal. In any event one has to be cautious in using these data to generalize to the validity of typical self-report inventories" (p. 57).

American Psychiatric Association's DSM-IV diagnostic criteria, drug use does not automatically constitute abuse or dependence on a drug (American Psychiatric Association, 1994). As a result, general prevalence levels established via official records and/or pharmacological data are often inappropriately cited. This is simply because these types of data are not able to assess "need for treatment," rather they are limited to simply establishing recent drug use (Miller & Lazowski, 1999). Furthermore, because of the complexity of addiction and associated diagnostic practices, straightforward self-report data extracted from respondents answering a single question such as "Are you currently in need of drug treatment?" would also not be sufficient for arriving at a finding of "need for treatment." Rather, as self-report methodology had proven valuable in generating insights into drug taking behaviors, this technique was next used in combination with clustered questions (screening instruments) in order to provide early insights into mental health syndromes (drug abuse and dependency disorders).

The Next Evolution – Screening via the Self-Report Methodology

> Self-report instruments are the most convenient and widely used forms of substance use assessment.
>
> (Richter & Johnson, 2001, p. 1)

Following the evolution of self-report methodology being employed in research on drug use as it relates to crime and criminality, this technique was next more fully considered within the criminal justice venue with respect to screening arrestees and inmates for "need for treatment." The assessment of personality, affect, attitudes, attributions, behavior, character, cognitive styles, emotion, temperament, values, and other psychological and personological aspects of individuals within the criminal justice system have represented significant domains of research for informing treatment modalities and institutional practices. Self-report has traditionally been the principal method for the assessment of personality (Angleitner & Wiggins, 1986). Research employing self-report methodology has directly advanced researchers' understanding of characteristics such as depression, anxiety, loneliness, self-concept, and other dimensions of the self that involve subjective feelings and self-evaluation (Reynolds, 1993). Therefore, the addition of diagnostic assessments for "need for treatment" within this unique population was the next natural application of self-report methodology. Many features of an individual's mental state are, to a great degree, subjective and therefore necessitate a domain for which self-report is the primary modality. Thus, it is here, with the assessment of an individual's "need for treatment," that self-report methodology provides a unique perspective and information about substance use and abuse in criminal justice populations.

Scope of the Problem

In order to more fully understand the growing necessity in criminal justice venues for the deployment of empirically grounded and valid diagnostic instrumentation based on self-report methodology, it will be necessary to first consider the scope of the problem. Research addressing criminal justice interactions with those who have a mental illness – with special attention on drug abuse and dependency disorders – is extensive and primarily centers on the institutions and practices of policing, jails, and prisons. Research has found that 7% of police contacts reported by major police departments involved mentally ill individuals in crisis (Deane, Steadman, Borum, Veysey, & Morrissey, 1998). In a similar instance, results from a survey drawing on a sample of police officers (n = 450) from 3 U.S. cities found that in the prior 30 days those surveyed had, on average, responded to 6 calls involving a mentally ill individual in crisis (Borum, Deane, Steadman, & Morrisey, 1998). With respect to detention centers, jails, and prisons, national research data has reported that between 6% and 15% of all detention/jail inmates and 10% to 15% of prison inmates presented with a severe mental illness (Lamb & Weinberger, 1998). Research has indicated that approximately 70% of mentally ill detainees also presented with a co-occurring (co-morbid) drug and/or alcohol abuse problem (Teplin, 1994; Abram and Teplin, 1991). Finally, researchers (Torrey et. al., 1993) have held that "since mentally ill individuals are admitted to jails at approximately eight times the rate at which they are admitted to public psychiatric hospitals, there are now more people with severe mental illness in U.S. jails than in state hospitals" (Broner, Borum, Whitmire, and Gawley, 2002, p. 290).

With these types of research findings representing the bulk of the literature, it becomes self-apparent that in order for effective management of these issues to be established to address such "at-risk" populations, the development of systematic evidence-based processes to screen for drug and alcohol disorders is necessary. With the immense populations and limited resources available to law enforcement institutions, the practice of triaging and classifying inmates might best be initiated by screening instruments grounded in self-report methodology. To this end, researchers have held that "self-report instruments are the most convenient and widely used forms of substance use assessment" (Richter & Johnson, 2001, p. 1). Unfortunately, this statement may not have yet grown to encompass the criminal justice populations as, "there are currently few jurisdictions that systematically screen for mental health problems [to include drug and alcohol disorders] upon arrest, prior to or following the arraignment process, or upon entrance into the jails" (Broner, Borum, Whitmire, and Gawley, 2002, p. 291).

Development of Self-Report-Based Screening Instruments

Employment of the self-report methodology within the general population as a means of gathering information on the assessment of psychological characteristics is not a recent development. In the early twentieth-century (1920s and 1930s), a series of multidimensional self-report measures of adjustment (e.g., Minnesota Multiphasic Personality Inventory – MMPI) were developed for application (Atkinson, Zibin, & Chuang, 1997) across an array of audiences drawn from the general population – adults, adolescents, and children. Many of these emerging practices were driven by the mental hygiene movement of the time which, as a bi-product, spurred the advancement of various psychological self-report-based measures for use by psychologists, counselors, teachers, and various other mental health professionals (Reynolds, 1993). While the development of measures grounded in self-report methodology continued throughout the twentieth-century, the impetus behind this progress changed from advancing a social movement to serving as a response to declining interests in "projective measures" (La Greca, 1990; Mills, 1999; Watson & Evans, 1990).[14]

[14] The psychological schools of Behaviorism (advanced by such researchers as Ivan Pavlov, John B. Watson, S. Smith Stevens, Clark Hull, Edward C. Tolman, and B.F. Skinner) grew to influence the methodologies used for the gathering of data from the early 1900s (rooted strongly in Watson's 1913 manifesto, "Psychology as the Behaviorist Views It") through its peak in the

Various researchers have agreed that while the value and use of measures grounded in self-report methodology have historically advanced and declined, it is likely that the enhanced interest in this method for gathering data was in part due to an appreciation of the limitations of behavioral assessment (much like the limitations of official data were understood in the social sciences during this same time period), coupled with the recognition of cognitions as a significant component for understanding the individual (Hilgard, 1989; Reynolds & Stark, 1983).

Screening Charges and Challenges

In the context of the current research, *screening* may be defined as "a preliminary evaluation that attempts to measure whether key or critical features of the target population area are present in an individual" (Winters & Zenilman, 2000, p. 3). The use and challenge of the self-report screening methodology has been to establish its efficacy for assessment of behaviors related to alcohol and drug use employing only a brief set of questions. More specifically, the chief concern has been the early detection of dependence, or the high probability of dependence, as this disorder has been held to be *the* most distinct condition by research on diagnostic typologies (Gastfriend, Najavits, & Reif, 1994; Hasin, Li, McCloud, & Endicott, 1996; Hasin, Van Rossem, McCloud, & Endicott, 1997; Winters & Zenilman, 2000). It is important to note that screening protocols are not intended to produce diagnosis, rather, they are charged with "flagging" individuals who need further assessment (Winters & Zenilman, 2000).[15] Researchers have held that,

---

1940s and 1950s, when it "reigned supreme in American psychology" ("Behaviorist," 1999, ¶ 5). However, in the 1960s the influence of Behaviorism on data collection techniques began to wane with the coming of the "cognitive revolution" (advanced by researchers like Piaget and Chomsky). To a great extent, researchers have held that Behavioristic theories were overly simplistic and inadequate, and psychologists sought something more to explain the complexity of the human condition (American Psychological Association, 1999).

[15] In contrast, comprehensive assessments are conducted by mental health professionals (rather than lay screening staff) for the specific purpose of establishing diagnosis. Moreover, this practice is informed by thorough

> ...the primary goal of an effective screening instrument is to identify the largest possible proportion of people who are likely to have a disorder. As a result, the number of people flagged will be somewhat over-inclusive. That is, although most of the people with a disorder will be flagged by the instrument, some of those flagged will be found not to have a disorder during a subsequent comprehensive assessment (Broner, Borum, Whitmire, & Gawley, 2002, p. 292).

In addition to providing diagnostic information on an individual respondent, the aggregate examination of screening instrument results might also provide estimates of prevalence rates for a particular population. As previously discussed, unlike recent use, dependence cannot be verified by a chemical assay test. Rather, self-report of behaviors and experiences are necessary to establish a diagnosis for addictions (Gastfriend, Najavits & Reif, 1994). Therefore, establishing dependence – the high probability of "need for treatment" – has also been more likely to substantiate the allocation of treatment resources at the individual-level of analysis, while simultaneously providing relevant data at the aggregate level that may influence specific issues related to correctional institutional management, as well as more far reaching criminal justice policies and practices.

Social Forces and the Enhanced Use of Self-Report-Based Screening

Although many self-report inventories and scales have been developed to assess an individual's need for substance abuse treatment, for the most part, these measures have not been specifically created for application within institutionalized criminal justice venues (Winters & Zenilman, 2000). Rather they have typically been engineered for primary application within the general population and are thereafter simply applied within criminal justice settings – most often without any pilot testing, modifications, or norming of the instrument(s). A reported weakness of most prior screening instruments used within criminal justice institutionalized populations has been that they were not well linked either to contemporary criminological theory or to the empirical

---

structured assessment methods and collateral and self-report information, in part informed by any "screening" information available to be integrated by the assessor (Peters & Hills, 1999; Spitzer, 1983; Steadman, Morris, & Dennis, 1995; Winters & Zenilman, 2000).

literature on the validation of risk factors (Brennan, 1987, 1993; Jones, 1994). Screening instruments are more useful when systematically linked to the major theories of criminality and current empirical research findings. This in turn assists users in making more sense of screen findings, developing clearer explanations, and selecting the most appropriate interventions.

The evolution of screening instruments, like those under consideration in the current study, in part came about in the early 1990s as the result of increased scrutiny by the U.S. Congress, which asked the Institute of Medicine (IOM) (1990) to study treatment services for persons with substance problems (Gastfriend, Najavits, & Reif, 1994).

> The IOM study noted…two questions that juxtapose costs and quality concerns: first, how to ensure that the sick receive needed medical care without spending so much that other social objectives are compromised; and, second, how to discourage unnecessary and inappropriate use of medical services without jeopardizing access to needed, high-quality care. The committee's report (IOM, 1990) defined a need for improvements in pretreatment assessment of alcohol problems as a means of facilitating appropriate treatment decisions (Gastfriend, Najavits & Reif, 1994, p. 1).

To this congressionally sponsored edict to the medical community, additional pressures were added as a result of the "War on Drugs." Here, efforts by law enforcement and government officials to address the growing drug epidemic had, as a by-product, generated growing awareness surrounding the subject of drug abuse and dependency. It became understood that criminal justice populations presented high prevalence rates for drug misuse and, as a result, much emphasis began to be placed on the use of screening instruments in these populations (Winters & Zenilman, 2000). Akin to this phenomenon, an exponentially increasing incarceration rate, beginning in the early 1980s, demanded a greater understanding of drug issues, and specifically called for a more efficient methodology by which to allocate the limited resources available for treatment. Within this increasingly crowded criminal justice system, brevity, efficiency, ease of administration, and the clear organization of key risk-needs data became critical.

Next, other historical pressures that certainly influenced the development of screening protocols included consideration and experimentation with "alternative" institutional philosophies across the criminal justice system. Throughout the 1990s, there was convincing evidence of practices within the criminal justice system having been influenced by an integration of the "Harm Reduction" and/or "Public Health" models (e.g., drug court, alternatives to incarceration). Finally, following the inception and effective utilization of self-report screening instruments as a means to triage cases in the medical and psychiatric communities (the Medical Model), their use also began to become progressively more widespread as standardized screening instruments within the criminal justice system.

Advantages of Using Screening Instrumentation

> Formal screening instruments may provide the standardization and credibility necessary for effective negotiation of treatment planning resources.
>
> (Gastfriend, Najavits, & Reif, 1994, p. 2)

With the development of uniform screening instruments to assess an individual's "need for treatment," several advantages over conventional clinical interviews have been realized. Specifically, valid screening instruments provide the opportunity for standardized inquiries, comprehensive coverage of essential criterion, quantification of collected information, and standardization of the interpretations of the data. Many researchers have gone as far as suggesting that objective statistical assessments were generally superior to human expert judgment (Grove & Meehl, 1996; Meehl, 1965; Swets, Dawes, & Monahan, 2000). Errors of classification, particularly false positive errors, are quite often lower with statistical procedures, which remain one of the primary reasons for their superiority over human judgment (Gottfredson, 1987).

> Assessments without instruments cannot provide these features, because interviewers may vary widely in study (e.g., use of open versus closed-ended questions), areas of inquiry (e.g., severity of substance dependence versus psychopathology), depth of inquiry (superficial screening in

> some areas versus detailed probing in others), units of measure (e.g., severity of drug use may be measured in terms of quantity, frequency, recency, and/or expenditures); most importantly, interviewers may vary widely in the assumptions they employ in interpreting test results (Gastfriend, Najavits and Reif, 1994, p. 1).

To the apparent advantages presented to researchers and institutional decision makers, there is also the innate advantage related to who may administer such an instrument. Most screening instruments have been designed for use by a wide variety of service providers, to include lay staff with minimal training. This attribute of the screening process allows for this practice to occur in the absence of highly trained (and typically highly paid) medical or psychiatric professionals, thereby reducing necessary resources. As the screening process is designed to delineate individuals who have a "high probability of need for treatment" from those who do not, here again, a cost savings might be realized as individuals are triaged to treatment modalities more efficiently.

Finally, research has provided evidence that self-report screening information can augment official data in predicting violent and general criminal recidivism (Motiuk, Motiuk, & Bonta, 1992). Self-report screening information may also serve to fill in data gaps that typically exist in official records, and to ensure greater objectivity by offsetting potential official biases.

Cautions Regarding the Use of Self-Report-Based Screening Instrumentation

Over the course of the 1990s to the present, the literature has increasingly acknowledged that the validity of report measures were matters of degree rather than absolute properties of a measuring device (Barbor, Brown, & Del Boca, 1990; Del Boca & Noll, 2000). While the goal of objectivity has been advanced in the scoring of assessment instrumentation derived from projective procedures (Exner & Weiner, 1982)[16], "interpretation is, in most cases, largely based on dynamic

[16] Projective procedures are intended to result in the respondent being unable to influence the meanings attributed by the interpreter.

interpretation of scores as "signs" of underlying psychological processes and pathologies...there are numerous issues specific to the validity and utility of self-report as a general assessment methodology" (Reynolds, 1993, p. 99; Epstein, 1979; Groves & Meehl, 1996; Meehl, 1965). In Meehl's (1954, 1965) research conducted some four decades ago, he made innovative efforts to understand the comparative efficacy of "human judges" in combining information to that of formalized ("mechanical," "statistical") procedures. While throughout his research Meehl (1965) held that "investigations involving several clinicians characteristically show significant differences in predictive skill," (p. 31) he nonetheless acknowledged some advantages to clinically grounded judgments.[17] In addition, Meehl (1965) held that:

> A pretty strong case can be made for an overarching decision-policy to predict by actuarial methods (screening instrumentation), except when empirical information is available as to the predictive efficiency of the clinicians functioning in an installation; and the specificity of abilities surely makes it dangerous to assume that these can be assessed by an indirect general method...instead of carrying out a major predictive study on each clinic's personnel. (p. 32)

Notwithstanding such cautions, research has more recently held that "the optimal diagnostic procedure for identifying substance use disorders is a comprehensive assessment conducted by a professional with relevant expertise" (Miller, 1999, p. 57). Researchers here went on to add that such assessments "should include one or more interviews, ideally with good rapport between client and professional. It should also take into account a range of other supportive information sources such as collateral contacts, test reports and legal history" (Miller & Lazowski, 1999, p. 57).

---

[17] In his review of prior research papers (specifically Lindzey) Meehl (1965) acknowledged the value of clinical judgments across unique populations as he stated, "whereas the clinical judges suffered some loss of predictive power in moving [from the student population] to the prisoner population, their attrition was not nearly as great as the attrition suffered by the sign-statistics [screening instruments], which collapsed to a clinically useless magnitude" (p. 29).

Two key validity issues, driven by four epidemiological criteria[18] (Peters, et. al., 2000; Winters & Zenilman, 2000) specific to understanding the strength and accuracy of self-report-based screening instruments include an assessment of this methodology's "sensitivity" and "specificity." Here, sensitivity may be held to be a methodology's ability to identify those individuals who actually are in "need of treatment" (i.e., to avoid false negatives). In opposition to this, specificity involves a methodology's ability to not identify as "in need of treatment" those individuals who are indeed not (i.e., to avoid false positives). Once measurements of sensitivity and specificity have been established for a screening instrument within a specific population, these data may be used to determine the screen's *positive* and *negative predictive value.*[19] Researchers have stated that:

> For any screening instrument to be effectively used, an evaluation of its *predictive value* is critical...should assess the scope and limitations of the instrument and should be carried out in the same manner as that used with clinical tests. One way to determine an instrument's sensitivity, specificity, effectiveness, and facility of use is through field testing...should take into account the prevalence of alcohol and drug abuse...in the population being tested (Winters & Zenilman, 2000, p. 7).

While self-report information derived via diagnostic screening instruments certainly seek to gather and estimate the "objective facts" with the greatest amount of sensitivity, specificity, and accuracy achievable, such endeavors surely suffer from limitations akin to (and probably greater than) verbally self-reported information, as there is no

---

[18] These epidemiological criteria are based on the four categories into which screening results are classified: two types of positive results (true positives and false positives) and two types of negative results (true negatives and false negatives) (Winters & Zenilman, 2000).

[19] Positive predictive value is an epidemiological concept that evaluates the likelihood that a positive test result is truly positive – that the condition is indeed present. Conversely, negative predictive value evaluates the likelihood that a negative result is truly correct – that the condition is indeed absent. "Positive and negative predictive values are determined by a test's sensitivity and specificity, as well as by the prevalence of the condition in the population being evaluated" (Winters & Zenilman, 2000, p. 7).

opportunity to qualify respondent answers by means of this later methodology (Meehl, 1954, 1965). Consider the following commentary regarding the problems associated with verbal self-report information collected within health service venues and focused upon addiction behaviors:

> Respondents may be asked to describe a "typical" or "usual" pattern of consumption, an exercise that may require them to summarize a large number of diverse drinking experiences, few of which may be particularly notable or salient in memory. Similarly, assessments of substance use problems are cognitively demanding in that some instruments call upon the respondent to make attributions regarding the causes of events. It is also important to underscore that response accuracy must be evaluated in terms of the information that the investigator seeks. Thus, specific questions may fail to elicit the data of interest because they are understood differently than intended. In this sense, the actual "facts" may be elusive even under circumstances in which a motivated respondent provides accurate answers to the questions posed (Del Boca & Noll, 2000, p. 348).

Researchers have held that, relative to the accuracy of self-report measures of most human behaviors, the accuracy of self-report responses of "sensitive" behaviors is more uncertain (Richter and Johnson, 2001; Turner, Ku, Rogers, Lindberg, Pleck, & Sonenstein, 1998). "A question is sensitive if it raises concerns about disapproval or other consequences (such as legal sanctions) for reporting truthfully or if the question itself is seen as an invasion of privacy" (Tourangeau, & Smith, 1996, p. 276). Therefore, due to the often uncomfortable nature of the subject matter of drug abuse and dependency, an obvious concern regarding the use of the self-report methodology rests in its potential to under and/or over-estimate the "need for treatment" in some populations, especially those that by their very nature are characteristically resistant to structure and authority (e.g., deviant and criminal populations). Nevertheless, as previous research has demonstrated, potential setting, case, and individual-level variables may influence screen findings; therefore it would seem appropriate to empirically determine which environments and/or types of individuals are more or less likely to misreport their substance use dynamics.

Richter and Johnson (2001) held that developing these understandings "is essential to do in a field such as substance abuse where systematic distortion of the primary dependent variable could create a wholly inaccurate picture of the underlying reality of the behavior being investigated" (p. 5). To this end, "unless the screening process is systematic, the target population may not be identified. As a result, they cannot be diverted into alternative programs or provided effective discharge planning – both of which may reduce recidivism" (Broner, Borum, Whitmire, and Gawley, 2002, p. 291).

Historical Summary

The synopsis of the historical use and development of self-report methodology presented above suggests a number of interesting commonalties and insights across time and over the venues in which it has been employed. First, the evolution of self-report methodology in the social, psychological, and criminological sciences appears to have followed similar timelines in terms of embracing the self-report method as a valuable technique for informing scientific inquiries by accessing otherwise untapped data. It is clear that beginning in the middle twentieth century, in part as a result of multiple "social pressures" and recognized limitations of the scientific data collection methodologies of the era, that self-report methodology was a major focus in the social sciences. By the late twentieth century, such efforts had culminated in the application of self-report-based diagnostic screening instruments applied within special populations (e.g., jails, prisons).

Furthermore, as the use of the self-report methodology progressed, so did its application across various populations and subject matter (e.g., deviant behavior, crime, drug use and abuse). It was this use across multiple settings that brought about the next set of realizations. Namely, it became understood that the role of the environment/setting and population dynamics from which self-report information was gathered might have often influenced the accuracy and value of collected data. Further inquiry revealed that individual and case-level variables may also have played a role in influencing the accuracy of data obtained by means of self-report methodology.

In order to begin exploring these concerns, the next chapter will discuss and define the types of validity of central concern herein.

Subsequently, various potential threats to validity as applicable to self-report methodology will be presented, as well as research strategies that have been previously used to examine such concerns. Finally, a discussion of issues potentially influencing the validity of diagnostic screening data grounded in the self-report methodology and collected from criminal justice populations will be offered.

CHAPTER 3

Self-Report Screening and Issues of Validity

In conjunction with the historical development and progressive applications of self-report methodology and its increased use across time, numerous potential influences requiring further investigation have come to light. Foremost among these is the issue of validity. To this end, the current chapter will explore, define and discuss various types of validity fundamental to the value and use of self-report information. Various threats to the validity of self-report methodology will be reviewed along with research strategies that have previously been employed to examine such concerns. In addition, an analysis of issues potentially influencing the validity of diagnostic screening data grounded in the self-report methodology and collected from criminal justice populations will be presented.

CONCERNS AND THREATS TO VALIDITY REGARDING THE USE OF THE SELF-REPORT METHODOLOGY VIA DIAGNOSTIC SCREENING INSTRUMENTATION

As previously noted, clinical practice and research endeavors have employed numerous methodological procedures (e.g., self-report screens) in attempts to produce a variety of accurate classifications involving criminal justice populations (e.g., "probability of need for treatment"); however, such efforts have often been less than fully successful as a result of the prior quality of data available (e.g., official data, observational information). Next, it was held that data derived by means of self-report methodology had in many cases been able to surmount many of its predecessors' limitations. Following its evolution across multiple populations, venues, and subject matter, self-report methodology arrived in the later twentieth century with its incorporation and use in producing diagnostically-grounded screening data within criminal justice populations. This contemporary practice in turn provided a new means for classification and allocation of institutional resources to address "need for treatment" triaging. Here, as with the previous use of self-report methodology, validity is imperative. Specifically, Gastfriend, Najavits, & Reif (1994) held that a prerequisite for effective treatment planning is the ability to conduct a valid assessment of the patient's illness and needs. With this the case, the need for empirical testing of self-report-based screening practices becomes self-apparent.

It is important to note that while such techniques have seemingly advanced the classification practices within criminal justice institutions, researchers have held that several concerns may affect the validity of such classification efforts, including such issues as: "measurement reliability, base rates (the relative frequency of an event in the study population), selection ratios (the proportion of events identified by the prediction method as belonging to the outcome class), sample representativeness (Meehl, 1965), and cross validation" (Gottfredson, 1987, p. 24). While several of these issues are given tangential attention in the present study, it is the later of these concerns that is the central focus of this research. Specifically, while questions of validity regarding screening data grounded in self-report methodology may be addressed from a variety of perspectives (e.g., content validity – the assessment of the degree to which a measure effectively reflects the full domain, or the full content of a concept being measured) (Carmines & Zeller, 1979), this research effort will focus on the issues of criterion validity and construct validity.

Criterion validity "refers to the relationship between test scores and some known external criterion that adequately indicates the quantity being measured" (Huizinga & Elliott, 1986, p. 308). In the current research effort, an examination (both at the aggregate and individual case levels of analysis) between screen findings and an accepted standard-criterion (clinical psychological assessments) will be conducted in order to assess general criterion validity for this methodological practice. Conversely, construct validity may be understood as "the extent to which the measure being validated is related in theoretically expected ways to other concepts or constructs" (Thornberry & Krohn, 2000, p. 51). To this end, construct validity will be examined herein as a comparison will be conducted between various self-reported data (e.g., frequency of drug use, primary route of drug administration) and screen findings across respondent groupings, to understand the extent to which expected theoretical findings are realized.

Factors Affecting the Validity of Self-Report Screening Data

> Survey researchers have concluded that many factors influence individuals' responses to survey questions, thereby affecting the accuracy or truthfulness of their self-reports, even in so-called "matters of fact." A body of evidence from studies supports this conclusion.
>
> (Wentland & Smith, 1993, p. 3)

While research has provided insights regarding various threats to validity stemming from corollary relationships with respondent attributes and/or settings in which self-report information was gathered, further inquiry throughout the literature has evidenced additional theoretical factors potentially impacting the value of self-report data – response effects.[20] Namely, factors are interaction dynamics that are not directly attributable to the respondent and/or setting but may nevertheless influence the accuracy of self-report information. A variety of factors have been examined with respect to their potential influences on the accuracy of information obtained by self-report methodology. Therefore, the recognition of such factors of potential

---

[20] Researchers often use the term *response effect* to refer to the amount of error in the response to a question associated with a particular factor (Sudman & Bradburn, 1974; Wentland & Smith, 1993).

influence upon self-report-based screening practices would seem prudent. These factors are not limited to, but have included, the particular data-gathering approach used in the survey (Begin & Boivin, 1980; Victorin, Haag-Gronlund, & Skerfving, 1998), question form (Del Boca & Noll, 2000), wording (Mauldin & Marks, 1950; Meyers et al., 1999), order (McFarland, 1981), survey sponsorship (Seltzer, 1983), characteristics and expectations of an interviewer – training and skill, probing answer and coding responses, transmission of biasing cues (Duncan, Rosenberg, & Finkelstein, 1969; Hurtado, 1994; Rosenthal, 1966; Johnson, Fendrich, Shaligram, Garcy, & Gillespie, 2000; Jones & Cooper, 1971; Magura, Goldsmith, Casriel, Goldstein, & Lipton, 1987; See & Ryan, 1998; Singer, Frankel, & Glassman, 1983; Willis, 1997), time interval considered for assessment (e.g., frequency of substance use during the past 30 days vs. the past year) (Gray, 1955), communication of the purpose of the assessment (e.g., triage to treatment, program evaluation, scientific research), format and mode of administration (e.g., personal interview, paper-and-pencil questionnaire, computer-assisted assessment)[21], procedures used to elicit information (e.g., clarity of instructions, sequencing of questions), type of information requested (salient, rare events vs. everyday occurrences; well-defined events versus ambiguous or subjectively defined states such as intoxication), complexity and duration of the task, number and range of response options (Del Boca & Noll, 2000), the extent of confidentiality implied in the procedure and the likelihood of future verification – anonymous versus identifiable (Malbin & Moskowitz, 1983), and the level of threat to the respondent posed by various types of questions or the sensitivity of the subject (Locander, Sudman, & Bradburn, 1976).

The current research effort would be remiss if it did not acknowledge the potential influences of the previously mentioned factors recognized throughout the literature as having been theoretically expected to influence the validity of data obtained via self-report; however, such factors are beyond the scope of the current research study. Nonetheless, the assorted testing procedures used to examine such variables as they potentially impacted the validity of self-report

[21] Research has found that respondents tend to report higher levels of socially undesirable or pathological behavior in computer-assisted assessments compared with other self-report methods (Turner et. al., 1998).

information may prove an asset herein. Specifically, both aggregate and individual level examinations of validity have been conducted systematically throughout the literature in an effort to assess issues of validity.

Assessing the Validity of Self-Report Screening Data at the Aggregate Level

Over the years, in an effort to assess the validity of information collected via self-report, researchers have frequently compared results obtained from dissimilar data sources. Such external data have been understood to represent an independent source of information (Gottfredson & Hindelang, 1977). Frequently, these endeavors involved comparing data at the aggregate level of analysis (see discussion in "Self-Report and Deviant Behavior-Crime" in Chapter 2) (Braithwaite, 1981; Elliott, Huizinga, & Morse, 1987; Gove, Hughes, & Geerken, 1985; Hindelang, Hirschi, & Weis, 1979; Hindelang, Hirschi, & Weis, 1981; Hirschi, Hindelang, & Weis, 1980; Thornberry & Farnworth, 1982). Often the central subject matter in such comparisons involved sensitive or threatening topics, such as respondents' involvement in illegal activities (Wentland & Smith, 1993). Because information collected by means other than self-report were capable of providing an independent source of data for comparison, such analyses were held to provide considerable insight into the value of self-report methodology (see discussion in Hindelang, Hirschi, & Weis, 1981, pp. 97-101). Researchers have held that a standard strategy to understand many validity issues (concurrent validity) included the use of multiple indicators (e.g., screening instruments) and multiple risk factors to balance out errors (Brennan, Fretz, & Wells, 2000). Yet another strategy often employed to assess the accuracy of self-report information (construct validity) involved comparing responses across groups known to differ along some specific dimension (e.g., age, education, race).

This same vein of thought served as the impetus for the extension of such examinations – the practice of reviewing aggregated self-report-based screening data against independently-based information (e.g., psychological assessments) (Gastfriend, Najavits, & Reif, 1994; Lazowski, Miller, Boye, & Miller, 1998; Millon, 1997). These objectives have proven to be differentially valuable when employing a self-report screening methodology as compared to that of a clinical judgment by a professional with access to face-to-face interactions and non-verbal information as part of their diagnostic decisions. The importance of clinical judgment is especially noteworthy in assessing individuals with drug use problems as it can assess nonverbal information and as respondents "may be poor historians due to denial, cognitive impairment secondary to their addiction, and feelings of shame and embarrassment about their past" (Gastfriend, Najavits, & Reif, 1994, p. 2).

Using such an aggregated model for examination, a limited amount of research has been conducted regarding the criterion validity of various self-report screening instruments (Gastfriend, Najavits, & Reif, 1994; Lazowski et al., 1998; Millon, 1997). However, it is important to note that while such comparisons across various aggregated data will surely provide important insights into issues of validity, such analyses are not capable of providing insights with respect to the accuracy of an individual's response. This limitation is a result of aggregated data potentially reflecting compensating errors that balance out (Wentland & Smith, 1993). Such a cancellation effect across error types would certainly be problematic; therefore it is essential to the understanding of various screening dynamics that individual-level analyses also be conducted.

Assessing the Validity of Self-Report Screening Data at the Individual Level

Numerous studies, employing a variety of distinct research designs and spanning a considerable array of subject matter, have been conducted in an effort to better understand individual-level response data collected by means of the self-report methodology as it influences issues of validity (Wentland & Smith, 1993). In such cases, information specific to each respondent was acquired (e.g., age, race, gender) and subsequent comparisons to some specified criterion were made in order to determine if any relationship existed between the accuracy of self-report-based data and a particular individual-level attribute. Often such individual-level research has involved sensitive subject matter (e.g., criminal activity, drug misuse) (Wentland & Smith, 1993). For example, with respect to the self-reporting of drug-using behavior, a significant amount of research has been conducted in an effort to more readily identify variables that influence response accuracy (Babor, Stephens & Marlatt, 1987; Babor et. al., 1990; Babor & Del Boca, 1992; Bradburn & Sudman, 1981; Cannell, Miller & Oksenberg, 1981; Del Boca & Noll, 2000; Sudman et. al., 1996). In a similar effort, several large scale research investigations (e.g., Epidemiological Catchment Area Study, National Comorbidity Study), having the capability to focus on specific mental disorders (instead of being limited to global impairment ratings) (Eaton et. al., 1981) have established that persons with different mental disorders tended to have different demographic characteristics, family histories, life events, and neurobiological correlates (Regier et al., 1984).

As the analysis of individual-level variables' impact on the accuracy of data collected by means of self-report proved valuable, it would likewise seem appropriate to extend such an examination to reviewing individual-level case variables' potential influences on self-report-based screen findings. While this type of individual-level investigation has not readily been extended to self-report-based screening data, there have however been a handful of studies examining this gap in the research (Wentland & Smith, 1993). Findings derived from such analyses continue to allow for the discovery of variables potentially correlated with higher levels of self-report screening accuracy, thereby providing insight into future screening instrumentation and practices.

Validity Issues in the Utilization of Self-Report Screening Data with Criminal Justice Populations

While previous sections of this chapter have identified numerous concerns and threats to validity regarding the potential value of screening data grounded in self-report methodology, subsequent discussions must address the special population of concern to this research – criminal populations. Beyond the more general concerns regarding the validity of self-report screening data, numerous issues relate, either directly or indirectly, to the use of this methodology as it is employed in the evaluation of need for substance abuse treatment for individuals housed in the criminal justice system. As has been realized in the prior research on self-report methodology discussed to this point, many of these issues are likely tied to individual or case-level influences, while others may be more related to the restrictive setting itself. In an effort to begin exploring several dynamics that may influence the accuracy of self-report-based screen findings, potentially influential issues and corresponding variables identified in the literature will be reviewed. To achieve this objective, such issues have been organized into subsequent sections of this chapter to include: 1) Evaluation Setting and Psychometric Qualities, 2) Competency and Development, 3) Social Desirability, and 4) Self-Disclosure. Moreover, within each of these sections, both psychological and sociologically oriented variables will be considered. While this review is certainly not exhaustive, it will address a myriad of variables and potential threats to validity that will later be available for testing and further consideration in the current study.

Evaluation Setting and Psychometric Qualities

Psychometric features, such as validity and normative data, are standard attributes and requirements for psychological tests and measures. Such information is fundamental in assessing the value of a self-report screening instrument for research and/or clinical practice (Andrews and Bonta, 1994; Winters and Zenilman, 2000). With this the case, it is essential that researchers and practitioners use instrumentation that has demonstrated significant levels of validity. Researchers have held that the interpretation of validity coefficients is, in part, "a function of the specific construct assessed, the nature of the instrument, the subjects, and the assessment situation" (Reynolds, 1993, p. 105).

For example, an important dynamic in self-report screening activity that has often been significantly influenced by the social environmental context involves the perceived role of the respondent in the question-answering process (Bradburn, 1983). "The question-answering process is embedded within a social context that is governed by prevailing cultural norms, forces associated with the organizational setting in which data are collected, and the constraints of the immediate interpersonal situation. The immediate context may include other people" (Del Boca & Noll, 2000, p. S350). Many contemporary screening instruments used in criminal justice institutionalized populations have been based on measures or constructs that were originally developed for respondents from a different environmental context – the general population. The extent to which these constructs are valid across differing populations and settings is often overlooked or disregarded. Thus, it is reasonable to assume that various institutional and cultural norms (e.g., difficult to recruit respondents – Cottler, Zipp, Robins, & Spitznagel, 1987) and task demands may influence the accuracy and value of self-report-based screening data. It is therefore imperative that, prior to its formal application, the self-report screening methodology be empirically tested and examined for threats to validity specific to the unique venue in which it is to be employed – institutionalized criminal justice settings.

A further significant psychometric attribute that deserves attention, but which is frequently overlooked or ineffectually considered, has been that of normative information. Norms are fundamental to the comprehension and proper interpretation of a self-report-based screen finding. Basic features of norms are representativeness and recency (Reynolds, 1993). Norms should be reflective of the population in which an instrument is to be applied. Instrument norming typically involves stratifying or differentiating across variables where significant differences in screen findings have been realized (e.g., demographics, drug use or treatment history, criminal justice experience). A potential exception to this assertion, which may further complicate this issue, may reasonably include the development of norms for clinical phenomena such as drug abuse and dependency. Reynolds (1993) held that:

> For some clinical disorders or problems, we generally consider the severity of symptoms as the primary feature. As an example, we generally find females demonstrating higher scores than males on depression measures. While separate norms for males and females may provide some additional information, the critical issue is not whether the individual is male or female, but the absolute magnitude of the score. To suggest that a score above a critical level for males is not critical for females, because different base rates ignore the reality that both males and females manifesting that level of symptom severity may be depressed. (p. 105)

Beyond the complexities involved in appropriately norming a screening instrument, research has found that the interpretation and explanation of norms grows more perplexing when it is understood that there exists variation in base rates and variability in the distribution of constructs across assorted "domains of personality and problem behavior." Here researchers have held that "statistical procedures used to develop standard score norms generally assume a reasonable degree of normality of raw score distribution. For many clinical disorders, raw score distribution on self-report and other report measures are quite skewed and far from normal" (Reynolds, 1993, p. 104). Therefore, as a result of previously discussed environmental differences, in combination with differences across base rates for various psychopathologies, screening instruments normed for use in the general population should not be deployed in criminal justice populations unless empirical evidence suggests that they present adequate levels of validity.

As previously suggested, recent research has held that the validity of report measures are matters of degree rather than absolute properties of a measuring device (Barbor, Brown & Del Boca, 1990) and that "evaluation of these psychometric qualities depends upon the researchers' purpose and the context within which data are collected" (De. Boca & Noll, 2000, p. 348). Therefore, "the objective of attaining a perfectly valid indicator – one that represents the intended, and only the intended, concept – is unachievable. Instead, validity is a matter of degree, not an all-or-none property" (Carmines & Zeller, 1979, p. 13). With this the case, it is essential that norming information specific to a criminal justice setting be established and further used in the development and deployment of self-report-based screening instruments. The current research will explore potential variables as a means to produce essential "norming information" to inform the development and application of the self-report screening methodology.

Competency and Development

Beyond the issue of a criminal justice setting, many of the concerns surrounding questions of validity with respect to self-report-based screen findings are specific to whether individuals adjudicated into criminal justice populations are readily competent reporters of their feelings, behaviors, attitudes and mental orientations. As such, an individual's intellectual and cognitive functioning plays a central role in delivering valid response data via self-report methodology (Meehl, 1965). Typically, adults housed in criminal justice populations, like individuals in the general population, are understood and expected to possess the skills necessary to effectively respond to self-report queries. Consequently, screen respondents are expected to accurately access and self-report such mental states in accordance with an established response format. This is evidenced by the widespread use of self-report-based screening instruments originally designed for application in the general population as they are employed within institutionalized criminal justice settings (e.g., Substance Abuse Subtle Screening Inventory – SASSI-3).

However, notwithstanding such expectations, criminal justice populations suffer from various shortcomings and deficiencies in competency and intellectual functioning at much higher rates than the general population. For example, issues of illiteracy (Haigler, Harlow, O'Connor, & Campbell, 1994; Stino & Palmer, 1999; Vacca, 2004), language comprehension (Torrens, Serrano, Astals, Perez-Dominguez, & Martin-Santos, 2004), differences in experiential factors (Richter and Johnson, 2001), episodic recall/memory[22] (Babor, Stephens, and Marlatt, 1987, Belli, 1998, Conrad, Brown & Cashman, 1998; Del Boca & Noll, 2000; Hippler, Schwarz, & Sudman, 1987; Spanier, 1976), intelligence level and cognitive impairment (Del Boca and Noll, 2000), and the psychosocial maturity (Reynolds, 1993) required to comprehend and respond appropriately to screening scale content make the express utilization of measures designed for use in the general population potentially inappropriate for institutionalized criminal populations. Research has suggested a number of conditions that may

[22] When considering the role of memory as it may influence the validity of information obtained by means of self-report methodology, Del Boca and Noll (2000) reported, "Recent theorizing regarding the structure of autobiographical memory, that part of memory in which life events are stored, is particularly relevant to understanding the retrieval of information needed to accurately report behaviors such as alcohol consumption and illicit drug use. Cognitive psychologists understand autobiographical memory to be hierarchically arranged with the most general types of memory comprising the top level (Belli, 1998)…the most detailed autobiographical memories make up the bottom level of the hierarchy. These memories are of specific events and are comprised of perceptual and episodic information (e.g., "drinking with the guys at the bar last weekend"). Accessing specific events therefore may require more than one pathway, a thematic pathway (e.g., drinking events) as well as temporal pathways (e.g., sequences of events)" (pp. 352-353).

prove especially relevant to criminal justice populations, and which may further hamper the ability to accurately access and report one's own mental state, to include incorrect adoption of feeling rules (e.g., convincing oneself that they feel happy when in fact the opposite is true), effects of self-analysis (e.g., self-reflection), and the amount and accessibility of processing preceding attitudes (Wilson, 1985).

To the variety of concerns surrounding the issue of competency, numerous developmental concerns must also be taken into account when employing self-report-based screening instruments in criminal justice populations. For example, an individual's cognitive self-awareness and capacity to differentiate between emotions, as well as appreciating that dissimilar, sometimes seemingly contradictory, emotions may occur concurrently is a developmental issue central to one's ability to meaningfully self-report screen information (Reynolds, 1993). The capacity to reliably self-monitor domains such as behavior, cognitions, and feelings is central to the validity of the self-report screening methodology.

In an effort to better understand issues of self-report survey errors, research conducted by Groves (1989) drew data from a variety of disciplines and perspectives in order to consolidate the literatures as they related to different types of survey errors. In his conclusion Groves noted that "cognitive processing appears to be central to survey measurement error" (p. 407). In a more recent review of cognitive functioning as it impacts one's ability to provide valid self-report information, Del Boca & Noll (2000) referenced a study conducted by Babor et al. (1990), stating that:

> The effects of cognitive and communication factors on responses have been extensively studied in recent years (see Sudman et al., 1996 for a review)…research has demonstrated that the cognitive and communication processes involved in answering clinical research questions are similar to those that characterize discourse in everyday social interaction. The respondent must attend to a request for information (attention), interpret the question (comprehension), recall from memory pertinent to drinking behaviors (retrieval), integrate information via comparative, inferential, or attributional processes (integration), and then decide (not necessarily in a

deliberate or conscious manner) how to respond (response selection). (p. S351)

Next, impairments to accurately self-monitoring various symptoms may itself be consistent with some disorders (e.g., drug abuse and dependency) that influence intellectual and cognitive development and have been found to exist at significantly higher rates in criminal justice populations than in the general population (Broner et al., 2002; Regier et al., 1984; Tonry and Wilson, 1990).[23] Research has also demonstrated that for individuals with either an alcohol or other drug disorder, the odds of having a co-morbid mental disorder were seven times greater than for the rest of the population (Broner et al., 2002; Regier et al., 1990).

Further research has regularly indicated that age at onset for many disorders was considerably earlier than had previously been believed (Burke, Burke, Rae, & Regier, 1991); again likely having a significant influence within a criminal justice population. In light of the limitations noted above regarding issues of competency and development, absent evidence-based-research and support specific to criminal justice populations, it would seem prudent that self-report screen measures designed for administration in general populations should be employed with extreme caution or not at all. To this end, data collection completed as part of the current research effort has the capacity to examine a variety of variables (i.e., cognitive functioning, age, education, and age at first drug use) related to competency and development as they may influence the validity of self-report screening data collected on institutionalized criminal justice populations.

---

[23] In a 1990 research finding analyzing data from the Epidemiological Catchment Area Study (ECA), Regier et al. (1990) concluded that although institutionalized populations represent only 1.3% of the total population, they expressed much higher rates of psychopathology than existed within the greater community. Among those institutions included in this same research, prisoners expressed the second highest lifetime rate of any disorder at 82%. This high rate among prisoners was primarily attributed to a remarkably high (72%) lifetime prevalence of substance abuse, in which 56.2% were found to have had an alcohol disorder and 53.7% had another drug disorder.

Social Desirability

In addition to the issues of environmental context and competency, the phenomenon of social desirability has been widely examined as it may affect the validity of self-reports across general social populations (Bauman & Ennett, 1994; Dadds, Perrin, & Yule, 1998; Presser & Stinson, 1998; Wilson, 2003), and to a more limited extent, across criminal justice drug-using populations (Paschall, Ornstein, & Flewelling, 2001; Sloan, Bodapati, & Tucker, 2004). Richter and Johnson (2001) defined social desirability as they held that "respondents tend to respond to self-evaluative questions in a socially approved manner to appear more socially desirable" (p. 811). Johnson and Fendrich (2002) stated that "social desirability is commonly thought of as the tendency of individuals to project favorable images of themselves during social interactions" (p. 1). More specifically, "social desirability operates as an editing process; participants retrieve the requested information and then evaluate it before responding" (Holtgraves, 2004, p. 1).

As such, it is reasonable that under a variety of conditions, individuals may desire to present themselves in a socially desirable light and, as a result, may modify their true responses to seem more acceptable to their audience (Victorin, Haag-Gronlund, & Skerfving, 1998). Conversely, circumstances and respondent motivations may result in counter strategies, where respondents' self-reported information may be engineered to produce a more dysfunctional image in order to achieve some anticipated outcome (Collins, Hubbard, Rachal, Cavanaugh, Craddock, and Kristiansen, 1982). With respect to the current research subject matter addressing self-report-based screening, researchers have also held that this typically would result in an underestimation of substance use (Bradburn, 1983; Schwarz, 1999). Modifying such an expectation, Klein (1989) held that because of the unique venue in which criminal justice is couched, the issue of social desirability produced additional threats to validity that were of concern when employing self-report methodology. Specifically, both under and over-reporting were more likely to be of concern in this population as advantages (enhancing one's self, access to treatment programming) and disadvantages (fear of consequences – legal, institutional, and social) were considered.

In an effort to alleviate or minimize respondents' social desirability from contaminating self-report-based findings, several strategies (e.g., question ordering) and measures have been introduced in an effort to "flag" such issues so that they might be controlled for as part of data analyses (Paulus, 1991). The scale most commonly used for this purpose has been the Marlowe-Crowne Social Desirability Scale (Crowne and Marlowe, 1964).[24] Even with the utilization of such scales, various difficulties in establishing validity have been acknowledged. While social desirability scale findings may provide promising insights into "less than accurate self-reports," controlling for social desirability may also unintentionally interfere with recognizing potentially valuable differentiating information in respondent populations. Research conclusions may also be open to widely divergent interpretations as a result of assumed response biases across respondents' gender, ethnic background (Johnson & Glassman, 1999), and prior experience (Richter & Johnson, 2001). Researchers have also held that responses to social desirability measures may often simply be interpreted as the personality characteristics of "need for approval" (Del Boca & Noll, 2000; Crowne, 1979). In addressing such concerns Richter and Johnson (2001) stated that "by controlling for individual motivations that might affect response styles, the instrument might hide or 'wash out' important cultural or demographic differences in respondents' thoughts, attitudes, or beliefs about the topic under investigation" (p. 811).

The literature has evidenced a number of insights and potential threats to validity with respect to social desirability in providing self-report-based information that may readily translate to diagnostic screen findings. Individual difference variables may confound scores on some measures. In research with hospital inpatient respondent samples, Mabe and Treiber (1989) and Reynolds (1993) found that mental age demonstrated a moderately high correlation with social desirability scores. Specifically, respondents evidencing younger mental ages gave higher socially desirable instrument responses. An indirect application of such findings might be understood for institutionalized criminal justice populations, as high prevalence levels for mental illness and

---

[24] Scores from the Marlowe-Crowne Social Desirability Scale, once established, may be integrated into analyses to control for individual difference in motivation for optimal social presentation.

cognitive deficits have been established (National Comorbidity Study), much of this certainly linked to drug using behaviors.

Another set of potentially confounding variables to establishing validity for self-report screen findings taken from within criminal justice populations may involve respondents' actual drug using dynamics as well as treatment histories. Research has found that an individual's severity of dependence, stage of recovery, and sobriety or withdrawal state may often impact the accuracy of self-reported information regarding drug behaviors (Babor et al., 2000; Brown, Kranzler, & Del Boca, 1992). Sobell and Sobell (1990) found that heavy drinkers tended to underestimate alcohol use when they had a positive blood alcohol level. Research has also suggested that respondents who were recent treatment participants may underreport consumption during evaluations following treatment (Del Boca & Noll, 2000).

The social desirability hypothesis assumes that all respondents, and not just those with a "need for treatment," will find questions about drug using behaviors threatening. While this proposition has not been supported by empirical evidence (Schwarz, 1999), it is nevertheless important to consider in light of the current research effort. In other words, the degree of threat or embarrassment associated with providing information may produce motivations quite different for an institutionalized criminal justice population than anticipated. Moreover, such motivations may be somehow correlated with individual attributes (e.g., age, education, race, religion). In light of such findings, it would seem necessary to empirically establish variables specific to the current research population that may be related to issues of social desirability (e.g., demographics, prior experiences), and as a consequence, impact the validity of the self-report screening methodology.

Self-Disclosure

Unlike social desirability which addresses the manner and related motives from which a respondent presents self-report information, scholars have defined self-disclosure as divulging information to others that they would not normally know, discover, or have readily shared (Borchers, 2005). More specifically, social desirability focuses on how data might be skewed as part of the self-report dynamic, where self-disclosure is principally related to an inmate actually providing self-report information at all. Self-disclosure involves risk and vulnerability on the part of the person sharing the information. The willingness of an inmate housed in the criminal justice system to self-disclose drug using information with respect to themselves, their friends, and family, or other related lifestyle dynamics has not been broadly examined. Across most research venues where data gathering is of central concern, it is unlikely that issues of respondent self-disclosure would present a significant problem, especially as practices of guaranteeing confidentiality/anonymity and assuring data aggregation prior to dissemination of findings has been employed. Research involving less threatening topics or critical findings as perceived by the respondents is also less likely to meet with such dilemmas. On the other hand, in a limited number of unique settings, such as those found within the criminal justice system, with respect to particular subject matters (e.g., criminal or deviant behaviors), a respondent's willingness to self-report possibly “self-damaging” information may present a significant concern (Feucht, Stephens, & Walker, 1994; Mieczkowski, Barzelay, Gropper, & Wish, 1991). Therefore, while such concerns are universal when gathering self-report information from respondents, it is in this unique setting and population dynamic that a respondent’s willingness to self-disclose drug-using information may pose the greatest threats to validity.

Researchers (Babor & DelBoca, 1992; Babor, Steinberg, Anton, & Del Boca, 2000; Broner, Borum, Whitmire, & Gawley, 2002; Klein, 1989; Wentland & Smith, 1993) have held that despite the apparent success of self-report-based questionnaires and screening instruments across various research subjects, there are significant problems in the use of this method to collect such personal information. In support of this notion, Thornberry and Krohn (2000) held that “based on the results of the [self-report based] tests of criterion validity [across various criminological data], there appears to be a substantial degree of either concealing or forgetting past criminal behavior” (p. 58).

To this end, researchers have suggested some linkage between respondent characteristics and their attitudes and beliefs. Specific to the current review of self-reported drug use/misuse, Del Boca and Noll (2000) suggested that beliefs regarding the causes and consequences of addiction may be linked to respondent characteristics. Moreover, these researchers held that the processes involved in motivation and denial may be linked to a respondent's willingness to self-disclose drug-using information, as by its nature denial is thought to distort the accuracy of information about drug use. In another setting, reporting on research on suicidal ideation in adolescents who had recently attempted suicide, Reynolds (1993) found that a number of hospitalized youth had self-reported low levels of ideation and, in follow-up information, indicated that their belief was that if they had self-reported that they had actually continued to think about suicide that they would not have been discharged. Reynolds stated that "this example illustrates how situational factors may limit or result in a lack of self-disclosure" (p. 105).

Beyond those propositions and instances previously mentioned as potentially providing insight into self-disclosing behaviors, it would seem reasonable to expect, that within an institutionalized criminal justice setting, a respondent's drug use dynamics (e.g., drug of choice, frequency of drug use, and route of administration) (Sloan et al., 2004; Paschall et al., 2001) and/or treatment history (e.g., substance abuse and/or mental health treatment, support group experiences) (Del Boca and Noll, 2000) along with previous experiences with the criminal justice system (e.g., prior lifetime incarcerations, number of adult incarcerations, current offense and sentence dynamics, institutional misconduct), would be especially relevant to self-disclosing practices. With this the case, it is essential that such considerations be empirically examined for influences on validity impacting self-report-based screening methodology.

SUMMARY

As this research has evidenced thus far, the self-report methodology has been used in diagnostic screening instruments to assess individuals in need of treatment since the later part of the twentieth century. The employment of self-report methodology has a deep history rooted in the psychological and social sciences; thereafter branching across time to arrive at incorporation within a variety of criminal justice practices to include screening for "need for treatment" in institutionalized populations. As part of this evolution and application across each new and more sensitive environment, an accumulation of progressive threats to validity also became apparent. Nevertheless, self-report screening as used within criminal justice venues provides for a rich source of data.

In reality, no self-report measure is infallible. Some measures are better than others, and some individuals are better than others at self-reporting their own thoughts, feelings, beliefs, behaviors, experiences, and psychological states. The use of institutionally housed individual criminals' self-reports for screening purposes should be tempered with respect to the evaluation setting, population under review, cognitive level of the respondent, social influences impacting response dynamics, willingness to self-disclose, and the accessibility and value of independent sources of data. Considering such innate limitations when gathering self-report-based screening data on prior experiences of substance use, it is easily foreseeable that errors in reporting (intentional or not) may lead users of such information to arrive at erroneous conclusions with respect to an individual's level of substance use and/or "need for treatment." Beyond the problematic use of this information at the individual level of analysis, such data could also negatively impact the building and evaluation of theoretical understandings. For example, invalid data might play a role in impeding a valuable understanding of the mechanisms fundamental to addiction as well as the dynamics of the self-report screening process itself.

All users of self-report screening data obtained from criminal justice institutionalized populations must be aware of the upper boundaries to the validity and accuracy of such information. As Hammond (1996) held, virtually all "indicators" are fallible to some degree. Researchers have acknowledged that data derived by means of self-report methodology are certainly available for critique as a result of "known contaminations" to self-report screening measures (Spector, 1994). However, many of these same authors have quickly pointed out that the fallibility of the self-report methodology is not in itself a cogent critique. Rather, it is important that possible threats to the validity of information grounded in self-report methodology be fully explored in order to arrive at a more accurate understanding of the screening data produced.

In support of this notion, Wentland and Smith (1993) held that much could be learned from a systematic examination and quantitative assessment of aggregated self-report data, as these might reveal patterns and help identify variables potentially affecting response accuracy. Here, the researchers drew heavily on studies and theories in the cognitive and social-psychological literature in order to begin identifying possible variables of influence on the self-report methodology.

While research reviewed as part of this chapter has repeatedly held that validity is not an absolute, understanding the degree to which various influences may pose threats to validity is nevertheless essential in developing, interpreting, and deploying self-report-based instrumentation. It is important to note that in the sections of this chapter, various issues were used as organizational tools by which to consider potential variables of influence upon the validity of self-report screening practices in institutionalized criminal justice venues. The current research will not attempt to specifically test such issues in and of themselves, but rather variables available for consideration herein and proving to impact validity may subsequently be discussed within such frameworks.

Research Purpose

The purpose of this study is to attempt to assess the utility of self-report screening instrumentation as an effective methodological tool for producing valid data regarding drug and alcohol disorders within institutionalized criminal justice venues – specifically, incoming prison populations. Because little research has directly addressed the general validity of self-report screening methodologies in these special populations, this study will use various data drawn from prison populations in order to accomplish such goals. Questions to be addressed in this research endeavor include: 1) Do screening instrument findings derived via self-report methodologies generate high levels of confidence (i.e., criterion validity, construct validity, and efficacy) when compared to forensic clinical psychological assessments, and 2) Does the value of the self-report screening methodology vary based on case attributes (i.e., demographics, cognitive functioning, drug use history, treatment history, criminal justice experiences)? While the current research is limited in its ability to fully estimate the value of the self-report screening methodology as it might be administered throughout the entire criminal justice system (e.g., probation, court settings, jails, detention centers, community corrections, parole), it does however begin to examine its possible utility with regard to institutionalized prison populations.

How is this Research Different?

Previous evaluations of self-report-based screening instruments have typically involved the testing of individual screens, rather than the underlying methodology itself. However, the testing of individual screening instruments has not been able to readily evaluate the aggregate validity of self-report-based screen findings, nor have such evaluations been able to address the common institutional practice of utilizing and consulting multiple screening instruments. When such evaluations are offered in the literature, they tend to employ relatively "weak" criterion measures, typically other DSM-IV-based self-report instruments. Finally, "most studies in this area were not designed to test directly hypotheses (atheoretical) regarding the utility of different assessment approaches. Rather, they have involved secondary analyses of data originally collected for different purposes" (Del Boca & Noll, 2000, p. 349).

Therefore, in order to address these gaps in the research, the current study employs a "meta-method" examination to assess issues of aggregate convergent validity between self-report screen findings and an optimal independent external criterion – forensic clinical psychological findings. Specifically, the culmination of three self-report-based screening instruments logistically available and serendipitously designed for different audiences and used within the Nebraska state prison system (Diagnostic Evaluation Center) to provide insights to institutional decisions are used. Employing this methodology, this study additionally examines theoretical relationships (construct validity) between screen outcomes and various indexes of substance misuse. Finally, individual and case level variables are analyzed against cumulative screen scores in order to ascertain potential variables influencing the validity of such findings.

Significance

To this point, the research literature has identified a variety of insights and limitations regarding the use of self-report-based information as it has developed with respect to each new application and venue in which it was used. However, as self-report-based information has begun to be used in a very critical mode – to screen individuals housed in institutional criminal justice settings for "need for treatment" – it is essential that a more in-depth understanding of potential threats to validity be developed. It is therefore anticipated that the current research effort will prove significant in that it produces an examination of a specific and unique sub-population which is beginning to heavily employ the use of the self-report screening methodology for variables of potential influence on self-report-based diagnostic screen outcomes. Moreover, as a result of aggregating a battery of self-report screen findings for criterion comparison, this research provides insight into the value of the self-report screening methodology overall. Finally, research findings may provide practical insights into evidence-based-policy for researchers and institutions involved in the designing, interpretation, and deployment of self-report-based screening instruments.

CHAPTER 4

Examining the Validity of Self-Report Screening in Prisons

This study attempts to assess the utility of self-report screening instrumentation as an effective methodological tool for producing valid data regarding drug and alcohol disorders within institutionalized criminal justice venues – specifically, incoming prison populations. Because to date, little research has directly addressed the general validity of the self-report screening methodology in these special populations, this study will use various data drawn from prison populations in order to accomplish this goal. Questions to be addressed in this research include: 1) Do screening instrument findings derived via self-report methodologies generate high levels of confidence (i.e., criterion validity, construct validity, and efficacy) when compared to forensic clinical psychological assessments; and 2) Does the value of the self-report screening methodology vary based on case attributes (i.e., demographics, cognitive functioning, drug use history, treatment history, criminal justice experiences)? While the current research is limited in its ability to fully estimate the value of the self-report screening methodology as it might be administered throughout the entire criminal justice system (e.g., probation and parole venues, court settings, jails, detention centers, community corrections institutions), it will, however, begin to examine its possible utility with regard to institutionalized prison populations.

The current study affords data to make quantified statistical comparisons between multiple diagnostic screening instruments generated via self-report methodology (i.e., the Simple Screening Instrument – SSI, the Substance Abuse Subtle Screening Inventory – SASSI-3, the 31 Question Substance Abuse Treatment Oriented Program Instrument – 31 Question SATOP), forensic clinical psychological assessments, a variety of other indexes of substance misuse, and variables gathered across inmate sample cases. These comparisons were conducted to establish the cumulative validity of screening instruments utilizing the self-report methodology as a means of generating diagnostic screening measures (i.e., case probability scores) for substance disorders within the criminal justice system. Following the inception and effective utilization of screening instruments as a means to triage cases in the medical and psychiatric communities, their use has become progressively more widespread as standardized screening instruments within the criminal justice system. However, notwithstanding the growing subscription in use of self-report screening instruments, there still remain questions regarding the validity of this methodology, especially as applied within criminal justice venues. In order to address such questions, data was collected on incoming prisoners from the state of Nebraska Department of Corrections (DOC) Diagnostic Evaluation Center (DEC) throughout the year 2001. Because data was collected on multiple screening instruments across all cases reviewed, the author was able to generate multiple data sets, each capable of providing some insight into the validity and influences on the screening instrument outcomes collected via self-report methodology.

Chapter Organization

The current chapter has been organized into three primary sections in order to facilitate the communication of research steps, methodological choices, and study rationales. First, general research questions and their related null hypotheses are presented along with the overall research design. The second primary section of this chapter provides insight into proposed data collection procedures, standards, and instrumentation. In addition, a discussion of indexes of substance misuse and case variables of central focus herein has been provided. To conclude, section three of this chapter demonstrates the various applications of research analyses to respective data. Specifically, the anticipated evaluation, analysis, scoring, and organization of self-report screening data is described and the subsequent means to be used in order to examine variable influences upon the validity of self-report methodologies is demonstrated.

Research Hypotheses

In order to begin to address the general research questions by means of a scientifically rigorous methodology, it is necessary to first delineate the specific null hypotheses to be tested. Therefore, listed below are the two primary research questions, each subsequently followed by their respective null hypotheses.

Research Question 1

Do screen findings derived via self-report methodologies in criminal justice institutionalized settings generate high levels of confidence (i.e., criterion validity when compared to forensic clinical psychological assessments, efficacy of findings, and construct validity as compared to other indexes of substance misuse)?

Null Hypotheses 1 thru 8 and Queries 1 thru 5

H1: Diagnostically based screen instrument findings (pooled scores produced by the screening instruments listed below) collected via self-report methodology within an institutional criminal justice venue do not significantly differ from findings derived via forensic clinical psychological assessments.

A. The Substance Abuse Subtle Screening Inventory (SASSI-3)
B. The 31 Question Substance Abuse Treatment Oriented Program Screen (31 Q. SATOP)
C. The Simple Screening Instrument (SSI)

Q1-5: What are the associated levels of efficacy (individually listed below) of diagnostically based screen instrument findings (pooled scores from the SASSI-3, 31 Q. SATOP, and the SSI) collected via self-report methodology within an institutional criminal justice venue?

Q1. Specificity
Q2. Sensitivity
Q3. Positive Predictive Power (PPP)
Q4. Negative Predictive Power (NPP)
Q5. Accuracy

H2-8: Diagnostically based screen instrument findings (pooled scores from the SASSI-3, 31 Q. SATOP, and the SSI) collected via self-report methodology within an institutional criminal justice venue do not demonstrate general theoretical support via construct validity when compared to other indexes (individually listed below) of substance misuse.

H2. Age of first drug use
H3. Frequency of drug use (i.e., daily, weekly, monthly)
H4. Primary route of drug administration (i.e., swallow, smoke, snort, injection)
H5. Previous substance abuse treatment
H6. Under the influence at time of arrest
H7. Current offense dynamics (e.g., drug related)
H8. Institutional misconduct specific to use of drugs

Research Question 2

Does the value of the self-report screening methodology administered in criminal justice institutionalized settings vary based on case attributes?

Null Hypotheses 9 thru 14

H 9-14: Case variables (listed below) do not significantly influence the validity of diagnostic screen instrument findings (pooled scores from the SASSI-3, 31 Q. SATOP, and the SSI) collected via the self-report methodology in criminal justice institutionalized venues.

H9. Demographics (i.e., age, race, education, marital status, religious affiliation, employment status)
H10. Intellectual Functioning (cognitive functioning typology)

H11. Drug Use History (i.e., age of first drug use, current primary drug of choice, frequency of drug use, primary route of drug administration)

H12. Treatment History (i.e., previous substance abuse treatment, previous mental health treatment, current community-based support)

H13. Criminal Justice Experiences (i.e., prior lifetime incarceration, number of prior adult incarcerations, current offense, current minimum/maximum sentence length, institutional misconduct)

H14. Indexes of Substance Misuse (i.e., under the influence at time of current offense

Research Design

This study employs cross-sectional analyses of secondary data – institutional inmate cases. While a cross-sectional study typically lacks the ability to generalize phenomena to a population over a long period of time, researchers (Campbell & Stanley, 1963; Hagan, 1997; Maxfield & Babbie, 1995; Neuman, 2000; Palys, 1997) have held that this methodological approach is extremely discerning for exploratory studies such as the one conducted herein.

Another principal gain of employing cross-sectional analyses in the current study involved the ability to compile and examine information regarding feasible similarities and/or differences between various data groupings (e.g., instrumentation indicating different diagnostic outcomes), with the prospect that further research ideas may have emerged. As previously mentioned, other advantages of using this method are that the study was expeditious, more economical, and required relatively fewer participants than other research designs (Babbie, 1992). One disadvantage of applying this design was that the researcher had to, in large part, depend on written reports produced by institutional personnel, allowing for the possibility of introducing some amount of bias into the research data. Other obstacles included the dilemma of properly segregating data into groups to be compared, and the challenge of controlling for extraneous variables.

DATA COLLECTIONS

Institutional Review Board Procedures Used

In November of 2001, The University of Nebraska Medical Center's (UNMC) Institutional Review Board (IRB) granted permission to conduct the current research (IRB #377-01-FB). Subsequently, the criminal justice institutions involved in this research endeavor were contacted to make them aware of the study's intentions and to receive proper permissions to access relevant populations and their corresponding data (State of Nebraska Department of Corrections – Diagnostic Evaluation Center). As required by IRB protocol, each institutional entity involved was provided with information regarding a) the purpose of the study, b) identification of the Principal Investigator (PI) for security clearance purposes, c) assurances that would be taken to ensure confidentiality of case file information, and d) the data collection procedures and corresponding timelines necessary to properly collect and house the information into data sets. In addition, the primary investigator agreed to make available research findings and/or to answer any questions or concerns of those institutions providing study data.

Data Collection Procedures

All information gathered for the purposes of the current research by means of institutional data sources was done so with the express permission of the criminal justice institutions involved. The PI contacted all organizational entities involved in the study in order to make specific arrangements as to how, when, where, and under what conditions any institutionally-housed data was to be accessed, reviewed, and collected. For purposes of working within the State of Nebraska Correctional Facility, this required meeting with the warden and research director for the Diagnostic Evaluation Center (DEC) located in Lincoln, Nebraska. In addition, several meetings with the Research Specialist employed by the Nebraska Department of Corrections (DOC) were held in order to develop an understanding of the state's post-adjudication process with respect to the administration, housing, coordination, and sharing of inmate diagnostic information. These meetings and investigative communications provided the PI with access to secondary prison data sources.

Sampling of Secondary Data Sources

One of the primary objectives of the current study was to generate research findings that would be generalizable to all State of Nebraska prison commitments for the year 2001. In order to achieve this objective, it was necessary to gain access to relevant data for a representative sample of all incoming prisoners during 2001. Therefore, the practice of employing post-hoc secondary data collections derived from the State of Nebraska's DOC DEC for research analyses was adopted. With respect to current research purposes, the DEC served as an essential institutional venue, as all newly adjudicated state inmates are originally sent there to receive subsequent institutional assignments within the state prison system. In addition, it is at the DEC that inmates are systematically assessed via clinical psychologists and self-report screening instrumentation – both essential data for the current study.

Access to these data sources was granted in November of 2001, therefore, in early 2002 the PI drew a random sample of (n = 424) inmate cases from the total incoming population for the year 2001 (N = 1,518). The total number of cases randomly selected for study inclusion consisted of 27.9% of the total available 2001 inmate population. This sampling strategy was selected as it provided a means to intermittently select and draw research cases within the timeframe and logistical constraints required to regularly visit the institution, access case files, code data, and consult with relevant staff regarding the interpretation of case file information (e.g. Substance Abuse Counselors, Psychologist, Case Managers, Research Specialists, Prison Warden and Associate Warden). It should be noted that as part of the data coding process, the PI removed DEC numbers and personal identifiers in order to assure confidentiality.

The analysis of case data for the purposes of the current research was limited to information collected, housed and available within the inmate DEC files. Information stemming from criminal justice contacts in other states or the federal system may not have been included in DEC case files. In a like fashion, case files may not have always contained juvenile criminal justice contact information for review as part of the institutional psychological assessment procedure. However, such limitations were not anticipated to have significantly biased research outcomes as institutional personnel reported such instances as very uncommon.

Study Sample Description – Demographics

A total of 424 male inmates housed at the State of Nebraska's DEC were randomly selected for case file reviews as part of the current research effort. Official data (e.g., arrest and court information, institutional adjustment, demographics census information), medical information, case management data and psychological evaluations (e.g. clinical psychological assessments and multiple self-report screen instrument findings) were obtained for all inmates selected. Gleaned from this data were the demographic attributes of the current research population presented in Table 1 (Research Sample 'Demographic' Information).

The sample of cases randomly drawn from the overall 2001 incoming prison population for current research purposes indicated a young population, as both the mean and median ages were 30.0 and 31.3 years of age respectively. Moreover, nearly half the sample population (49.3%) were under the age of 30, while only 9.9% were 45 years of age or older. The sample of cases consisted of only male respondents and was predominantly comprised of Caucasian (58.0%) inmates, with Blacks constituting the largest minority population at 22.2%. Hispanics and American Indians comprised 12.7% and 5.5% of the sample respectively.

On average, sample cases rated poorly on the various measures of mainstream attainment. Many inmates did not have a high school degree (37.5%), and it was relatively rare that an inmate had obtained a college degree (3.8%) of some sort. Moreover, the unemployment rate immediately prior to incarceration, at 37.7% among this sample, was disproportionately high relative to the general citizen population. Official data held that 49.5% of the inmates had full-time employment immediately prior to their current incarceration, while another 12.7% were reported to have been working part-time.

Most of the study sample was single and had never been married (59.0%). An additional percentage was single (18.9%) as a result of being separated, divorced or widowed. Only 21.2% of the sample reported that they were married or had been co-habitating prior to their current incarceration. Additionally, official data evidenced that the majority of inmates in the sample (50.4%) had 1 or more children. Specifically, the number of children ranged from 0 to 10 with a mean of 1.4 children per inmate.

Data provided from inmate case files also furnished information regarding the assessed intellectual cognitive functioning of each inmate in the current research sample. Each inmate was evaluated and assigned a percentile rating which in turn was used to classify them within a four-prong classification system. Specifically, 16.3% of the sampled inmates were found to be operating at a 'Low/Borderline' level of cognitive functioning. The majority of cases sampled (52.8%) demonstrated an 'Average' level of functioning while almost one-third (30.9%) of the inmates demonstrated 'High Average' or 'High/Superior' cognitive abilities.

Finally, case file demographic information revealed that most inmates in the current sample described themselves as having a religious affiliation/belief system. The majority of inmates reported themselves to specifically be a Catholic (37.0%) or a Baptist (16.7%). Other faiths consistently reported included Christian (13.7%), Lutheran (6.1%), Protestant (5.2%), Methodist (4.7%), and Native American (3.8%). Only 4.7% of the inmate sample population declared no religious affiliation.

Table 1

Research Sample 'Demographic' Information

Age

Range: 45 (17 to 62)

Mean = 31.25 Median = 30

Age	%
16 – 21	21.5%
22 – 24	12.3%
25 – 29	15.6%
30 – 34	15.6%
35 – 39	13.4%
40 – 44	11.8%
45 – 49	4.2%
50 – 54	2.8%
55 – 59	1.4%
60+	1.4%

Marital Status

Single/Never Married	59.0%
Married/Cohabitating	21.2%
Divorced/Separated	18.9%
Widowed	0.9%

Inmates' Number of Children

Range: 10 (0 to 10)

Mean = 1.38 Median = 1.0

Children	%
0	40.6%
1	21.0%
2	18.2%
3	10.8%
4	4.7%
5	1.7%
6	0.9%
7	1.7%
8	0.2%
9	0.0%
10	0.2%

Race

White	58.0%
Black	22.2%
Hispanic	12.7%
American Indian	5.2%
Asian/Other	1.9%

Education

No Formal Education	0.5%
Less than 8th grade	3.3%
8th grade	3.8%
9th grade	7.8%
10th grade	7.8%
11th grade	14.4%
12th grade or GED	41.7%
1 year post high-school	10.1%
2 year college degree	6.8%
3 years college	1.4%
4 year college degree	2.4%

Employment

Unemployed	37.7%
Part-time	12.7%
Full-time	49.5%

Intellectual Cognitive Functioning

Low/Border Line	16.3%
Average	52.8%
High Average	19.3%
High/Superior	1.6%

Religious Affiliation

Asatru	1.2%	Episcopal	0.2%	Pentecostal	0.7%
Assembly of God	0.5%	Islam/Muslim	1.9%	Presbyterian	1.4%
Baptist	16.7%	Lutheran	6.1%	Protestant	5.2%
Buddhist	0.5%	Methodist	4.7%	Seventh-Day Adventist	0.9%
Catholic	37.0%	Native American	3.8%	Wicca	0.5%
Christian	13.7%	Nazarene	0.2%	None	4.7%

Study Sample Description – Alcohol/Drug Information

In addition to basic demographic data, information on the sample population was also collected with respect to issues of prior use and abuse of alcohol and other drugs – see Table 2 (Research Sample 'Alcohol/Drug' Information). To this end, it was found that only 2.8% of the sample self-reported having never used alcohol/drugs in their lifetimes. Of those individuals having reported some use of alcohol/drugs during the course of their lifetime (97.2%) the mean age of first use was 16.9 years with a median of 14. These initial uses of alcohol/drugs were highly concentrated between the ages of 10 and 19 years old (79.3%).

Of those inmates who self-reported a current 'primary drug of choice' (96.7%), the leading substance was methamphetamine (37.0%), followed by alcohol (27.8%) and marijuana (19.8%). In addition, information reported on a 'secondary drug of choice' (72.4% of inmate cases) evidenced that marijuana (30.7%) was used most often, followed by alcohol (23.3%) and cocaine/crack (10.8%). This data also found that the primary route of administration of drug users in the sample population was smoking (42.9%), followed by oral consumption (29.2%). Inmates' also self-reported injection (16.5%) and snorting (8.0%) as routes of administration. The majority of inmates reported using alcohol/drugs daily (66.0%) or weekly (24.5%).

Data was also collected from inmate records regarding their most recent arrest dynamics. In particular, the majority of the inmates (65.1%) had self-reported being under the influence of alcohol/drugs at the time of their arrest. Many of the inmates' (40.6%) had been charged with drug-related offenses. Similarly, 42% of the sample inmates had been charged with a violent crime.

Information dealing with prior treatment experienced by inmates found that 46.2% of inmates had experienced some form of prior alcohol/drug abuse treatment, with 22.2% self-reporting having been part of a community-based support group at some time prior to their current incarceration. Finally, it is worth noting that many of the inmates (29.7%) in this study sample had undergone some form of mental health treatment in their lifetime.

Table 2

Research Sample 'Alcohol/Drug' Information

Age of First Alcohol/Drug Use (SR)

Range: 28 years (4 to 32)

Mean = 16.9 Median = 14

SR has not used alcohol/drugs 2.8%

Less than 5 years of age	0.5%
5 to 9 years of age	7.5%
10 to 14 years of age	45.5%
15 to 19 years of age	33.8%
20 to 24 years of age	6.3%
25 to 29 years of age	2.6%
30 to 34 years of age	1.0%

Under the Influence at Time of Arrest (SR)

No	34.9%
Yes	65.1%

Primary Drug of Choice (SR)

SR no primary drug	3.3%
Alcohol	27.8%
Marijuana	19.8%
Cocaine/Crack	9.7%
Methamphetamine	37.0%
Heroin	2.4%

Secondary Drug of Choice (SR)

SR no secondary drug	27.6%
Alcohol	23.3%
Marijuana	30.7%
Cocaine/Crack	10.8%
Methamphetamine	6.1%
Heroin	1.4%

Primary Route of Administration (SR)

Not a current user	3.3%
Oral / Swallow	29.2%
Smoke	42.9%
Snort	8.0%
Inject	16.5%

Frequency of Alcohol/Drug Use (SR)

Don't use	3.3%
Daily	66.0%
Weekly	24.5%
Monthly	6.1%

Current Offense – Drug Related?

Non-drug related	59.4%
Drug related	40.6%

'Most Serious' Current Offense – Violent?

No	58.0%
Yes	42.0%

Prior Substance Abuse Treatment (SR)

No	53.8%
Yes	46.2%

Prior Mental Health Treatment (SR)

No	70.3%
Yes	29.7%

Attended a Community Based Support Group (SR) (immediately prior to incarceration)

No	77.8%
Yes	22.2%

SR = Self Report

Table 3

Research Sample 'Criminal Justice Experience' Information

Current Sentence Length (in months) –	Minimum	Maximum
12 or less	36.8%	11.3%
12+ to 24	34.7%	20.0%
24+ to 36	9.9%	21.7%
36+ to 48	6.6%	10.8%
48+ to 60	0.7%	14.2%
60+ to 72	1.9%	4.5%
72+ to 84	0.5%	1.9%
84+ to 96	0.9%	2.8%
96+ to 108	0.0%	0.5%
108+ to 120	2.4%	3.8%
120+ to 132	0.0%	0.5%
132+ to 144	0.0%	0.0%
144+ to 156	0.5%	0.0%
156+ to 168	0.5%	0.9%
168+ to 180	0.5%	1.4%
180+ to 192	0.0%	0.0%
192+ to 204	0.0%	0.0%
204+ to 216	0.9%	0.0%
213+ to 228	0.5%	0.0%
228+ to 240	0.5%	0.0%
240+ to life	2.4%	5.7%

Prior Lifetime Incarceration?	
No	56.6%
Yes	43.4%

Number of Adult Felony Incarcerations?	
0	57.3%
1	24.5%
2	11.6%
3	2.8%
4	1.9%
5	1.4%
6	0.5%

Institutional Misconduct – Drugs	
No	94.3%
Yes	5.7%

Institutional Misconduct – Escape Attempts	
No	92.5%
Yes	7.5%

Study Sample Description – Criminal Justice Experiences

Finally, institutional information provided across all case files in the current study population was examined to demonstrate criminal justice related experiences – see Table 3 (Research Sample 'Criminal Justice Experience' Information). It was found that nearly half (43.4%) of the inmate case files randomly drawn for inclusion in this study evidenced a 'prior lifetime incarceration.' Moreover, 42.7% of the sampled cases indicated that the inmate had previously been incarcerated as an adult. Information on sentence dynamics (minimum and maximum sentence lengths) for each case was also recorded and analyzed collectively. The majority (71.5%) of sampled inmates had received a minimum sentence of 24 months or less, while only 22.0% had received a maximum sentence of 60 months or more. With respect to issues of institutional adjustment, only 5.7% of the sampled inmates had been reprimanded for a drug-related issue and 7.5% for an escape attempt.

Assembling Research Data Sets by Means of Secondary Collections

As previously discussed, the screening data produced as a result of self-report methodology was central to the current research effort with respect to demonstrating levels of criterion validity, construct validity, and efficacy with forensic psychological assessments derived from criminal populations. While the development and attributes of these instruments is discussed in the following sections of this chapter, it is in the current section that the methodology involved in collecting research information from the study's institutional criminal justice populations will be discussed – to include, forensic psychological assessment findings, multiple self-report screen findings, information on indexes of substance misuse, and individual inmate case variables. The aforementioned information for this study was gathered entirely by means of secondary data collection.

First, as previously mentioned, essential information was made available for this research effort as part of an arrangement with the Nebraska DOC to, in part, collect self-report-produced screening data. As with the clinical assessment, the SASSI, SATOP, and SSI screen inventories had been previously completed by incoming male inmates to the state correctional system with the categorical exceptions of juveniles and "death row" inmates. In order to promote of investigative results and enhance relevant comparability of data sets, inmate cases were randomly selected for inclusion in the study parameters (i.e., male inmates adjudicated within the State of Nebraska and processed at the DEC during the 2001 calendar year).

Following this, matching case files to those selected were drawn from various institutional data sources (e.g., from counselor's files, psychologist's files, medical records) in an effort to correlate case level information. In other words, the author constructed multiple data sets involving corresponding cases, to include the clinical psychological assessment findings (n = 424), the SASSI (n = 424), the SATOP (n = 424), the SSI (n = 424), substance abuse indexes (n = 424), and case level variable data (n = 424) for inmate cases that had originally been randomly selected for study inclusion. This meant that, in total, an examination across 424 (the number of cases containing all relevant information for comparison) inmate files was now possible in an effort to represent the total incoming male correctional population in the State of Nebraska throughout the year 2001. All clinical psychological assessment findings were recorded along with substance misuse indexes and individual case variables. Finally, all self-report methodology-based screening instruments were scored and subsequently recorded in data sets for later examination.

Clinical Psychological Assessments

For the purposes of this study, the most practical and valuable means for establishing the validity of individual and cumulative screening instrument data collected by means of self-report methodology was to generate comparisons between findings from screening instrument outcomes and the corresponding clinical psychological assessments for these same inmate cases. Psychologists operated under the generally accepted criteria of the Diagnostic and Statistical Manual, 4th Edition (DSM-IV), of the American Psychiatric Association (1994). In addition, because of the professionalism, care, and diligence exercised by the psychologists producing each inmate's psychological review, combined with the careful scrutiny of each record on the part of the PI, the use of clinically-based assessments in this study was considered acceptable as a reasonable amount of confidence was established in their accuracy. This procedure for assessing the clinical value of screening inventories has previously been used throughout the literature as a criterion measure to identify participants with substance abuse and dependence disorders (Bohn, Babor, & Kramzler, 1995; Gastfriend, Najavits, & Reif, 1994; Lazowski et al., 1998; Miller & Lazowski, 1999; Millon et al., 1997; Torrens et al., 2004).

The clinical assessments were conducted by experienced forensic psychologists employed by the State of Nebraska DOC DEC and were done so independently of any screening outcome information. In other words, the psychologists did not use any screening information in order to arrive at their conclusions. In addition, the sequence of screening and psychological assessment was randomly administered to respondents, with some individuals having been screened before a clinical evaluation and others after. As a result of this serendipitous institutional practice, various possible threats to internal validity (e.g., history, testing, selection biases, experimental mortality) and external validity (e.g., multiple treatment interferences) that may have otherwise become confounding to study outcomes were minimized (Campbell & Stanley, 1963) – see Appendix A.

The total number of clinical psychological assessments that were collected with the objective of comparison to self-report screening instrument outcome data was equal to the number of cases randomly selected for review (n = 424). In the year 2001, there were a total of 1,518 inmate admissions to the Nebraska DOC via the DEC. Therefore the sample of psychological assessments drawn for the purposes of the current study represents 27.9% of the overall incoming population for the year.

Multiple Self-Report-Based Screening Inventories

In order to maximize confidence in the research findings central to the current study – validity of the self-report diagnostic screening methodology – the use of a battery of self-report screening tools proved beneficial, thereby providing opportunities to explore issues of validity (criterion and construct) and case variable influences as a function of the self-report screening methodology rather than specific instrumentation. To meet this need, three instruments were configured as a "model" screening package. In addition, the review of this cumulative information was a direct test of the actual practice employed by the Nebraska DOC DEC, in that the combined results of the screening instruments reviewed in this study were directly related to the allocation of various institutional treatment resources. Moreover, in a review of several other state and county-level jail and prison practices, the use of multiple screening instruments has also been found to be a common practice in determining "probability of need for treatment" (e.g., State of Michigan Department of Corrections, Kent County Correctional Facilities – Michigan, Pottawattamie County Jail – Iowa, and State of Minnesota Department of Corrections).

While no single screening instrument has proven capable of generating the exact same study results for a substantial population of respondents as those produced through psychological assessments performed by a clinical psychologist (Meehl, 1965), classifications generated by such diagnostically-based instruments have nevertheless proven valuable and have been widely used in medical treatment fields (Broner, Borum, Whitmire, & Gawley, 2002; Crawley & Wakefield, 2002; Crawley, 2003; Letteri, Nelson, & Sayers, 1985). Therefore, it was because of such recognized limitations that three distinct screening tools were used as concurrent validators (Blanchard et al., 2003) for the purposes of the current research. It was anticipated that through the use of multiple diagnostic tools, not only would confidence in findings increase as each instrument would have the opportunity to sustain the others' conclusions, but that the spotlight of the research would also remain centered on the issue of validity and value of self-report diagnostic screening methodologies rather than the assessment of a specific screening instrument.

Consequently, in addition to the clinical psychological assessments previously discussed, three substance use inventories, each employing self-report methodology, and each based on the American Psychiatric Association's DSM-IV criterion, were used in this research effort – the Substance Abuse Subtle Screening Inventory (SASSI), the 31-Question Substance Abuse Treatment Oriented Program (SATOP) screen, and the United State's Department of Health and Human Service's Simple Screening Instrument (SSI). These instruments were selected for their current utilization in correctional treatment planning (i.e., State of Nebraska Diagnostic Evaluation Center), their sound psychometric properties, and their ready availability to the current research effort. While these self-report screening instruments were developed with unique considerations (e.g., primary populations), relations among and between outcomes of these substance inventory screening instruments could provide research evidence with respect to issues of validity, methodological efficacy, and inductive theory building. The following three chapter sub-sections provide a summary of each specific screen, a brief discussion regarding its target populations, support in the literature, and method by which its data was collected for purposes of the current study.

The Substance Abuse Subtle Screening Inventory (SASSI)

One of the three screening instruments used to address issues of validity with full psychological assessments was the SASSI-3, which was administered in the prison population of the current study. The SASSI, a screening instrument grounded in self-report methodology, was developed in the mid-1980s and has since undergone multiple revisions and enhancements (Lazowski et. al., 1998; Miller, 1995, 1985; Rapp et. al., 1999; Rogers, 1997) to arrive at the version used in the present study – the SASSI-3 (Miller & Lazowski, 1999). This most recent version of the SASSI included two face valid scales consisting of 26 items and eight sub-scales consisting of 67 true/false items.

The SASSI-3 screening inventory was specifically designed to identify individuals with a high probability of a substance use disorder. Moreover, the SASSI-3 was developed with the unique objective of identifying individuals who had a substance problem irrespective of whether they recognized and/or acknowledged pertinent symptoms. This was accomplished by the SASSI-3 as it employed both face-valid and subtle screening questions in order to classify individuals appropriately. It was this instrument's declared ability to all but overcome the problem of denial (Creager, 1989) that makes the SASSI-3 an instrument of considerable value with respect to this study.

The originator of the SASSI, Dr. Frank Miller, has held that the instrument is an objective tool for a variety of human service settings (1998). The most recent research effort to evaluate the SASSI-3 found the overall accuracy of the instrument in distinguishing individuals with substance abuse disorders from those without such disorders to be 94% (Lazowski et al., 1998). As this research was conducted in multiple settings, a range of validity-values were produced, spanning from 93 to 95%. This same set of research findings also described the SASSI-3 as a reliable and valid measurement tool and provided evidence of criterion (convergent/concurrent) validity with other substance-use screening measures, to include – the Michigan Alcohol Screening Test (MAST), the Minnesota Multiphasic Personality Inventory-2 (MMPI-2), Addiction Potential and Addiction Acknowledgement Scales, the MMPI-2 MacAndrew Alcoholism Scale-Revised, and the Millon Clinical Multiaxial Inventory-II Alcohol Dependence and Drug Dependence Scales (Lazowski et al., 1998). Its logistical availability and the evidence of empirical research support in the literature for the SASSI-3 made it a practical instrument to use for the current objective of exploring cumulative screening instrument outcomes collected via self-report methodology for issues of validity.

The SASSI-3, as all other data in this study, was available for review by means of secondary data collections within the prison populations included in this study. As previously stated, in order to ensure maximum generalizability of research findings and also maintain the ability to make relevant comparisons, matching cases (that included SASSI-3 screening data) to those previously selected with respect to clinical assessment data were gathered. In other words, the researcher had now acquired two corresponding data sets for each of the randomly selected inmate cases in the study – the clinical assessment findings and the SASSI-3 data. Specifically, of the 424 cases providing forensic psychological assessment information, SASSI-3 data from all 424 (100% of the randomly selected study population) of these inmate files were also available from the total incoming male correctional population throughout the year 2001. This again meant that 27.9% of the total inmate population under review was available via both clinical information and SASS-3 screening data. Subsequent to reviewing the SASSI-3 instruments for each of the randomly selected inmate cases, the instruments were next scored and recorded in a data set for later analyses.

The 31-Question Substance Abuse Treatment Oriented Program (SATOP) Screen

The SATOP screen, also employing self-report methodology, was another screening inventory already administered to the prison population of this study. Like the previous instrument discussed, this screen data was also used to address issues of validity with forensic psychological assessments conducted on the same population. The SATOP instrument has been used by the State of Nebraska's DEC since the mid-1990s in order to provide clinical support for "routing decisions" made on inmate cases regarding future drug treatment needs and requirements. While the SATOP has been used by the State of Nebraska DOC for a significant period of time, the investigator was not able to determine the origination of the instrument, nor how or why it was adopted by the institution. Nevertheless, the SATOP inventory instrument was designed as a straight-forward screening tool containing 31 yes/no face valid questions, directly representing domain criterion for drug and alcohol disorders listed in the DSM-IV.

The SATOP scores 12 of the 31 questions it presents to its respondent in an index fashion, accumulating one point for each question answered "yes" on the screen – see Appendix B. The results of the screening tool are dichotomous in nature with a score of 3 or more indicating that the respondent is likely to be in need of treatment for a substance disorder. While this instrument doesn't seem to have been directly explored or empirically tested in the literature, because of its direct relationship to the DSM-IV – see Appendix C – the criteria for drug and alcohol disorders, and its ready availability as collateral screening data in the prison sample drawn for this study, it was included to further explore issues of validity related to self-report screening methodologies.

Like the SASSI-3 data previously discussed, the SATOP screening data was also made available for this study by means of secondary data collections. Identical to the methods previously discussed concerning the gathering of SASSI-3 data, maximum generalizability of research findings were ensured while still facilitating appropriate comparability between data sets, as those same cases that had previously been randomly selected with respect to clinical assessment and SASSI-3 data were again matched up. In other words, the examiner was now able to add corresponding SATOP screening data to the case files containing an inmate's clinical assessment and SASSI-3 data. Consequently, 424 (100% of the randomly selected study population) inmate files, or 27.9% of the total incoming male correctional population throughout the year 2001 were again reviewed, this time specifically examining the SATOP screening inventory findings. Finally, the instruments were again scored and recorded in a data set for later investigation.

The Simple Screening Instrument (SSI)

The third and final set of screening instrument data collected for purposes of demonstrating levels of criterion validity with the clinical psychological assessments in this study's population was the SSI. The SSI is a 16-question screening instrument grounded in self-report methodology and designed to identify individuals with a high probability of need for substance abuse treatment. This instrument was created under the sponsorship of the Substance Abuse and Mental Health Service Administration (SAMHSA) in the mid-1990s (Winters & Zenilman, 2000). The SSI was developed based on several other "successful" screens found throughout the treatment literature – see Appendix D. Because the creators of the instrument drew upon many other pre-existing screens, like them, the SSI also contains DSM-IV face valid items used to inventory life experiences commonly associated with substance dependence (Broner, Borum, Whitmire & Gawley, 2002).

The creation of the SSI was accomplished through work conducted by a panel of experts assembled from various fields of specialization and with several key objectives central to its implementation. For example, one objective involved that it be capable of addressing all substances of abuse. In addition, the SSI was created with the intention of being administered and scored in a very short time period by both professionals and individuals with no specific drug abuse training. The instrument was also developed to be applicable to diverse populations – to include criminal justice populations – with respect to age, gender, socioeconomic status, ethnicity, level of education, etc. (Winters & Zenilman, 2000, p. 3). To date there have been no reliability studies conducted on the SSI, however, various researchers (Peters & Greenbaum, 1996; Winters, 1995) have found this instrument to produce high levels of sensitivity for alcohol or drug dependence among inmate populations.

The SSI scores 14 of the 16 questions presented to the respondent, accumulating one point for each question answered "yes" on the screen. The cumulative results of this index scoring process identify those individuals who exhibit a high probability of need for substance abuse treatment. Specifically, screen scores of 4 or more are categorized on the SSI as "moderate to high: possible need for further assessment."

Like the SATOP screening instrument previously discussed, the ready availability of SSI screening data in the current study population, in combination with the fact that the instrument directly reflects DSM-IV criterion for substance abuse disorders, makes SSI data valuable for inclusion in the current research. Specifically, these data were used to further enhance the examination of validity and issues of efficacy between the self-report-based screening methodology and full clinical assessment findings.

Like the prior two screening instruments discussed herein, the SSI data was also available for examination in the current study by means of secondary data collections through the Nebraska DOC. Again, this information had previously been completed by adult male inmates entering the state prison system via the DEC. Collection methods to obtain SSI case data followed the formerly explained processes to ensure maximum generalizability of research findings while still making comparability across data sets possible. In other words, SSI data was collected from the same cases that had formerly been drawn from the research population with respect to clinical psychological assessment information, SASSI-3, and SATOP screening data. Again, in this case all 424 (100% of the randomly selected study population) cases originally used to provide clinical psychological assessment information also provided SSI screen findings (27.9% of the total study population). Next, the instruments were scored and recorded in a data set for analyses. Finally, with the accumulated research data, it was now viable for the research investigator to examine issues of validity derived via multiple self-report-based screening instruments and full forensic psychological assessments.

Other Indexes of Substance Misuse

In addition to the collection of clinical psychological evaluations and findings from three distinct self-report-based screening instruments, the PI also collected case data on other "Indexes of Substance Misuse." In other words, systematically collected and available institutional inmate case information that was anticipated to be theoretically related to "need for treatment" for substance abuse was collected and recorded for subsequent comparison to collective self-report screen findings.

Data were available from the same inmate cases entering the Nebraska Correctional System during the year 2001 which had also produced the self-report-based screens and psychological assessments sampled as part of the current research effort. Case data included both self-report information and official data produced and reported by various state agencies. Therefore, these cases were again examined in order to survey cases for "Indexes of Substance Misuse" information. This information was examined to explore the theoretical relationships between identified substance misuse data and the cumulatively scored self-report-based screening instrument's categorical findings (i.e., high probability of "need for treatment" vs. low probability of "need for treatment"). This was done in order to provide more insight into the value of the self-report screening methodology under examination in the current study – construct validity (Carmines & Zeller, 1979; Thornberry & Krohn, 2000).

The following 'Indexes of Substance Misuse' were selected for analysis across cases and for subsequent comparison to self-report-based instrument findings:

1) Age of first drug use (self-reported age)

2) Frequency of recent drug use (self-reported = daily, weekly, monthly, etc.)

3) Primary route of drug administration (self-reported = swallow, smoke, snort, inject)

4) Previous substance abuse treatment (self-report and official data)

5) Under the influence of drugs/alcohol at the time of current offense (self-report)

6) Current offense (official data = drug vs. non-drug)

7) Institutional misconduct report specific to the use of drugs (self-report and official data)

Again, it was expected that once the cumulatively indexed self-report-based instrument findings were divided into "need for treatment" categories (i.e., high or low probability of "need for treatment") that the "Indexes of Substance Misuse" information would theoretically support their findings. Specifically, it was anticipated by the investigator that indexes indicating younger first use of substances, more "intensive" drug use, more severe histories of problematic behavior, and other "negatively associated behaviors" would be more likely to correlate with the group of participants identified by self-report diagnostic instruments as likely to be in "need of treatment," rather than those who had been categorized with less significant "predictor scores" by the combined instrument scores. In other words, when reviewing cumulative screen findings across cases, it was expected that the inmate cases that were classified as demonstrating a "high probability of need for treatment" via the self-report-based screening methodology would also produce:

1) a lower mean age of first drug use

2) a greater frequency of recent drug use

3) a more invasive route of administration in drug use

4) a higher prevalence of prior substance abuse treatment

5) a higher prevalence of having been under the influence of alcohol/drugs at the time of arrest

6) a higher prevalence of convictions for drug related offenses

7) a higher prevalence of institutional misconduct reports specific to drug use

All of the inmate cases (n = 424) previously selected into the study sample included information regarding the presence or absence of the aforementioned "Indexes of Substance Misuse," making the exploration of theoretical research comparisons viable.

Case Variables Collected

The final data gathered via secondary data collection for the current research study involved individual-level variables systematically available across all inmate cases (n = 424). Such variables were collected and subsequently classified into the following groupings:

1) Demographics
    a. Age
    b. Race
    c. Education
    d. Marital status
    e. Religious affiliation
    f. Employment status immediately prior to incarceration

2) Intellectual Functioning
    a. Cognitive functioning classification

3) Drug Use History
    a. Age of first drug use
    b. Primary drug of choice (current)
    c. Frequency of drug use
    d. Route of drug administration

4) Treatment History
    a. Previous substance abuse treatment
    b. Previous mental health treatment
    c. Experience having attended a community-based support group (e.g., AA, NA)

5) Criminal Justice Experiences
    a. Prior lifetime incarceration
    b. Number of adult incarcerations
    c. Current offense classification (e.g., violent, drug-related)
    d. Current sentence dynamics (minimum and maximum lengths)
    e. Institutional misconduct issues (case summary of escape attempts and drug-related misbehavior)

These previously listed variables were gathered across cases to determine if they produced a statistically significant influence on the self-report methodology as it had been used via diagnostic screening instrumentation. In other words, the investigator wanted to address the research question "Does the value of the self-report screening methodology vary based on case attributes?" with the available institutional data. This was an express attempt to assess the use of self-report screening instrumentation as an effective methodological tool for producing valid data regarding drug and alcohol disorders within institutionalized criminal justice venues – specifically incoming prison populations.

DATA ANALYSES

Exploring Criterion Validity, Construct Validity, and Influential Affects

The final sections of this chapter explain the various research analyses used in the current study. Specifically, the evaluation of the collected research sample and the methodology employed in the scoring and organization of self-report screening data is conveyed. Moreover, the analysis of criterion (convergent/concurrent) and construct validity, self-report screening efficacy, and the analysis of presented case variable influences upon self-report screening methodologies are demonstrated.

A Representative Research Sample? – A Goodness of Fit Test

In order to advance the generalizability of research findings produced by the current study, a random sampling methodology for case selection was employed. To explore the success of this process in selecting a representative sample from the incoming prison inmate population, statistical analyses were conducted to compare the sample drawn to the total inmate population. Specifically, a chi-square 'Goodness of Fit' analysis of the percentages of cases in these populations (2001 DEC inmate population and research sample population) as a function of demographic variables (i.e., age, race, marital status, sentencing lengths – minimum and maximum) was conducted. The obvious exception of comparison categories in these populations was, of course, gender, as all inmates in this study were male.

Comparative information for these statistical tests were derived from institutional census data on incoming DEC inmates (generated monthly) during the study's temporal parameters (the year 2001), and via information gathered by the researcher on inmate cases that had been methodologically selected for research participation. It is worth noting that the variables selected to compute statistical group comparisons were driven by available DEC inmate census data. In other words, institutional classifications had to be adhered to when comparing categories. The conclusion of these analyses is established and further examined in the subsequent chapter designated "Research Questions and Results" (Chapter 5).

The Standard – Prevalence Rate of 'Clinically Diagnosed Substance Abuse' for the DEC Sample Population

In order to advance the current study for further analysis, it was first necessary to identify a standard (a criterion) by which to compare self-report data. As suggested thus far in the current study, the clinically-based psychological findings served as this standard. The first use of this standard was to establish the prevalence rate of "need for treatment" among the study sample population. In order to acquire this prevalence rate, an examination of the frequency and percentage of inmate cases sampled for this study in which the institutional psychologist recommended substance abuse treatment was conducted. This finding, derived from the identified standard, was used thereafter in order to conduct additional analyses (e.g., positive and negative predictive powers for self-report-based screen assessments).

Cumulative Scoring of Sample Cases by Number of Positive Screen Findings

Following the identification of a standard (a prevalence rate based on clinical psychological assessments), it was next necessary to employ a method by which the aggregated utilization of the self-report screening method might be assessed, rather than simply evaluating each individual diagnostic instrument. Therefore, each case was subsequently indexed into groupings based on overall case scores. The score for each sample case was generated by summing the number of positive (i.e., a case evidencing a high probability of "need for treatment") self-report screen findings for each case (each positive screen weighted equally at one point). In other words, it was possible for a case to receive a discrete score of 0, 1, 2 or 3 – as a result of the number of self-report screening instruments that found the inmate to be in need of further assessment and/or treatment. This new "scoring variable" was next used to more closely examine the aggregated values of the self-report methodology as employed via diagnostic screening instruments, especially as they were employed within a criminal population.

Examining Criterion Validity – Clinical Psychological Assessments vs. Cumulative Self-Report Diagnostic Screen Findings

Following an assessment of the generalizability of the research sample used herein, the identification of an analytical standard for comparison, and the calculation of individual case scores, the next point of analysis involved calculating criterion (convergent/concurrent) validity values for the collective diagnostic screening instruments grounded in the self-report methodology. Research has often employed various types of forward-reverse and cross-record checks in studies attempting to determine issues of criterion validity (Carmines and Zeller, 1979; Hindelang, Hirschi, and Weis, 1981; Huizinga and Elliott, 1986; Wentland and Smith, 1993). In order to begin to gain insight into the value of the self-report methodology as used in the production of diagnostic screen findings, it was necessary to evaluate the convergence of the cumulative screen instrument outcomes against the DEC forensic psychological assessments for corresponding inmate cases. In order to attain this information, the researcher used data from the 424 randomly selected inmate cases previously described, each providing self-report-based findings for three distinct diagnostically-grounded screening instruments (i.e., the SASSI-3, the 31 Question SATOP, and the SSI) and a clinically-based DSM-IV diagnosis.

To this end, these data were subsequently used to calculate a series of chi-square concordance tables as a means to cross-validate cumulative screen findings (categorized by the previously discussed discrete cumulative scoring categories of 0, 1, 2 or 3 – each representing a progressively higher probability of "need for treatment" as determined by the self-report-based screening methodologies employed) against clinical psychological findings (simply divided into the findings of criterion positive – "treatment recommended," and criterion negative – "no treatment recommended"). Multiple concordance tables were used in order to explore relationships between the external criterion (psychological assessment findings) and various self-report-based screen scoring schemata. The resulting insights into the criterion validity evidenced between the cumulative self-report screening methodology and the findings of full psychological evaluations are presented in the subsequent chapter entitled "Research Questions and Results" (Chapter 5).

Efficacy of the Self-Report Screening Methodology

In addition to the examination of general issues of criterion validity by means of constructing concordance tables evaluating self-report screen findings versus clinical assessment findings, it was also important to empirically measure the efficacy of the self-report screening methodology as applied within the criminal justice institutionalized populations examined herein. Research has demonstrated that the prevalence of substance misuse and abuse varies (e.g., geographically, temporally, by drug type) greatly across criminal justice venues and therefore may need to be adjusted accordingly. For example, when examining the prevalence rates of overall drug use in arrestee populations across different cities at the same points in time, the Department of Justice's (DOJ) Arrestee Drug Abuse Monitoring Program (ADAM) found that the prevalence of arrestees testing positive (both pharmacologically and through self-report) for recent drug use significantly varied, depending on the city in which the data was collected (National Institute of Justice, 1999, 2000, 2001, 2001a, 2001b, 2002, 2002a). Moreover, ADAM data has also evidenced changes over time in criminal drug use prevalence rates within the same geographic data collection points (same cities) and also as a function of different drugs of use (National Institute of Justice, 2001a, 2001b, 2002). Similar to these data, research assessing the "need for treatment" across multiple criminal justice Institutionalized venues has also demonstrated variability (Crawley, 2003; Peters et. al., 2000).

With this the case, it was important to establish efficacy values of the self-report screening methodology in the current research venue.

Specifically, two case scoring classifications were used (a dichotomous classification termed "extreme" – cases scoring 0 or 3 only, and a dichotomous classification termed "majority" – cases scoring 0 or 1, versus 2 or 3) to disaggregate sample cases for analysis. These tables thereafter had the capacity to facilitate various matches between self-report-based screen findings and the conclusions derived via clinical assessments. To this end, the efficacy of the self-report screening methodology was subsequently measured via six accuracy indices/queries (Lazowski, et al., 1998; Miller et al., 1999; Peters, et. al., 2000; Winters & Zenilman, 2000) – prevalence, sensitivity, specificity, positive predictive power, negative predictive power, and accuracy.

Definitions and Utilization of Terms of Analysis

The efficacy of the self-report methodology used by means of diagnostic screening instruments is discussed in terms of the following six accuracy indices and the definitions they assume for the purposes of this study (an example of the classifications corresponding to each index may be found Appendix E):

1) **Prevalence** – refers to the number of cases that demonstrate a specific attribute ("need for treatment") in a given population divided by the total population assessed for the attribute.

2) **Sensitivity** – refers to respondents who are clinically identified as having a substance use disorder and the probability that they will screen positive ("need for treatment") by means of the self-report methodology. In other words, this refers to the percentage of actual clinically-based criterion positives that were also classified as screen positive via the self-report methodology; errors here produce "false negative" classifications. This measure is therefore used to assess how sensitive the self-report screening methodology is in detecting the presence of a clinically diagnosed substance use disorder.

3) **Specificity** – refers to respondents who have been clinically diagnosed as not having a substance use disorder and the probability that they will screen negative (no "need for

treatment") by means of the self-report methodology. This refers to the percentage of clinically-based criterion negatives that were also classified as screen negative via the self report methodology; errors here produce "false positive" classifications. This measure is therefore used to assess how capable the self-report screening methodology is in discriminating the absence of the disorder.

4) **Positive Predictive Power (PPP)** – refers to respondents who screen positive ("need for treatment") via the self-report methodology and the probability that a clinical psychological assessment would also reveal that they meet diagnostic criteria for a substance use disorder. This refers to the percentage of self-report-based screen positives that were also clinically identified as criterion positive; an estimate of the confidence warranted by a positive self-reported screen result. This measure is therefore used to assess when the instrument produces a positive self-report-based screen result, and how likely is that result to be correct? In general, the greater the positive predictive power demonstrated by the self-report screening methodology, the more valuable it is in identifying individuals in need of treatment.

5) **Negative Predictive Power (NPP)** – refers to respondents who screen negative (no "need for treatment") via the self-report methodology and the probability that a clinical psychological assessment would also reveal that they do not meet diagnostic criteria for a substance use disorder. This refers to the percentage of self-report-based screen negatives that were also clinically identified as criterion negative; an estimate of the confidence warranted by a negative self-reported screen result. This measure is therefore used to assess when the instrument produces a negative self-report-based screen result, and how likely it is that result will be correct. In general, the greater the negative predictive power demonstrated by the self-report screening methodology, the more valuable it is in identifying individuals not in need of treatment.

6) **Accuracy** – refers to the number of cases (both "need for treatment" and no "need for treatment") that demonstrate correct classifications by both the clinical psychological findings and the self-report screening methodology divided by the total sample population. This measure is therefore used to describe the degree to which the self-report screening methodology agrees with the standard used herein – clinical psychological assessments.

(Miller & Lazowski, 1999, pp. 14-51)

Assumptions

With respect to the above discussed analyses, the underlying assumption here was that the standard (the criterion) to which screen outcomes were compared – the forensic clinical psychological assessments – was in fact accurate. In other words, discrepancies between self-report screen outcomes and clinical outcomes to be used as criterion measures could have resulted because of an inaccuracy or factual error in either the screen or the psychological assessment. In addition to possible instrumentation problems (on the part of either the self-report screens or the forensic assessments), as indicated in the current study's review of the literature, it was expected that a number of DEC inmates would be unable to recall, or reluctant to admit, information essential for self-report screening instruments to obtain accurate outcome results. Conversely, it was also estimated that over reporting would be infrequent as it was improbable that inmates would self-report a socially undesirable behavior (perhaps even considered a weakness) that was not genuine, unless the individual was attempting to influence the screening and/or psychological assessment outcomes. Such inaccuracies are more discernibly examined in the subsequent analyses concerning instrumentation efficacy.

Examination of Theoretical Relationships between Cumulatively Scored Sample Cases and Other Indexes of Substance Misuse – Construct Validity

Data analysis is defined as "…a learning process achieved through comparing empirical evidence with theoretical expectations" (Singleton et al., 1988, p. 379). Therefore, in addition to establishing aggregate criterion validity values between self-report screen findings and clinical assessment findings, and thereafter examining the efficacy of the self-report screening methodology, data was next examined to determine the relationships between cumulative case scores (based on the number of positive screen findings) and "other indexes of substance misuse." This examination, referred to as construct validity, simply involved comparing self-reported information to screen findings across respondent groupings to understand the extent to which expected theoretical findings were realized (Carmines & Zeller, 1979; Thornberry & Krohn, 2000). Such variables of theoretical interest and logistically available across all study sample cases included:

1) Age of first drug use (self-reported age)

2) Frequency of drug use (self-reported = daily, weekly, monthly, etc.)

3) Primary route of drug administration (self-report = swallow, smoke, snort, inject)

4) Previous substance abuse treatment (self-report and official data = yes/no)

5) Current offense dynamics (official data = drug vs. non-drug)

Once all inmate cases were categorized into discrete classifications based on cumulative scores (0, 1, 2, or 3), comparisons to "indexes of substance misuse" were correlated across categories to reveal any meaningful or significant relationships in the data. Frequency tables were used so that information could be grouped and presented in the most meaningful manner (Hagan, 1997). When appropriate, mean scores and standard deviations (of cumulative screen scores) were computed for each substance misuse index for classification groups and then compared to one another.

As previously stated, it was anticipated by the investigator that indexes indicating greater substance use, more severe histories of problematic behavior (e.g., intravenous drug use, drug related arrests), and other "negatively associated behaviors" would theoretically be more likely to correlate with the group of participants that had been classified as expressing a greater probability of "need for treatment," rather than those who had been found to produce less significant "predictor scores." These results were next converted into table format in order to assess the general relationship between these substance misuse indexes and self-report-based instrument findings. In addition, ANOVA[25] and Chi-square[26] analyses were conducted in order to test for significant differences evidenced across research groupings (examining the mean scores of each index as a function of screening classifications). This was expected to assess general theoretical support for the findings based on the self-report screening methodology, or conversely challenge its construct validity and ability to properly target the population of interest. The results of these analyses are detailed in the following chapter entitled "Research Questions and Results" (Chapter 5).

Classification of Sample Cases by Convergent/Divergent Scoring Schemata

In addition to scrutinizing the self-report screening methodology by means of investigating convergence and issues of efficacy, it is also worth noting that the accuracy of the self-report screening methodology could have been affected by other variables (e.g., demographic variables, drug-related variables, and variables related to indexes of substance misuse). However, prior to identifying variables that may significantly influence the self-report-based screening methodology, it was first necessary to once again employ a scoring practice in order to distinguish between inmate cases where screenings grounded in self-report were convergent with clinical assessment findings and cases in which these findings were divergent. In order to promote optimal

---

[25] A summary table of the analysis of variances includes: SS (sum of squares), df (degrees of freedom), MS (mean square), and F (interactional value to determine significance of effects), P (probability at the level of significance less than .05).

[26] Chi-square tests are used when an investigator wants to know if the number of responses that fall in two or more categories are due to chance – whether a significant difference exists between those individuals' self-report-based screen findings actually indicating "high probability of need for treatment" and those expected, based on some theoretically driven variable. To accept or reject a null hypothesis there has to be a significant difference between the observed "screen findings" and the expected findings at or below the .05 level of significance.

sensitivity in research findings, each inmate case was again assigned a discrete score of 0, 1, 2, or 3. While previous case scores were derived from the cumulative number of positive ("need for treatment") screen findings per case, here scores were the function of the number of screens per case which were convergent (in agreement) with the clinical assessment findings. Therefore, the score for each inmate case evidenced a demarcated level of convergence between clinical and self-report screen findings.

Power Analysis

Because scores for inmate research cases ranged from 0 to 3, it was possible to group case variables across these scores for the purposes of subsequent analyses. Once each of the groupings had been constructed into a research model and data arranged accordingly (e.g., dummy coding of categorical variables), a power analysis was conducted in order to estimate the number of cases required per research model (i.e., based on "effect-size" and "alpha level") in order to produce statistically significant findings (Cohen & Cohen, 1983; Cohen, 1988; Sedlmeier & Gigerenzer, 1989).

Disriminant Analysis

In order to begin to understand the value of the self-report screening methodology, testing for the significant influence of variables on the level of criterion validity of self-report driven screen findings was undertaken. To this end, discriminant (also known as discrimination) analysis[27] was used to determine if theoretically selected and logistically available variables across study sample cases did indeed significantly influence the accuracy of self-report-produced screen

---

[27] Discriminant analysis is often used in situations where a criterion variable may have more than two values but be qualitative in nature (Manly, 1994). In this case discriminant analysis seeks to demonstrate whether values on various predictor variables are related to the alternative values on the qualitative criterion variable. "The benefits of such a technique are the same as for regression analysis...we can learn which variables are related to the criterion variable, and...we will be able to predict values on the criterion variable when given values on the predictor variables" (Kachigan, 1991, p. 216).

findings[28] One full statistical model, followed by three partial models were run where independent variables included:

1) Demographics (age, race, education, marital status, number of children, religious affiliation, employment status immediately prior to incarceration) and Intellectual Functioning (cognitive functioning classification).

2) Drug Use History (age of first drug use, current primary drug of choice, current secondary drug of choice, frequency of drug use, primary route of drug administration) and Treatment History (previous substance abuse treatment, previous mental health treatment, attending community-based support group immediately prior to incarceration).

3) Criminal Justice Experiences (prior incarceration, under influence at time of current offense, current offense type, length of current sentence, institutional misconduct) and "Other Indexes of Substance Misuse" (under the influence at time of current offense, current offense dynamics).

Prior to the analysis of these partial models, a full model was run which included all variables under consideration for potential influence on the criterion validity of self-report-based screen findings. In addition to this, rather than only entering all variables into one equation, and in order to allow maximum opportunity for each variable to demonstrate a significant effect on the accuracy of the self-report screening methodology, multiple analyses were conducted based on variable

---

[28] While effectiveness of discriminant analysis will be found to rest on the existence of predictor variables which differ in mean value from one criterion group to another, there are two key assumptions with regard to the variances of the predictor variables and their inter-correlations – 1) it is assumed that the variance of a given predictor variable is the same in the respective populations from which any groups of objects have been drawn (different predictor variables can have different variances, but the variance of a given variable must be the same in each criterion group population), and 2) it is necessary that the correlation between any two predictor variables is the same in the respective populations from which alternative criterion groups have been sampled (the correlation matrix of predictor variables must be the same in each group) (Kachigan, 1991, p. 219).

classifications (i.e., individual level attributes, drug-related experiences, and development level attributes). This was particularly important once categorical variables within each statistical model had been further dummy coded for analysis. In addition, separate models provide for a more theoretically bounded consideration of findings.

Because it is frequently the case that the use of dummy coded variables in combination with discriminant analysis produces potential artificial covariance problems (Hair, et. al., 1998), both "pooled" and "unpooled" covariance structures were calculated, with follow-up discussions of the more predictive findings. In addition, the discriminant analysis of each partial model was conducted twice – once using all four possible cumulative screen scoring classifications as the dependent variable (0, 1, 2, and 3), and once with a dichotomous dependent variable (using a cumulative screen scoring classification of 0, 1 versus 2, 3). The results of the aforementioned power analyses and the various discriminate analyses are further examined in the subsequent chapter titled "Research Questions and Results" (Chapter 5). In addition, a "methodological visual" of research strategies is available for review in Appendix F.

CHAPTER 5

Research Questions and Results

In the current chapter a recently adjudicated prison population, drawn from the State of Nebraska Department of Corrections (DOC) Diagnostic Evaluation Center (DEC), is analyzed to assess the utility of self-report screening instrumentation as an effective methodological tool for producing valid data regarding drug and alcohol disorders within institutionalized criminal justice settings – specifically incoming prison populations. Questions to be addressed in this research include: (1) Do screening instrument findings derived via self-report methodologies generate high levels of confidence (i.e., criterion validity, efficacy, and construct validity) when compared to forensic clinical psychological assessments; and (2) Does the value of the self-report screening methodology administered in criminal justice institutionalized settings vary based on case attributes (i.e., demographics, cognitive functioning, drug use history, treatment history, criminal justice experiences)?

Chapter Organization

The current chapter has been organized into four primary sections in order to facilitate the communication of research analyses and findings. First, the overall findings from this study's analyses will be presented in aggregate form in the 'Comprehensive Findings' section of this chapter. Second, an examination of the attributes of the sample population available for analytical comparison to institutional inmate census data will be considered as a means to establish the potential value of subsequent research findings. The third primary section of this chapter imparts detailed findings related to the initial research question above – results related to criterion validity, efficacy, and construct validity. To conclude, section four of this chapter conveys detailed findings related to the later of the above listed research questions – testing of case attribute influences on the validity of self-report screen findings.

Comprehensive Findings

Data was obtained from institutional files of 424 inmates incarcerated during the year 2001 at the State of Nebraska's DOC DEC. Analyses were conducted in order to assess the validity, efficacy and potential influences on self-report screening instrumentation deployed in criminal populations in relationship to clinical psychological assessments. First, it was ascertained through multiple chi-square 'Goodness of Fit' analyses that there were no statistically significant differences between the sample population (n = 424) and the DEC institutional population (N = 1,518) from which it was drawn with respect to a variety of variables (i.e., age, race/ethnicity, marital status, minimum and maximum sentences).

Next, criterion validity of self-report screen findings was assessed utilizing clinical psychological assessment information as an external standard. Here, similar findings were generated by both means of assessment indicative of an estimated equivalence across raters. Moreover, chi-square analyses generated across the external criterion and multiple cumulative screen score classifications indicated the existence of a significant statistical relationship across all scoring schemata. Therefore, significant results were obtained in assessing the relationship between screening outcomes and an 'optimal' external criterion in this study's setting as findings supported the criterion validity of the self-report screening methodology at the aggregate level of analysis.

In addition to an examination of criterion validity at the aggregate level of analysis, self-report screen results were also explored in terms of efficacy. Two scoring classifications were used to disaggregate sample cases for analysis, essentially producing information for a 2-by-4 (*extreme*) and a 2-by-2 (*majority*) concordance table. Six epidemiological criteria were explored by means of these analyses – prevalence, sensitivity, specificity, positive predictive power, negative predictive power, and accuracy. Here, both extreme and majority sensitivity were found to be relatively high (83.0% and 94.3% respectively). Counter to these findings, both extreme and majority specificity were found to be relatively low (25.0% and 44.4% respectively). Next, positive predictive power demonstrated relatively high values across both extreme and majority models (95.4% and 89.2% respectively). Negative predictive power findings were mixed with the extreme model resulting in 90.0% and the majority model resulting in 61.5%. Finally, accuracy also presented somewhat mixed findings with extreme accuracy analysis demonstrating findings of 73.1% and majority accuracy at 85.8%. Overall, the self-report screening methodology was found to demonstrate mixed levels of epidemiological efficacy. Specifically, statistical evidence described a methodology highly accurate in identifying those in need of treatment, however, also demonstrating a tendency to produce overly conservative findings with respect to those individuals clinically found to not be in need of treatment.

Subsequent to examining criterion validity and efficacy, issues of construct validity were explored. Variables under analysis here included 1) age of first drug use, 2) frequency of drug use, 3) primary route of drug administration, 4) previous substance abuse treatment, 5) under the influence at time of current offense, 6) current offense dynamics, and 7) institutional misconduct specific to use of drugs. The information related to these variables was theoretically assessed and statistically analyzed (via analysis of variance and chi-square analyses) against pooled self-report screening score results for applicable inmate cases. Five of the seven relationships under review with respect to the construct validity of self-report screen results were found to support, both theoretically and statistically, the use of the self-report screening methodology. Only the first (age of first drug use) and seventh (institutional misconduct specific to use of drugs) variable relationships presented some disagreement between theoretical expectations and statistical findings. However, ultimately six out of the seven relationships explored were found to produce significant results. Therefore, support was found for the construct validity of the self-report screening methodology as used in this study population.

Finally, the potential influence of case and individual-level variables on the criterion validity of self-report-based screen findings was examined by means of a series of discriminant analyses. Variables were grouped into research models for statistical analyses that included 1) individual level attributes (demographics and intellectual functioning), 2) drug-related experiences (drug use history and treatment histories), and 3) developmental attributes (criminal justice experiences and other indexes of substance misuse). In addition to these three partial models, an initial full model containing all variables was also conducted. Statistical analyses established that several variables failed to produce any significant discriminant capacity across dependent variable categories (e.g., age of onset, prior mental health treatment, and sentence minimums), while at the same time other variables demonstrated a recurring ability to produce correct classifications of grouped cases (e.g., primary drug of choice, religious affiliation, institutional misconduct, employment status, race, under the influence at time of offense, and current offense). Built on the foundation of these results, evidence was established for a number of the case variables and individual-level research variables examined throughout the current study to demonstrate moderate capacities to discriminate across categorical self-reported screened "need for treatment" findings.

GOODNESS OF FIT TESTS

As previously stated in Chapter 4, one of the primary objectives of the current study was to generate research findings that might be extrapolated to all State of Nebraska prison commitments for the year 2001. To this end, and in order to promote the value, in terms of generalizability of research findings generated by the current study, a random sample of inmate cases (n = 424) from the total population for the year 2001 (N = 1,518) were selected (27.9%). Subsequently, to assess that this process was successful in selecting a representative sample of the population under study, statistical analyses were conducted to compare the two groups. Specifically, chi-square 'Goodness of Fit' test analyses of the percentage of cases in these populations (incoming prison population and research sample population), as a function of available institutional data (age, race/ethnicity, marital status, minimum sentence, and maximum sentence), was conducted. Comparative information for these tests was derived from institutional census data on prisoners housed at the DEC during the year 2001 (generated monthly) and information gathered by the researcher on individuals who had been methodologically selected into the research sample (see Table 4 Chi-Square 'Goodness of Fit Test).

Table 4: Goodness of Fit Test -- Nebraska Department of Corrections (DOC) Diagnostic Evaluation Center (DEC) 2001 vs. Research Sample -- DEC Census Data

	Jan.	Feb.	March	April	May	June	July	Aug.	Sept.	Oct.	Nov.	Dec.	Total	Sample
New Admits	n=137	n = 113	n = 122	n = 123	n = 14	n = 134	n = 135	n = 131	n = 93	n = 138	n = 141	n =104	N = 1,518	N = 424
Current Holdings	n = 445	n = 423	n = 418	n = 433	n = 437	n = 444	n = 448	n = 427	n = 406	n = 418	n = 435	n = 384		
Age														
16-21	22.2% 99/445	20.7% 88/423	20.3% 85/418	21.8% 94/431	24.3% 106/437	23.2% 103/444	22.3% 100/448	22.7% 97/427	18.7% 76/406	21.5% 90/418	21.4% 93/435	20.8% 80/384	21.7% 1,111/5,116	21.5% 91/424
22-24	13.3% 59	14.7% 62	12.7% 53	13.2% 57	11.9% 52	13.5% 60	11.8% 53	13.1% 56	13.1% 53	10.0% 42	12.0% 52	9.9% 38	12.5% 637	12.3% 52
25-29	14.6% 65	14.7% 62	14.6% 61	14.8% 64	16.0% 70	13.3% 59	14.1% 63	12.2% 52	13.8% 56	14.6% 61	14.9% 65	18.0% 69	14.6% 747	15.6% 66
30-34	15.3% 68	14.7% 62	17.2% 72	15.3% 66	14.2% 62	13.7% 61	15.0% 67	14.1% 60	13.8% 56	13.9% 58	16.3% 71	16.9% 65	15.0% 768	15.6% 66
35-39	13.0% 58	12.3% 52	13.2% 55	13.0% 56	12.4% 54	13.1% 58	13.4% 60	13.8% 59	16.0% 65	15.8% 66	13.3% 58	12.8% 49	13.5% 690	13.4% 57
40-44	10.8% 48	10.9% 46	10.3% 43	12.5% 54	12.6% 55	14.9% 66	14.5% 65	14.8% 63	13.8% 56	12.4% 52	11.0% 48	9.6% 37	12.4% 633	11.8% 50
45-49	5.6% 25	5.9% 25	6.2% 26	4.4% 19	4.1% 18	2.5% 11	3.1% 14	3.5% 15	4.2% 17	4.8% 20	5.3% 23	7.3% 28	4.7% 241	4.2% 18
50-54	2.7% 12	2.6% 11	2.2% 9	2.1% 9	1.8% 8	2.7% 12	3.3% 15	3.7% 16	3.9% 16	3.8% 16	3.4% 15	3.1% 12	3.0% 151	2.8% 12
55-59	1.3% 6	2.1% 9	2.2% 9	1.2% 5	1.8% 8	1.8% 8	1.3% 6	0.9% 4	1.0% 4	1.2% 5	1.4% 6	1.0% 4	1.4% 74	1.4% 6
60 & +	1.1% 5	1.4% 6	1.2% 5	1.6% 7	0.9% 4	1.4% 6	1.1% 5	1.2% 5	1.7% 7	1.9% 8	0.9% 4	0.5% 2	1.3% 64	1.4% 6
Missing	0	0	0	2	0	0	0	0	0	0	0	0		

* **Test Statistic = ChiSquare = .6183 -- df = 6 -- p-value = .9961 -- No Significant difference**

** Please note that all demographics were collected via official agency data (census and individual inmate case files).

** Note, all variables selected to compute statistical group comparisons were limited to available census data.

** Age categories of '45-49, 50-54, 55-59, and 60 & Over' were collapsed for statistical comparison as a required conditions of the Chi Squared test (expected count in each category must be at least 5%).

Table 4 (Cond't): Goodness of Fit Test -- Nebraska Department of Corrections (DOC) Diagnostic Evaluation Center (DEC) 2001 vs. Research Sample -- DEC Census Data

Race / Ethnicity	Jan.	Feb.	March	April	May	June	July	Aug.	Sept.	Oct.	Nov.	Dec.	Total	Sample
White	60.9%	63.4%	60.8%	57.9%	57.9%	59.5%	60.6%	60.0%	62.6%	62.4%	59.5%	58.5%	**60.3%**	**58.0%**
	271/445	268/423	254/418	250/432	253/437	264/444	271/447	256/427	254/406	261/418	259/435	224/383	**3,085/5,115**	**246/424**
Black	20.0%	18.2%	19.6%	22.2%	23.6%	24.1%	21.3%	21.5%	19.5%	21.8%	21.1%	21.9%	**21.3%**	**22.2%**
	89	77	82	96	103	107	95	92	79	91	92	84	**1087**	**94**
Hispanic	13.9%	12.1%	11.7%	11.3%	11.4%	10.6%	12.3%	13.8%	13.3%	11.0%	13.3%	14.4%	**12.4%**	**12.7%**
	62	51	49	49	50	47	55	59	54	46	58	55	**635**	**54**
American	4.9%	5.9%	7.2%	8.3%	7.1%	5.9%	5.8%	4.2%	4.2%	4.5%	5.7%	5.2%	**5.8%**	**5.2%**
Indian	22	25	30	36	31	26	26	18	17	19	25	20	**295**	**22**
Asian/Other	0.2%	0.5%	0.7%	0.2%	0.0%	0.0%	0.0%	0.5%	0.5%	0.2%	0.2%	0.0%	**0.3%**	**1.9%**
	1	2	3	1	0	0	0	2	2	1	1	0	**13**	**8**
Missing	0	0	0	1	0	0	1	0	0	0	0	1		

* **Test Statistic = ChiSquare = .1.2165 -- df = 3 -- p-value = ..74911 -- No Significant difference**

** Ethnic categories of 'American Indian, and Asian/Other' were collapsed for statistical comparison as a required conditions of the ChiSquared test (expected count in each category must be at least 5%

Table 4 (Cond't): Goodness of Fit Test -- Nebraska Department of Corrections (DOC) Diagnostic Evaluation Center (DEC) 2001 vs. Research Sample -- DEC Census Data

	Jan.	Feb.	March	April	May	June	July	Aug.	Sept.	Oct.	Nov.	Dec.	Total	Sample
Marital Status														
Single / Never Married	60.4% 269/445	60.4% 255/422	60.5% 251/415	62.0% 263/424	63.4% 276/435	63.1% 268/425	61.9% 258/417	59.6% 251/421	58.5% 233/398	59.2% 241/407	59.2% 250/422	59.3% 223/376	**60.7%** **3,038/5,007**	**59.0%** **250/424**
Married / Cohabitating	22.7% 101	21.1% 89	20.5% 85	21.9% 93	23.2% 101	24.0% 102	24.0% 100	25.4% 107	23.3% 93	23.6% 96	24.4% 103	22.6% 85	**23.1%** **1,155**	**21.2%** **90**
Divorced / Separated	16.2% 72	17.8% 75	18.3% 76	15.8% 67	13.1% 57	12.7% 54	14.1% 59	15.0% 63	17.8% 71	16.5% 67	15.9% 67	17.6% 66	**15.9%** **794**	**18.9%** **80**
Widowed	0.7% 3	0.7% 3	0.7% 3	0.2% 1	0.2% 1	0.2% 1	0.0% 0	0.0% 0	0.3% 1	0.7% 3	0.5% 2	0.5% 2	**0.4%** **20**	**0.9%** 4
Missing	0	1	3	9	2	19	31	6	8	11	13	8	**60.7%**	**59.0%**

* Test Statistic = ChiSquare = 4.0624

** Marital categories of 'Divorced/Separated, and Widowed' were collapsed for statistical comparison as a required conditions of the ChiSquared test (expected count in each category must be at least 5%).

Table 4 (Cond't): Goodness of Fit Test -- Nebraska Department of Corrections (DOC) Diagnostic Evaluation Center (DEC) 2001 vs. Research Sample -- DEC Census Data

Minimum Sentence (in months)	Jan.	Feb.	March	April	May	June	July	Aug.	Sept.	Oct.	Nov.	Dec.	Total	Sample
12 or less	32.8%	33.3%	35.9%	32.8%	30.0%	32.0%	30.4%	29.7%	30.8%	36.6%	37.0%	34.9%	**33.0%**	**36.8%**
	146/ 445	141/ 423	150/ 418	142/ 433	131/ 437	142/ 444	136/ 448	127 /427	125/ 406	153/ 418	161/ 435	134/ 384	**1,688/ 5,118**	**156/ 424**
12+ to 24	33.3%	33.1%	33.0%	37.2%	37.8%	32.4%	32.1%	35.1%	32.5%	31.6%	32.4%	38.0%	**34.0%**	**34.7%**
(1-2 yrs.)	148	140	138	161	165	144	144	150	132	132	141	146	**1,741**	**147**
24+ to 36	11.0%	9.2%	7.7%	8.8%	10.8%	11.5%	12.1%	11.0%	10.8%	9.3%	9.7%	9.1%	**10.1%**	**9.9%**
(2-3 yrs.)	49	39	32	38	47	51	54	47	44	39	42	35	**517**	**42**
36+ to 48	6.3%	6.4%	5.5%	4.4%	5.0%	7.4%	8.7%	8.0%	8.1%	7.2%	6.7%	5.5%	**6.6%**	**6.6%**
(3-4 yrs.)	28	27	23	19	22	33	39	34	33	30	29	21	**338**	**28**
48+ to 60	4.3%	4.3%	3.3%	3.9%	3.4%	4.5%	3.6%	5.2%	4.4%	3.8%	2.3%	2.9%	**3.8%**	**0.7%**
(4-5 yrs.)	19	18	14	17	15	20	16	22	18	16	10	11	**196**	**3**
60+ to 72	2.9%	2.6%	3.3%	2.3%	1.6%	2.5%	2.9%	3.0%	3.2%	1.9%	2.8%	2.9%	**2.7%**	**1.9%**
(5-6 yrs.)	13	11	14	10	7	11	13	13	13	8	12	11	**136**	**8**
72+ to 84	1.1%	0.9%	0.5%	0.5%	0.7%	0.9%	2.0%	1.4%	1.2%	0.5%	0.9%	0.3%	**0.9%**	**0.5%**
(6-7 yrs.)	5	4	2	2	3	4	9	6	5	2	4	1	**47**	**2**
84+ to 96	0.4%	1.4%	1.7%	1.6%	1.6%	2.5%	1.8%	0.9%	1.2%	1.4%	0.9%	0.3%	**1.3%**	**0.9%**
(7-8 yrs.)	2	6	7	7	7	11	8	4	5	6	4	1	**68**	**4**
96+ to 108	0.0%	0.2%	0.2%	0.2%	0.5%	0.7%	0.9%	0.2%	0.5%	0.2%	0.2%	0.3%	**0.4%**	**0.0%**
(8-9 yrs.)	0	1	1	1	2	3	4	1	2	1	1	1	**18**	**0**
108+ to 120	2.2%	2.4%	2.2%	1.6%	2.1%	1.4%	1.8%	1.4%	2.0%	2.6%	2.3%	1.6%	**2.0%**	**2.4%**
(9-10 yrs.)	10	10	9	7	9	6	8	6	8	11	10	6	**100**	**10**
120+ to 132	0.2%	0.2%	0.5%	0.2%	0.0%	0.0%	0.0%	0.0%	0.5%	0.0%	0.0%	0.3%	**0.1%**	**0.0%**
(10-11 yrs.)	1	1	2	0	0	0	0	0	2	0	0	1	**7**	**0**
132+ to 144	0.2%	0.2%	0.2%	0.2%	0.2%	0.2%	0.2%	0.2%	0.5%	0.5%	0.2%	0.3%	**0.3%**	**0.0%**
(11-12 yrs.)	1	1	1	1	1	1	1	1	2	2	1	1	**14**	**0**
144+ to 156	0.2%	0.0%	0.0%	0.0%	0.0%	0.2%	0.2%	0.2%	0.2%	0.2%	0.2%	0.0%	**0.1%**	**0.5%**
(12-13 yrs.)	1	0	0	0	0	1	1	1	1	1	1	0	**7**	**2**
156+ to 168	0.2%	0.5%	0.2%	0.0%	0.0%	0.0%	0.0%	0.0%	0.0%	0.2%	0.5%	0.0%	**0.1%**	**0.5%**
(13-14 yrs.)	1	2	1	0	0	0	0	0	0	1	2	0	**7**	**2**
168+ to 180	0.4%	0.5%	0.7%	1.4%	1.6%	1.1%	0.2%	0.0%	0.5%	0.7%	0.7%	1.3%	**0.8%**	**0.5%**
(14-15 yrs.)	2	2	3	6	7	5	1	0	2	3	3	5	**39**	**2**
180+ to 192	0.2%	0.2%	0.2%	0.5%	0.5%	0.7%	0.2%	0.0%	0.0%	0.0%	0.2%	0.5%	**0.3%**	**0.0%**
(15-16 yrs.)	1	1	1	2	2	3	1	0	0	0	1	2	**14**	**0**
192+ to 204	0.0%	0.0%	0.2%	0.2%	0.0%	0.0%	0.2%	0.2%	0.0%	0.0%	0.0%	0.0%	**0.1%**	**0.0%**
(16-17 yrs.)	0	0	1	1	0	0	1	1	0	0	0	0	**4**	**0**
204+ to 216	0.4%	0.2%	0.5%	0.2%	0.2%	0.2%	0.2%	0.5%	0.5%	0.2%	0.5%	0.5%	**0.4%**	**0.9%**
(17-18 yrs.)	2	1	2	1	1	1	1	2	2	1	2	2	**18**	**4**
216+ to 228	0.2%	0.5%	0.5%	0.5%	0.0%	0.2%	0.2%	0.0%	0.0%	0.0%	0.0%	0.0%	**0.2%**	**0.5%**
(18-19 yrs.)	1	2	2	2	0	1	1	0	0	0	0	0	**9**	**2**
228+ to 240	0.9%	0.9%	0.5%	0.5%	0.5%	0.2%	0.7%	0.7%	0.5%	0.5%	0.7%	0.3%	**0.6%**	**0.5%**
(19-20 yrs.)	4	4	2	2	2	1	3	3	2	2	3	1	**29**	**2**
240 +	2.5%	2.6%	2.9%	3.2%	3.4%	1.1%	1.1%	1.4%	1.7%	1.7%	1.1%	1.0%	**2.0%**	**2.4%**
(20+ yrs.)	11	11	12	14	15	5	5	6	7	7	5	4	**102**	**10**
Life	0.0%	0.2%	0.2%	0.0%	0.2%	0.2%	0.4%	0.7%	0.7%	0.7%	0.7%	0.3%	**0.4%**	**0.0%**
	0	1	1	0	1	1	2	3	3	3	3	1	**19**	**0**

* Test Statistic = ChiSquare = 10.2749

** Sentence categories of '48+ to 60, thru 144+ to 156' were collapsed for statistical comparison as a required conditions of the ChiSquared test (expected count in each category must be at least 5%).

** Sentence categories of '156+ to 168, thru life' were collapsed for statistical comparison as a required conditions of the ChiSquared test (expected count in each category must be at least 5%).

Table 4 (Cond't): Goodness of Fit Test -- Nebraska Department of Corrections (DOC) Diagnostic Evaluation Center (DEC) 2001 vs. Research Sample -- DEC Census Data

Maximum Sentence	Jan.	Feb.	March	April	May	June	July	Aug.	Sept.	Oct.	Nov.	Dec.	Total	Sample
12 or less	15.3%	14.7%	17.7%	15.9	11.0%	16.0%	17.6%	13.1%	13.5%	18.4%	16.8%	14.8%	**15.4%**	**11.5%**
	68/	62/	74/	69/	48/	71/	79/	56/	55/	77/	73/	57/	**789/**	**48/**
	445	423	418	433	437	444	448	427	406	418	435	384	**5,118**	**424**
12+ to 24	16.6%	15.1%	14.4%	14.3%	16.5%	13.1%	10.0%	14.1%	15.0%	16.5%	19.5%	19.0%	**15.3%**	**20.0%**
(1-2 yrs.)	74	64	60	62	72	58	45	60	61	69	85	73	**857**	**85**
24+ to 36	16.9%	20.1%	19.4%	19.2%	19.7%	15.3%	15.0%	17.1%	17.2%	17.5%	17.0%	19.3%	**17.8%**	**21.7%**
(2-3 yrs.)	75	85	81	83	86	68	67	73	70	73	74	74	**883**	**92**
36+ to 48	7.4%	6.6%	8.1%	11.5%	12.4%	11.7%	11.8%	11.7%	11.6%	8.4%	8.0%	10.7%	**10.0%**	**10.8%**
(3-4 yrs.)	33	28	34	50	54	52	53	50	47	35	35	41	**507**	**46**
48+ to 60	16.6%	14.7%	13.9%	15.0%	16.5%	14.6%	15.4%	13.6%	12.1%	12.2%	13.8%	12.2%	**14.3%**	**14.2%**
(4-5 yrs.)	74	62	58	65	72	65	69	58	49	51	60	47	**675**	**60**
60+ to 72	5.4%	4.5%	3.8%	3.9%	4.3%	8.1%	9.2%	8.2%	6.7%	4.5%	6.2%	7.6%	**6.0%**	**4.5%**
(5-6 yrs.)	24	19	16	17	19	36	41	35	27	19	27	29	**298**	**19**
72+ to 84	3.1%	2.4%	2.2%	1.6%	1.6%	2.0%	1.8%	3.0%	3.0%	3.6%	1.4%	1.8%	**2.3%**	**1.9%**
(6-7 yrs.)	14	10	9	7	7	9	8	13	12	15	6	7	**108**	**8**
84+ to 96	2.7%	4.3%	2.6%	2.3%	2.7%	3.6%	2.9%	4.7%	4.2%	4.1%	3.4%	2.6%	**3.3%**	**2.8%**
(7-8 yrs.)	12	18	11	10	12	16	13	20	17	17	15	10	**161**	**12**
96+ to 108	0.9%	0.9%	1.0%	0.7%	0.0%	0.7%	1.1%	0.7%	1.7%	0.7%	0.7%	0.8%	**0.8%**	**0.5%**
(8-9 yrs.)	4	4	4	3	0	3	5	3	7	3	3	3	**38**	**2**
108+ to 120	4.7%	5.2%	4.5%	3.5%	3.2%	4.3%	4.2%	4.4%	3.7%	4.1%	3.9%	4.2%	**4.2%**	**3.8%**
(9-10 yrs.)	21	22	19	15	14	19	19	19	15	17	17	16	**202**	**16**
120+ to 132	0.7%	0.2%	0.5%	0.2%	0.5%	0.5%	0.4%	0.7%	0.5%	0.5%	0.2%	0.0%	**0.4%**	**0.5%**
(10-11 yrs.)	3	1	2	1	2	2	2	3	2	2	1	0	**19**	**2**
132+ to 144	0.4%	1.2%	1.9%	1.4%	0.9%	2.0%	2.2%	0.5%	1.0%	0.7%	1.1%	0.8%	**1.2%**	**0.0%**
(11-12 yrs.)	2	5	8	6	4	9	10	2	4	3	5	3	**60**	**0**
144+ to 156	0.2%	0.2%	0.5%	0.2%	0.5%	0.7%	0.9%	0.2%	0.5%	0.5%	0.7%	0.5%	**0.5%**	**0.0%**
(12-13 yrs.)	1	1	2	1	2	3	4	1	2	2	3	2	**24**	**0**
156+ to 168	0.0%	0.2%	0.5%	0.5%	0.2%	0.0%	0.7%	0.9%	0.5%	0.5%	0.5%	0.3%	**0.4%**	**0.9%**
(13-14 yrs.)	0	1	2	2	1	0	3	4	2	2	2	1	**21**	**4**
168+ to 180	1.1%	0.9%	0.7%	1.6%	1.8%	2.3%	1.6%	2.8%	3.0%	1.4%	0.5%	0.3%	**1.5%**	**1.4%**
(14-15 yrs.)	5	4	3	7	8	10	7	12	12	6	2	1	**74**	**6**
180+ to 192	0.0%	0.2%	0.0%	0.0%	0.5%	0.5%	0.4%	0.0%	0.7%	1.2%	0.7%	0.3%	**0.4%**	**0.0%**
(15-16 yrs.)	0	1	0	0	2	2	2	0	3	5	3	1	**20**	**0**
192+ to 204	0.0%	0.0%	0.0%	0.0%	0.0%	0.0%	0.2%	0.0%	0.0%	0.0%	0.0%	0.0%	**0.0%**	**0.0%**
(16-17 yrs.)	0	0	0	0	0	0	1	0	0	0	0	0	**1**	**0**
204+ to 216	0.2%	0.0%	0.2%	0.2%	0.0%	0.0%	0.2%	0.0%	0.2%	0.0%	0.0%	0.0%	**0.1%**	**0.0%**
(17-18 yrs.)	1	0	1	1	0	0	1	0	1	0	0	0	**6**	**0**
216+ to 228	0.0%	0.0%	0.0%	0.0%	0.0%	0.0%	0.0%	0.0%	0.0%	0.0%	0.0%	0.0%	**0.0%**	**0.0%**
(18-19 yrs.)	0	0	0	0	0	0	0	0	0	0	0	0	**1**	**0**
228+ to 240	2.2%	2.6%	1.7%	1.4%	1.1%	0.7%	0.7%	0.5%	0.7%	1.0%	1.6%	1.6%	**1.3%**	**0.0%**
(19-20 yrs.)	10	11	7	6	5	3	3	2	3	4	7	6	**61**	**0**
240 +	4.7%	5.4%	5.5%	5.3%	5.3%	3.4%	3.1%	3.0%	3.4%	3.6%	3.2%	2.9%	**4.1%**	**5.7%**
(20+ yrs.)	21	23	23	23	23	15	14	13	14	15	14	11	**199**	**24**
Life	0.7%	0.5%	1.0%	1.2%	1.4%	0.7%	0.4%	0.7%	0.7%	0.7%	0.7%	0.5%	**0.8%**	
	3	2	4	5	6	3	2	3	3	3	3	2	**36**	

* Test Statistic = ChiSquare = 22.6981

** Sentence categories of '60+ to 72, thru 96+ to 108' were collapsed for statistical comparison as a required conditions of the ChiSquared test (expected count in each category must be at least 5%).

** Sentence categories of '108+ to 120, thru 228+ to 240' were collapsed for statistical comparison as a required conditions of the ChiSquared test (expected count in each category must be at least 5%).

** Sentence categories of 240+ and life' were collapsed for statistical comparison as a required conditions of the ChiSquared test (expected count in each category must be at least 5%).

Chi-Square Findings

All tests for comparison revealed no statistically significant differences between the research sample selected for study and the larger population of DEC inmates. It is, however, worth noting that the variables selected to compute statistical group comparisons were driven by available DEC census data. In other words, institutional classifications had to be adhered to when comparing categories. For example, while researchers gathered data regarding ethnicity using several categories, it was however necessary to collapse some of these together to reflect the institutional data it was to be statically compared to (i.e., Asian and Other [meaning any ethnicity not White, Black, Hispanic, or American Indian] were collapsed together in the 'Goodness of Fit' test for this reason). This was not seen as overly problematic, as the statistical differences between groups were quite small overall. Moreover, these categories were only collapsed for purposes of statistical sample comparisons (to demonstrate methodological soundness) and all other research analyses were capable of returning to the more sensitive and/or group specific data collected by the researcher.

In addition to collapsing variables into categories in order to reflect institutional data practices, it was also necessary to collapse some variables together in order to avoid violating assumptions of the chi-square 'Goodness of Fit' test. Specifically, it was necessary to collapse variables to achieve an *expected count* of at least 5% for each compared attribute of a variable across populations. To this end, age categories of '45-49, 50-54, 55-59, and 60 & Over' were collapsed for statistical comparison. Next, ethnic categories of 'American Indian, and Asian/Other,' and marital categories of 'Divorced/Separated, and Widowed' were collapsed respectively. Finally, minimum sentence categories of '48+ to 60, thru 144+ to 156' and '156+ to 168, thru life,' and maximum sentence categories of '60+ to 72, thru 96+ to 108,' '108+ to 120, thru 228+ to 240,' and '240+ and life' were collapsed into single attributes within their respective variables for statistical comparison as a required condition of the chi-squared 'Goodness of Fit' test (expected count in each category must be at least 5%).

While these modifications to the data did produce less sensitive comparisons across populations, there were nevertheless a suitable number of variables and associated attributes to arrive at a reasonable understanding with respect to the representativeness of the current research sample. More specifically, the inmates information sampled during this research period *are* representative of the entire DEC inmate population during the year 2001 (see Table 4 Chi-Square 'Goodness of Fit Test').

CRITERION VALIDITY AND EFFICACY

The first of two primary research questions to be informed by the following analyses has been stated as "Do screen findings derived via self-report methodologies in criminal justice institutionalized settings generate high levels of confidence?" The standard (criterion) used throughout the current study were forensic clinical psychological assessments. The results produced by clinical assessments, both at the aggregate and individual level of analysis, served as an external criterion by which to compare and assess the validity of corresponding inmate self-report screen findings. In order to establish comparable prevalence rates of "need for treatment" among the study sample population herein, a separate standard frequency and percentage of inmate cases was conducted for both clinical findings and self-report screen findings (see Table 5 'Forensic Clinical Psychological Assessment Findings,' and Table 6 'Cumulative Screen Scores').

Frequency Table Findings (criterion validity)

Table 5

Forensic Clinical Psychological Assessment Findings
Nebraska DOC DEC, 2001
(n = 424)

Clinical Findings	n	%	Cumulative %
No "Need for Treatment" Recommended	72	17.0	17.0
"Need for Treatment" Recommended	352	83.0	100.0

Figure 1

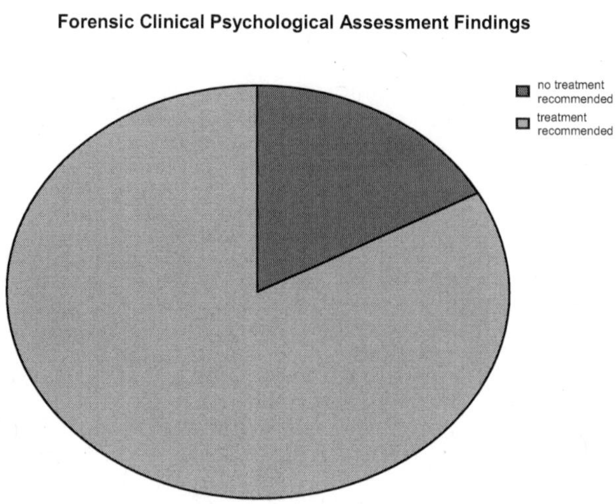

Table 6

Cumulative Screen Score Findings
Nebraska DOC DEC, 2001
(n = 424)

Cumulative Screen Score Values	n	%	Cumulative %
0	20	4.7	4.7
1	32	7.5	12.3
2	66	15.6	27.8
3	306	72.2	100.0

Figure 2

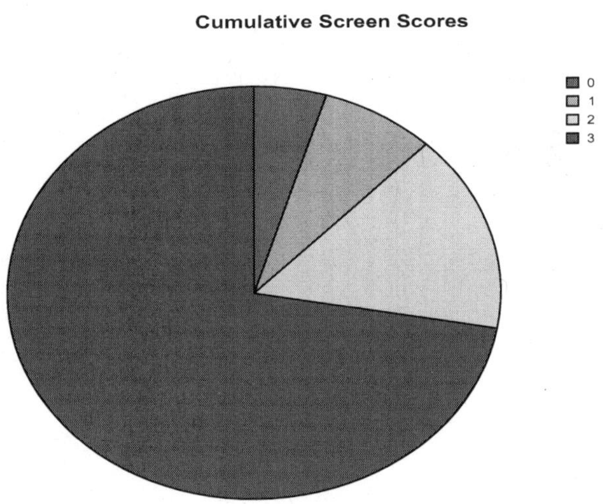

Analysis of clinical assessment information produced an 83% prevalence rate of "need for treatment" in the study sample population.

Findings from the cumulative screen scores grounded in self-report methodology generated separate prevalence levels for each possible scoring outcome, 0 thru 3. Here, a finding for the highest cumulative screen score classification – 3 – was 72.2%. When this cumulative screen score category was combined with the next highest category – 2 – the total prevalence level for the study population was determined to be 87.8% in "need of treatment." This combined total was relatively similar to the observed external criterion employed herein (the clinical assessment findings), with only a 4.8% (conservative) margin of error.

Chi-Square Findings (criterion validity)

Table 7

Clinical Assessment Findings by Scoring Schemata
Nebraska DOC DEC, 2001
(n = 424)

	Scoring Schemata (screen scoring categories in agreement by %)		
Clinical Assessment Findings	0,1,2 vs. 3	0,1 vs. 2,3	0 vs. 1,2,3
Negative	80.6%	44.4%	25%
Positive	83%	94.3%	86.6%
Pearson Chi-Square	120.039	83.468	79.386
p-value	<.001	<.001	<.001
Relationship	*significant*	*significant*	*significant*

* note: all tests are based on $df = 1$

* note: *significance* here supports rejecting the statistical null hypothesis that there is a statistical differences in findings across cumulative scoring classifications and clinical assessment findings.

Following the construction of frequency tables above, chi-square statistics were next produced for each possible self-report screen scoring classification-combination (0, 1, 2 vs. 3 – 0, 1 vs. 2, 3 – 0 vs. 1, 2, 3) to examine their relationships to clinical assessment findings (see Table 7 'Clinical Assessment Findings by Scoring Schemata').

Null Hypothesis 1 – Self-Report Screen Results by Clinical Findings

Diagnostically based screen instrument findings (pooled screening scores) collected via self-report methodology within an institutional criminal justice venue do not significantly differ from findings derived via forensic clinical psychological assessments.

As a result of the considerable agreement across the positive scoring categories in Table 7, and the statistical significance of the associated chi-square findings for each of the possible cumulative screen scoring classifications above, which confirms that there is a significant relationship between the self-report-based screen findings (across all three scoring classifications) and the clinical psychological assessments, the researcher accepts the first null hypothesis.

Concordance Table Findings (convergent validity and efficacy)

Collected research data were used to develop a 2-by-4 concordance table as a means to cross-validate cumulative screen findings (categorized by discrete cumulative scoring categories of 0, 1, 2 or 3 – each representing a progressively higher probability of "need for treatment") against clinical psychological findings (divided into the findings of criterion positive – "treatment recommended," and criterion negative – "no treatment recommended"). Calculations produced by the concordance table were used in order to explore the more specific efficacy values of self-report-based screen findings at differing levels of sensitivity. Here, two case scoring classifications were used (a dichotomous classification termed "extreme" – cases scoring 0 or 3 only, and a dichotomous classification termed "majority" – cases scoring 0 or 1, versus 2 or 3) to disaggregate sample cases for analysis. These tables thereafter have the capacity to facilitate various matches between self-report-based screen findings and the conclusions derived via clinical assessments in order to demonstrate various insights with respect to efficacy (see Table 8 'Examining Convergent Validity').

Table 8

'Examining Convergent Validity'
Self-Report Diagnostic Screen-Findings

Clinical Psychological Diagnostic Findings	Screened Positive ("need of treatment") 3	2	Screened Negative ("no need of treatment") 1	0	Total
Criterion Positive	292 (a)	40 (b)	18 (c)	2 (d)	352 (e)
Criterion Negative	14 (f)	26 (g)	14 (h)	18 (i)	72 (j)
Total	306 (l)	66 (m)	32 (n)	20 (o)	424 (p)

Analytical Terms, Formulas, and Findings:

Prevalence = e / p = 352 / 424 = **83.0%** (the 'standard' identified by assessment findings for the DEC sample population in the current study)

Extreme Sensitivity = a / a + b + c + d = 292 / 292 + 40 + 18 + 2 = **83.0%**

Majority Sensitivity = a + b / a + b + c + d =
292 + 40 / 292 + 40 + 18 + 2 = **94.3%**

Extreme Specificity = i / f + g + h + i = 18 / 14 + 26 + 14 + 18 = **25.0%**

Majority Specificity = i + h / f + g + h + i =
18 + 14 / 14 + 26 + 14 + 18 = **44.4%**

Extreme Positive Predictive Power (PPP) = a / a + f =
292 / 292 + 14 = **95.4%**

Majority PPP = a + b / a + b + f + g =
292 + 40 / 292 + 40 + 14 +26 = **89.2%**

Extreme Negative Predictive Power (NPP) = i / d + i =
18 / 2 + 18 = **90.0%**

Majority NPP = h + i / c + d + h + i =
14 + 18 / 18 + 2 + 14 + 18 = **61.5%**

Extreme Accuracy = a + i / p = 292 + 18 / 424 = **73.1%**

Majority Accuracy = a + b + h + i / p =
292 + 40 + 14 + 18 / 424 = **85.8%**

Efficacy 1 – Sensitivity

What are the associated levels of efficacy (sensitivity) of diagnostically based screen instrument findings (pooled screening scores) collected via self-report methodology within an institutional criminal justice venue?

The resulting efficacy values for the epidemiological criterion of *sensitivity* calculated from the 2-by-2 (extreme sensitivity) and 2-by-4 (majority sensitivity) concordance tables were 83.0% and 94.3% respectively. In consideration of the clinical prevalence findings for this study population also resulting in 83.0%, the resulting correlations (validity coefficients) evidenced that those respondents clinically identified as having a substance use disorder also had a high probability of being screened positive ("need for treatment") by means of the self-report methodology. However, it should be noted that these similar findings were derived at the aggregate level of analysis, and therefore may not represent the same individual respondents from the research population. Nevertheless, because this measure is used to indicate how *sensitive* the self-report screening methodology is in detecting the presence of a clinically diagnosed substance use disorder, these findings strongly support its utility in this population with respect to this efficiency criterion.

Efficacy 2 – Specificity

What are the associated levels of efficacy (specificity) of diagnostically based screen instrument findings (pooled screening scores) collected via self-report methodology within an institutional criminal justice venue?

The resulting efficacy values for the epidemiological criterion of *specificity* calculated from the 2-by-2 (extreme specificity) and 2-by-4 (majority specificity) concordance tables were 25.0% and 44.4% respectively. The resulting correlations evidenced that those respondents clinically identified as not having a substance use disorder had a relatively low probability of being screened negative ("no need for treatment") by means of the self-report methodology. Because this measure is used to indicate how *specific* the self-report screening methodology is in discriminating the absence of a clinically diagnosed substance use disorder, these findings do not support its utility in this population with respect to this efficiency criterion.

Efficacy 3 – Positive Predictive Power (PPP)

What are the associated levels of efficacy (positive predictive power) of diagnostically based screen instrument findings (pooled screening scores) collected via self-report methodology within an institutional criminal justice venue?

The resulting efficacy values for the epidemiological criterion of *positive predictive power* (*PPP*) calculated from the 2-by-2 (extreme positive predictive power) and 2-by-4 (majority positive predictive power) concordance tables were 95.4% and 89.2% respectively. The resulting correlations evidenced that those respondents screened positive ("need for treatment") by means of the self-report methodology also had a high probability of being clinically identified as having a substance use disorder. Because this measure is used to estimate the confidence warranted by a positive self-reported screen result (*PPP*) these findings strongly support its utility in this population with respect to this efficiency criterion.

Efficacy 4 – Negative Predictive Power (NPP)

What are the associated levels of efficacy (negative predictive power) of diagnostically based screen instrument findings (pooled screening scores) collected via self-report methodology within an institutional criminal justice venue?

The resulting efficacy values for the epidemiological criterion of *negative predictive power* (*NPP*) calculated from the 2-by-2 (extreme negative predictive power) and 2-by-4 (majority negative predictive power) concordance tables were 90.0% and 61.5% respectively. The resulting correlations evidenced that those respondents screened negative ("no need for treatment") by means of the self-report methodology had a mixed probability, depending on the scoring schemata employed, of being clinically identified as not having a substance use disorder. Because this measure is used to estimate the confidence warranted by a negative self-reported screen result (*NPP*) these findings demonstrated mixed support for its utility in this population with respect to this efficiency criterion.

Efficacy 5 – Accuracy

What are the associated levels of efficacy (accuracy) of diagnostically based screen instrument findings (pooled screening scores) collected via self-report methodology within an institutional criminal justice venue?

The resulting efficacy values for the epidemiological criterion of *accuracy* calculated from the 2-by-2 (extreme accuracy) and 2-by-4 (majority accuracy) concordance tables were 73.1% and 85.8% respectively. The resulting correlations evidenced that those respondents clinically identified as having, and not having, a substance use disorder had a relatively high probability of also being similarly screened positive ("need for treatment") or negative ("no need for treatment") by means of the self-report methodology. Because this measure is used to describe the degree to which the self-report screening methodology agrees with the standard used herein (clinical psychological assessments), these findings would lend support to its utility in this population with respect to this efficiency criterion.

CONSTRUCT VALIDITY

Data was next examined to determine the relationships between cumulative case scores (based on the number of positive screen findings) and "other indexes of substance misuse." This examination, referred to as construct validity, simply involved comparing self-reported information to screen findings across respondent groupings to understand the extent to which expected theoretical findings were realized (Carmines & Zeller, 1979; Thornberry & Krohn, 2000).

Descriptive Data

The first analyses conducted to assess construct validity involved the production of descriptive statistics from inmates who had self-reported *ever* having used drugs or alcohol (n = 412) in order to review the mean age of inmate's self-reported first alcohol/drug use (age of onset) by progressive screen score categories. Here, mean age data did not support the theoretical expectation that inmates self-reporting an earlier age of onset were also more likely to be screened as "in need of treatment" (see Table 9 'Self-Report Age at First Alcohol/Drug Use – Descriptives' and Figure 3).

Table 9

Self-Report Age at First Alcohol/Drug Use – Descriptives
Nebraska DOC DEC, 2001
(*n* = 412)

					95% Confidence Interval for Mean		Range
Screen Score Values	*n*	Mean	Standard Deviation	Standard Error	Lower Bound	Upper Bound	Min/Max
0	14	14.43	2.533	.677	12.97	15.89	10/18
1	28	12.29	4.250	.803	10.64	13.93	4/18
2	64	14.92	4.634	.579	13.76	16.08	8/32
3	306	14.76	4.179	.239	14.29	15.23	5/32

Figure 3

Self-Report Age at First Alcohol/Drug Use
By Cumulative Screen Score

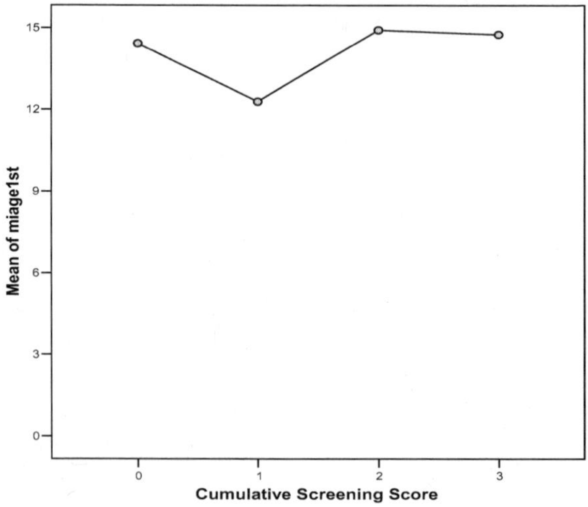

Levene Tests of Homogeneity of Variance

Following an inspection of the descriptive data above, it was next appropriate to statistically examine potential differences across cumulative scoring categories of self-report screen findings by inmate mean ages of first alcohol/drug use. The preferred method for this examination is to calculate an analysis of variance (ANOVA). However, prior to this, it was first important to assess the data for assumptions necessary to calculate an ANOVA – 1) homogeneity of variance, 2) independence, and 3) normality.

Table 10

Test of Homogeneity of Variances
for Self-Report Age at First Alcohol/Drug Use
Nebraska DOC DEC, 2001
(n = 412)

Levene Statistic	*df*1	*df*2	Significance Statistic	Finding
1.000	3	408	.393	*Significance*

* note: *significance* here supported accepting the statistical null hypothesis that there was no statistical difference in variance across cumulative screen scoring classifications.

Therefore, in association with the research variables under review above, a Levene Statistic was calculated as a test of homogeneity of variance. This in turn indicated that the variances of ages across categories of self-report screen findings were equal (see Table 10 'Test of Homogeneity of Variance'), thereby meeting the first necessary assumption for an ANOVA.

Statistics of Normality

Following the production of the Levene Statistic, the assumption of independence was considered. Because each research subject's age was collected independently, on a case-by-case basis, and there was little likelihood of corruption of such information, the second assumption of independence for an ANOVA calculation was considered to have been met.

Finally, normality, or the assumption that the distribution of ages followed a normal bell curve for each cumulative self-report scoring category was examined (see Table 11 'Statistics of Normality'). In addition, data were also charted on histograms for visual inspection (see Appendix G 'Assumptions of Normality'). Here, the assumption of normality was somewhat questionable, however, because homogeneity and independence had previously been satisfied, an ANOVA calculation was next conducted.

Table 11

Statistics of Normality
for Self-Report Age at First Alcohol/Drug Use
Nebraska DOC DEC, 2001
(n = 412)

Screen Score Value	n	Mean	Median	Skewness	Standard Error of Skewness	Kurtosis	Standard Error of Kurtosis
0	14	14.43	15.00	-.631	.597	-.567	1.154
1	28	12.29	13.00	-.491	.441	-.843	.858
2	64	14.92	14.50	1.538	.299	4.366	.590
3	306	14.76	14.00	1.304	.139	2.561	.278

ANOVA Findings

An ANOVA was conducted which demonstrated a statistically significant difference across inmates mean ages of first alcohol/drug use by categories of self-report screen findings (see Table 12 'Self-Report Age at First Alcohol/Drug Use').

Table 12

ANOVA
Self-Report Age of First Alcohol/Drug Use
Nebraska DOC DEC, 2001

ANOVA Classifications	Sum of Squares	*df*	Mean Square	F	Significance
Between Groups	164.655	3	54.885	3.08	.027
Within Groups	7249.857	408	17.769		
Total	7414.512	411			

* note: *significance* here supported rejecting the statistical null hypothesis that there was no statistical difference in mean age of first use across cumulative screen scoring classifications.

Scheffe Test of Comparisons

Subsequent to these mixed results, in order to review the relationships between ages of onset and self-report screen findings more closely across all category combinations (6 combinations were possible), a Scheffe calculation was conducted. Here, it was most explicitly understood which categories in combination with one another evidenced statistically significant differences. Specifically, only one combination of categories was found to demonstrate statistically significant difference – '1 and 3' (see Table 13 'Scheffe's Multiple Comparison Test for Self-Report Age at First Alcohol/Drug Use). Therefore, it is important to note in the prior ANOVA that findings of significance may have been an artifact of the sample sizes across the combined categories of '1' ($n = 28$) and '3' ($n = 306$).

Table 13

Scheffe's Multiple Comparison Test for Self-Report Age at First Alcohol/Drug Use Nebraska DOC DEC, 2001

Cumulative Screening Score	Comparative Cum. Screen Scores	Mean Difference	Standard Error	Significance	95% Confidence Interval Lower Bound	95% Confidence Interval Upper Bound
0	1	2.143	1.380	.492	-1.73	6.02
	2	.493	1.244	.984	-3.9	3.00
	3	-.330	1.152	.994	-3.56	2.90
1	0	-2.143	1.380	.492	-6.02	1.73
	2	-2.636	.955	.056	-5.32	.05
	3	-2.472 *	.832	.033	-4.81	-.14
2	0	.493	1.244	.984	-3.00	3.98
	1	2.636	.955	.056	-.05	5.32
	3	.164	.579	.994	-1.46	1.79
3	0	.330	1.152	.994	-2.90	3.56
	1	.472 *	.832	.033	.14	4.81
	2	-.164	.579	.994	-1.79	1.46

* note: the mean difference is significant at the .05 level.

Null Hypothesis 2 – Age of First Drug Use

Diagnostically based screen instrument findings (pooled screening scores) collected via self-report methodology within an institutional criminal justice venue do not demonstrate general theoretical support via construct validity when compared to other indexes (age of first drug use) of substance misuse.

Because the descriptive data analyses above do not support a theoretical expectation that a lower mean age of first alcohol/drug use travels with higher "probability of need for treatment," and as a result of multiple analyses (ANOVA, Scheffe) presenting a weak case for a statistically significant difference in mean age of first alcohol/drug use across self-report screen instrument findings, the researcher accepts the second null hypothesis.

Chi-Square Findings

The next analysis conducted to assess construct validity involved the production of a chi-square cross-tabulation of cumulative self-report screen score findings and inmates' frequency of drug use (immediately prior to incarceration). Here it was theoretically anticipated that inmates reporting a greater frequency of drug use would also be more likely to be screened "in need of treatment." In order to avoid violating chi-square assumptions (i.e., a maximum of 20% of cells may have expected counts less than 5%) it was necessary to collapse 'monthly' and 'don't use' reports of recent alcohol/drug use (for comparison to 'daily' and 'weekly'). Moreover, it was also necessary to dichotomize self-report screen findings where cumulative scores of '0 or 1' were compared to '2 or 3' (see Table 14 'Frequency of Recent Drug Use by Cumulative Screen Scores'). Therefore, the resulting calculation involved the analysis of a 2-by-3 concordance table.

Table 14

Frequency of Drug Use
by Cumulative Screening Scores
Nebraska DOC DEC, 2001
(*n* = 424)

Self-Reported Frequency of Drug Use	**Cumulative Screen Score Classifications** "no treatment" 0 & 1	"need treatment" 2 & 3	Total
Don't Use or Monthly	22 (55.0%)	18 (45.0%)	40 (100.0%)
Weekly	20 (19.2%)	84 (80.8%)	104 (100.0%)
Daily	10 (3.6%)	270 (96.4%)	280 (100.0%)

* Pearson Chi-Square = 92.248 $(df = 2)$ $p < .001$
* Likelihood Ratio = 72.427 $(df = 2)$ $p < .001$
* Linear-by-Linear Association = 86.437 $(df = 1)$ $p < .001$

Null Hypothesis 3 – Frequency of Drug Use

Diagnostically based screen instrument findings (pooled screening scores) collected via self-report methodology within an institutional criminal justice venue do not demonstrate general theoretical support via construct validity when compared to other indexes (frequency of drug use) of substance misuse.

Because the cross-tabulated data in Table 14 reflects a substantial theoretical relationship between a greater frequency of recent drug use and higher cumulative screen scores (suggesting a "high probability of need for treatment"), and on the basis of the strength of the Pearson Chi-Square correlations (X^2 = 92.248, *df* = 2, p <.001) across these same categories, the researcher rejects the third null hypothesis.

Table 15

Primary Route of Drug Administration by Cumulative Screening Scores Nebraska DOC DEC, 2001 (*n* = 424)

Self-Report Primary Route of Drug Administration	Cumulative Screen Score Classifications: "no treatment" 0 & 1	Cumulative Screen Score Classifications: "need treatment" 2 & 3	Total
Not a Current User	12 (85.7%)	2 (14.3%)	14 (100.0%)
Oral / Swallow	20 (16.1%)	104 (83.9%)	124 (100.0%)
Smoke	20 (11.0%)	162 (89.0%)	182 (100.0%)
Snort	0 (0.0%)	34 (100.0%)	34 (100.0%)
Inject	0 (0.0%)	70 (100.0%)	70 (100,0%)

* Pearson Chi-Square = 86.728 (*df* = 4) $p < .001$
* Likelihood Ratio = 68.489 (*df* = 4) $p < .001$
* Linear-by-Linear Association = 41.024 (*df* = 1) $p < .001$

In order to next assess the theoretical relationship between more invasive routes of administration being related to progressively higher cumulative self-report screen score findings, a chi-square cross-tabulation across the respective variables was conducted. As was the case in the previous chi-square analysis, in order to avoid violating this statistical technique's assumptions (i.e., a maximum of 20% of cells may have expected counts less than 5%) it was again necessary to dichotomize self-report screen findings where cumulative scores of '0 or 1' were compared to '2 or 3' (see Table 15 'Primary Route of Drug Administration by Cumulative Screen Scores').

Null Hypothesis 4 – Primary Route of Drug Administration

Diagnostically based screen instrument findings (pooled screening scores) collected via self-report methodology within an institutional criminal justice venue do not demonstrate general theoretical support via construct validity when compared to other indexes (primary route of drug administration) of substance misuse.

Because the cross-tabulated data in Table 15 supports a substantial theoretical relationship between a more invasive primary route of drug administration and higher cumulative screen scores, and on the basis of the strength of the Pearson Chi-Square correlations (X^2 = 86.728, df = 4, $p < .001$) across these same categories, the researcher rejects the fourth null hypothesis.

The next assessment of construct validity in the current study involved examining the theoretical relationship between previous substance abuse treatment and cumulative self-report screen score findings. Here inmates who had received prior treatment were theoretically expected to also be more likely to be screened "in need of treatment." Again, a chi-square cross-tabulation across the respective variables was produced (see Table 16 'Previous Substance Abuse Treatment by Cumulative Screen Scores').

Table 16

Previous Substance Abuse Treatment
by Cumulative Screening Scores
Nebraska DOC DEC, 2001
(*n* = 424)

Self-Reported Previous Substance Abuse Treatment	Cumulative Screen Score Classifications				
	0	1	2	3	Total
No	18 (7.9%)	24 (10.5%)	49 (21.5%)	137 (60.1%)	228 (100.0%)
Yes	2 (1.0%)	8 (4.1%)	17 (8.7%)	169 (86.2%)	196 (100.0%)

* Pearson Chi-Square = 37.460 (*df* = 3) $p < .001$
* Likelihood Ratio = 40.218 (*df* = 3) $p < .001$
* Linear-by-Linear Association = 33.129 (*df* = 1) $p < .001$

Null Hypothesis 5 – Previous Substance Abuse Treatment

Diagnostically based screen instrument findings (pooled screening scores) collected via self-report methodology within an institutional criminal justice venue do not demonstrate general theoretical support via construct validity when compared to other indexes (previous substance abuse treatment) of substance misuse.

Because the cross-tabulated data in Table 16 demonstrates a substantial theoretical relationship between previous treatment for substance abuse and higher cumulative screen scores (suggesting a "high probability of need for treatment"), and on the basis of the strength of the Pearson Chi-Square correlations (X^2 =37.460, *df* = 3, $p < .001$) across these same categories, the researcher rejects the fifth null hypothesis.

To next assess the theoretical relationship between an individual having been under the influence at the time of the offense for which they are currently sentenced and higher cumulative self-report screen score findings, a chi-square cross-tabulation across the respective variables was conducted (see Table 17 'Under the Influence at Time of Offense by Cumulative Screening Scores').

Table 17

Under the Influence at Time of Offense by Cumulative Screening Scores Nebraska DOC DEC, 2001 (*n* = 424)

Self-Reported Under the Influence at Time of Offense	Cumulative Screen Score Classifications 0	1	2	3	Total
No	17 (11.5%)	28 (18.9%)	35 (23.6%)	68 (45.9%)	148 (100.0%)
Yes	3 (1.1%)	4 (1.4%)	31 (11.2%)	238 (86.2%)	276 (100.0%)

* Pearson Chi-Square = 92.253 (*df* = 3) $p < .001$
* Likelihood Ratio = 92.083 (*df* = 3) $p < .001$
* Linear-by-Linear Association = 87.057 (*df* = 1) $p < .001$

Null Hypothesis 6 – Under the Influence at Time of Current Offense

Diagnostically based screen instrument findings (pooled screening scores) collected via self-report methodology within an institutional criminal justice venue do not demonstrate general theoretical support via construct validity when compared to other indexes (under the influence at time of arrest) of substance misuse.

As a result of the cross-tabulated data in Table 17 demonstrating a considerable theoretical relationship between being under the influence at the time of the current offense for which they had been sentenced and higher cumulative screen scores, and on the basis of the strength of the Pearson Chi-Square correlations ($X^2 = 92.253$, $df = 3$, $p < .001$) across these same categories, the researcher rejects the sixth null hypothesis.

The next assessment of construct validity in the current study involved examining the theoretical relationship between current offense dynamics, specifically if it was drug-related, and the cumulative self-report screen score findings. Here, inmates who had been convicted of a drug-related crime were theoretical expected to also be more likely to be screened "in need of treatment." Again, a chi-square cross-tabulation across the respective variables was produced (see Table 18 'Current Offense – Drug Related – by Cumulative Screening Scores').

Table 18

Current Offense (Drug Related)
by Cumulative Screening Scores
Nebraska DOC DEC, 2001
(n = 424)

Recorded Current Offense	**Cumulative Screen Score Classifications** 0	1	2	3	Total
Non-Drug Related	19 (7.5%)	24 (9.5%)	41 (16.3%)	168 (66.7%)	252 (100.0%)
Drug Related	1 (0.6%)	8 (4.7%)	25 (14.5%)	138 (80.2%)	172 (100.0%)

* Pearson Chi-Square = 16.514 (df = 3) $p < .002$
* Likelihood Ratio = 19.836 (df = 3) $p < .001$
* Linear-by-Linear Association = 15.671 (df = 1) $p < .001$

Null Hypothesis 7 – Current Offense Dynamics (drug related)

Diagnostically based screen instrument findings (pooled screening scores) collected via self-report methodology within an institutional criminal justice venue do not demonstrate general theoretical support via construct validity when compared to other indexes (current offense dynamics – drug related) of substance misuse.

Because the cross-tabulated data in Table 18 supports a substantial theoretical relationship between drug-related offenses and higher cumulative screen scores, and on the basis of the strength of the

Pearson Chi-Square correlations ($X^2 = 16.514$, $df = 3$, $p < .002$) across these same categories, the researcher rejects the seventh null hypothesis.

The last analyses conducted to assess construct validity herein involved examining the relationship between drug specific institutional misconduct and "need for treatment." Here, individuals who had been reprimanded for drug specific institutional misconduct were theoretically expected to be more likely to be progressively scored via self-report screening instrumentation as "in need of treatment." In order to avoid violating chi-square assumptions (i.e., a maximum of 20% of cells may have expected counts less than 5%) it was necessary to collapse the self-report screen cumulative scoring categories of '0 and 1' and '2 and 3' (see Table 19 'Institutional Misconduct Regarding Drugs by Cumulative Screening Scores').

Table 19

Institutional Misconduct Regarding Drugs by Cumulative Screening Scores Nebraska DOC DEC, 2001 (*n* = 424)

Documented Criminal Justice Experiences	**Cumulative Screen Score Classifications** "no treatment" 0 & 1	"need treatment" 1 & 2	Total
No	52 (13.0%)	348 (87.0%)	400 (100.0%)
Yes	0 (0.0%)	24 (100.0%)	24 (100.0%)

* Pearson Chi-Square = 3.556 ($df = 1$) $p < .060$
*Continuity Correction = 2.451 ($df = 1$) $p < .118$
* Likelihood Ratio = 6.478 ($df = 1$) $p < .012$
* Linear-by-Linear Association = 3.548 ($df = 1$) $p < .061$

Null Hypothesis 8 – Institutional Misconduct Specific to Use of Drugs

Diagnostically based screen instrument findings (pooled screening scores) collected via self-report methodology within an institutional criminal justice venue do not demonstrate general theoretical support via construct validity when compared to other indexes (institutional misconduct specific to use of drugs) of substance misuse.

While negligible, the strength of the Pearson Chi-Square correlations ($X^2 = 3.556$, $df = 1$, $p < .060$) does not demonstrate statistical significance for the cross-tabulated data in Table 19; nevertheless, the direction of the data demonstrates strong support for a theoretical relationship between inmates with prior records of institutional misconduct specific to drugs and higher cumulative screen scores (suggesting a "high probability of need for treatment"). Therefore, the researcher rejects the eighth null hypothesis.

INDIVIDUAL-LEVEL, DRUG-RELATED, AND DEVELOPMENTAL INFLUENCES ON CRITERION VALIDITY

The second of two primary research questions to be informed by analyses in the current study has been stated as "Does the value of the self-report screening methodology administered in criminal justice institutionalized settings vary based on case attributes?" As was the case in all analyses to this point in the current research, the standard (external criterion) used were forensic clinical psychological assessments. Here, this criterion also served as the dependent variable. With this the case, and in order to examine the potential influences of case and individual-level variables on the validity of self-report-based screen findings, a series of discriminant analyses were conducted on one full model and three partial models (models presented below). However, prior to the execution of these functions, it was first important to estimate the required number of cases necessary for each statistical model to produce significant findings.

1. **Individual Level Attributes** = Demographics (age, race, education, marital status, religious affiliation, employment status immediately prior to incarceration)

and Intellectual Functioning (cognitive functioning classification).

2. **Drug-Related Experiences** = Drug Use History (age of first drug use, current primary drug of choice, frequency of drug use, primary route of drug administration) and Treatment History (previous substance abuse treatment, previous mental health treatment, attending community-based support group immediately prior to incarceration).

3. **Developmental Attributes** = Criminal Justice Experiences (prior lifetime incarceration, number of prior adult incarcerations, current offense type, minimum/maximum length of current sentence, drug-related institutional misconduct) and "Other Indexes of Substance Misuse" (under the influence at time of current offense).

Power Analysis

In order to arrive at an informed understanding regarding the number of cases necessary for each partial model to be analyzed, a resource derived from the literature on *power analysis* in the social sciences was used – A Power Primer (Cohen, 1988). Here, it was possible to combine across tables, information regarding the types of statistical analyses to be conducted in association with the number of variables, alpha levels, and effect sizes, to arrive at the number of cases necessary to produce statistically significant findings (see Table 20 'A Power Primer,' and Table 21 'Statistical Test Criterion Selection by required N).

Table 20

'A Power Primer'
(Indexes and their Values for Small, Medium, and Large Effects)

Test	ES index	Effect Size Small	Medium	Large
*m*A vs. *m*B for Independent Means	$d = \frac{mA - mB}{\sigma}$	.20	.50	.80
Chi-square for Goodness of Fit and Contingency	$w = \sqrt{\sum_{i=1}^{k} \frac{(P1i - Poi)^2}{Poi}}$	.10	.30	.50
Multiple and Multiple Partial Correlation	$f^2 = \frac{R^2}{1 - R^2}$	.02	.15	.35

(Cohen, 1988, p. 157)

Table 21

Statistical Test Criterion Selection by required N
(N for Small, Medium and Large ES at Power = .80 for α = .01, .05, and .10)

	α								
	.01			.05			.10		
Test	Sm	Med	Lg	Sm	Med	Lg	Sm	Med	Lg
1. Mean diff	586	95	38	393	64	26	310	50	20
6. X^2									
1df	1,168	130	38	785	87	26	618	69	25
2df	1,388	154	56	964	107	39	771	86	31
3df	1,546	172	62	1,090	121	44	880	98	35
4df	1,675	186	67	1,194	133	48	968	108	39
5df	1,787	199	71	1,293	143	51	1,045	116	42
6df	1,887	210	75	1,362	151	54	1,113	124	45
8. Mult *R*									
2k [b]	698	97	45	481	67	30			
3k [b]	780	108	50	547	76	34			
4k [b]	841	118	55	599	84	38			
5k [b]	901	126	59	645	91	42			
6k [b]	953	134	63	686	97	45			
7k [b]	998	141	66	726	10	48			
8k [b]	1,039	147	69	757	107	50			

(Cohen, 1988, p. 158)

In review of Tables 20 and 21, information provided for multiple regression was used as a proxy for discriminant analysis requirements. From this data, it was initially determined that because the full model proposed for discriminant analysis was comprised of 21 variables, that it would not be possible to guarantee statistically significant findings with the limited number of sample cases. However, because each of the three partial models contained only 7 variables, a .05 alpha level was to be used, and a medium effect size was acceptable for research findings, that the minimum number of cases necessary for analysis was only 102 for each of the proposed research models. However, because several of the independent variables under consideration herein were categorical in nature, the utilization of discriminant analysis required that they be dummy coded (see Appendix H – Discriminant Analysis Modeling). This, of course, increased the number of actual variables under consideration in each of the statistical models under review. Specifically, subsequent to the process of dummy coding, the three models included 15, 15, and 7 variables respectively[29]. Furthermore, for this method of analysis the statistical literature has suggested a minimum of 5 observations (with a preference of 20) for each variable in the model (Hair, Anderson, Tatham, & Black, 1998). However, because each model had access to a representative set of 424 cases, it was anticipated that analytical findings derived by means of discriminant analyses would have the capacity to produce statistically significant findings for all partial models.

Discriminant Analysis Findings

Next, in order to explore the value of the self-report screening methodology, testing for the significant influence of variables on the level of criterion validity of self-report driven screen findings was undertaken. Discriminant analysis was used to determine if theoretically selected and logistically available variables across study sample cases significantly influenced the accuracy of self-report-produced screen findings. Multiple analyses were conducted based on variable classifications (i.e., individual level attributes, drug-related experiences, and development level attributes) in order to provide for a more theoretically bounded consideration of findings. Following the

---

[29] It is important to note that the number of variables referenced for each partial discriminant analysis model (7, 16, and 15 respectively) were the maximum number of variables for potential inclusion; however, it was expected that following a diagnostic examination of each model, that some initially considered variables may be removed from the model based on findings of multicolinearity. Here, multicolinearity is the degree of correlation between independent variables in a model. It is an important consideration when using discriminant analysis on data that has been collected without the aid of a design of experiment. A high degree of multicolinearity produces unacceptable uncertainty (large variance) in model coefficient estimates. Specifically, the coefficients can change drastically depending on which terms are in or out of the model and also the order in which they are placed in the model.

analyses of the full model, three partial models were run which included theoretically clustered variables under consideration for potential influence on the criterion validity of self-report-based screen findings.

Convergent screen scores (i.e., the number of screens per case in agreement with the external criterion) were used as the dependent variable in the analyses (arranged into either 4 or 2 categories), and furthermore, models were run both with "pooled" and "unpooled" covariance structures in order to avoid potential issues of multicolinearity in the model. However, prior to introducing variables into each of the models for analysis, an examination of variable significance and measures of association were conducted.

The Full Model

Variables originally introduced for analysis in the full model included all variables from the previously considered partial models – 1) Individual Level Attributes, 2) Drug-Related Experiences, and 3) Developmental Attributes (see Appendix H – Discriminant Analysis Modeling). The cumulative self-report-based screen scores across cases, and resulting four categories of convergent classification, were used here as the dependent variable in the full model.

Significance levels associated with variables to be introduced into the full model were reviewed. Subsequent to conducting a "Tests of Equality of Group Means" for the full model, it was determined that multiple variables were not significant in their individual contributions to the model ($p > .100$). As several of the variables in the full model were dummy coded, it was necessary to not only consider variables individually but also within the context of the collateral dummy coded variables derived from common original model variables. From this inspection it was determined that ten variables, or sets of variables, from the model were not significant in their contributions, and therefore were removed prior to further analysis of the partial model – 1) Current Age, 2) Education (Education 8th – 11th, Graduated, and Some College), 3) Marital Status (Married, No Longer-Married), 4) Cognitive Functioning, 5) Age of First Use, 6) Mental Health Treatment, 7) Lifetime Incarceration, 8) Number of Adult Incarcerations, 9) Sentence

Minimum, and 10) Sentence Maximum (see Table 22 'Tests of Equality of Group Means for the Full Model – extreme').

Following the removal of variables for insignificant contributions to the full model, it was held that five variables remained that also did not significantly contribute to the model in isolation; rather, the group of variables they were associated with as a result of dummy coding did significantly contribute to the value of the model. Therefore, it was held that these variables would be included in the analyses of the full model.

Table 22

Tests of Equality of Group Means for the Full Model (extreme) (*n* = 424)

	Wilks' Lambda	*F*	*df*1	*df*2	Significance
1) Current Age	.998	.335	3	420	.800
2) Caucasian	.929	10.694	3	420	.000
3) Black	.932	10.294	3	420	.000
4) Hispanic	.989	1.555	3	420	.200
5) Education 8th-11th	.991	1.244	3	420	.293
6) Graduated	.988	.292	3	420	.831
7) Some College	.986	2.012	3	420	.112
8) Married	.997	.417	3	420	.741
9) No Longer-Married	.988	1.702	3	420	.166
10) Catholic	.998	.282	3	420	.838
11) Baptist	.980	2.795	3	420	.040
12) Other-Christian	.981	2.675	3	420	.047
13) Part-Time	.965	5.136	3	420	.002
14) Full-Time	.994	.862	3	420	.461
15) Cognitive-Functioning	.996	.526	3	420	.665
16) Age of First Use	.989	1.615	3	420	.185
17) Alcohol	.988	1.750	3	420	.156
18) Marijuana	.929	10.712	3	420	.000
19) Cocaine/Crack	.973	3.891	3	420	.009
20) Meth	.941	8.850	3	420	.000
21) Heroin	.995	.654	3	420	.581
22) Daily User	.960	5.906	3	420	.001
23) Weekly User	.974	3.723	3	420	.012
24) Oral	.996	.554	3	420	.646

Table 22 *continued...*

	Wilks' Lambda	*F*	*df*1	*df*2	Significance
25) Smoke	.993	1.032	3	420	.378
26) Snort	.972	4.079	3	420	.007
27) Inject	.966	4.97	3	420	.002
28) Substance Abuse Treatment	.930	10.605	3	420	.000
29) Mental Health Treatment	.988	1.725	3	420	.161
30) Community Based Treatment	.939	9.045	3	420	.000
31) Lifetime Incarceration	.994	.870	3	420	.457
32) Number of Adult Incarcerations	.997	.369	3	420	.775
33) Current Offense	.985	2.112	3	420	.098
34) Sentence Minimum	.994	.815	3	420	.486
35) Sentence Maximum	.990	1.484	3	420	.218
36) Institutional Misconduct	.978	3.120	3	420	.026
37) Under the Influence at Time of Offense	.871	20.692	3	420	.000

Next, measures of association for the remaining variables to be introduced into the full model were reviewed. A "Within-Groups Matrices" evaluation established that while there were relatively few statistical results demonstrating elevated correlations across variables ($x > .400$), such variables were theoretically appropriate for inclusion in analysis of the full model (see Table 23 'Within-Groups Matrices for the Full Model – extreme'). Thus, it was held that all the remaining variables under consideration would be introduced into the pooled and unpooled analyses of the full model.

Table 23

Within-Groups Matrices for the Full Model (extreme)
(n = 424)

	1	2	3	4	5	6	7	8	9	10	11	12	13	14	15	16	17	18	19	20	21	22	23	24
Caucasian (1)	1.000	-.600	-.451	-.049	-.152	.267	-.014	.020	-.165	-.194	.094	.216	.143	.074	-.079	-.158	-.104	.076	.286	.013	.113	.091	.057	.104
Black (2)		1.000	-.227	-.052	-.317	-.125	.081	-.036	-.061	.196	-.030	-.074	-.089	.007	.013	-.074	.184	-.041	-.149	.092	-.113	-.009	-.103	-.137
Hispanic (3)			1.000	-.239	-.145	-.064	-.031	.111	.209	-.007	-.034	-.150	-.066	-.126	.094	.221	-.073	.006	-.179	-.221	-.081	-.005	-.034	-.050
Catholic (4)				1.000	-.343	-.554	-.016	.035	.049	-.092	-.020	.027	.077	-.090	.015	.067	-.074	.059	-.013	-.190	-.029	-.086	-.020	-.158
Baptist (5)					1.000	-.312	-.049	.018	.008	.128	-.093	-.098	.010	.014	-.079	-.005	-.024	-.022	.003	.069	.022	.073	-.069	-.078
Other-Christian (6)						1.000	.066	.031	-.007	.032	.084	-.056	-.049	.002	.070	-.012	.098	-.075	-.061	.081	.027	.058	-.023	.161
Part-Time (7)							1.000	-.379	-.019	.051	.025	.009	-.052	.044	.038	-.052	.101	.017	-.042	-.046	-.039	-.049	.087	-.052
Full-Time (8)								1.000	.070	.026	-.123	.012	-.097	-.066	.002	.099	-.046	.044	-.103	-.118	.011	.080	-.227	-.002
Alcohol (9)									1.000	-.346	-.191	-.470	-.095	-.208	.125	.945	-.528	-.186	-.263	.021	.066	-.194	-.047	.014
Marijuana (10)										1.000	-.126	-.344	-.069	.115	-.063	-.346	.524	-.047	-.185	-.040	.010	-.019	-.035	-.031
Cocaine/Crack (11)											1.000	-.302	-.058	-.070	.131	-.205	.052	.257	.018	.147	-.064	-.080	.177	-.038
Meth (12)												1.000	-.127	.208	-.083	-.405	.146	.081	.301	-.039	-.027	.288	-.013	.106
Heroin (13)													1.000	.105	-.082	-.405	.146	.081	.301	-.039	.104	-.072	-.042	.043
Daily User (14)														1.000	-.797	-.258	.302	-.050	.071	.079	.009	.178	.108	.256
Weekly User (15)															1.000	.188	-.171	.060	.004	.020	.008	-.077	-.081	-.080
Oral (16)																1.000	-.564	-.187	-.281	-.025	.058	-.158	-.060	.025
Smoke (17)																	1.000	-.255	-.381	-.025	-.112	.070	-.080	.024
Snort (18)																		1.000	-.141	-.075	.049	.112	-.006	-.073
Inject (19)																			1.000	.190	.092	.039	.200	.097
Substance Abuse Treatment (20)																				1.000	.234	-.026	.083	.100
Community Based Treatment (21)																					1.000	-.087	-.034	.059
Current Offense (22)																						1.000	-.074	.286
Institutional Misconduct (23)																							1.000	-.001
Under the Influence at Time of Offense (24)																								1.000

* note: Column numbers correspond with row numbers and variable names.

Results from the pooled discriminant analysis demonstrated that the full model was able to correctly classify 63.7% of the original grouped cases (see Table 24 'Pooled Covariance Structure Classification Results for Extreme Cumulative Categorization of the Full Model'). A follow-up unpooled discriminant analysis conducted on the full model evidenced an equivalent finding of 63.7% (see Table 25 'Unpooled Covariance Structure Classification Results for Majority Cumulative Categorization of the Full Model – extreme').

Table 24

Pooled Covariance Structure Classification Results for Extreme Cumulative Categorization of the Full Model ($n = 424$)

	Full Divergence	Partial Divergence	Partial Convergence	Full Convergence	Total
Original					
Full Divergence	13 (81.3%)	1 (6.3%)	0 (0.0%)	2 (12.5%)	16 (100.0%)
Partial Divergence	4 (9.1%)	19 (43.2%)	13 (29.5%)	8 (18.2%)	44 (100.0%)
Partial Convergence	3 (5.7%)	13 (43.2%)	27 (50.9%)	10 (18.9%)	53 (100.0%)
Full Convergence	21 (6.8%)	40 (12.9%)	39 (12.5%)	211 (67.8%)	311 (100.0%)
Cross-Validated					
Full Divergence	8 (50.0%)	4 (25.0%)	0 (0.0%)	4 (25.0%)	16 (100.0%)
Partial Divergence	4 (9.1%)	17 (38.6%)	13 (29.5%)	10 (22.7%)	44 (100.0%)
Partial Convergence	3 (5.7%)	17 (32.1%)	21 (39.6%)	12 (22.6%)	53 (100.0%)
Full Convergence	26 (8.4%)	41 (13.2%)	48 (15.4%)	196 (63.0%)	311 (100.0%)

* note: 63.7% of original grouped cases correctly classified.
* note: 57.1% of cross-validated grouped cases correctly classified.

Table 25

Unpooled Covariance Structure Classification Results for Extreme Cumulative Categorization of the Full Model ($n = 424$)

Original	Full Divergence	Partial Divergence	Partial Convergence	Full Convergence	Total
Full Divergence	15 (93.8%)	1 (6.3%)	0 (0.0%)	0 (50.0%)	16 (100.0%)
Partial Divergence	4 (9.1%)	19 (43.2%)	13 (29.5%)	8 (18.2%)	44 (100.0%)
Partial Convergence	2 (3.8%)	14 (26.4%)	28 (52.8%)	9 (17.0%)	53 (100.0%)
Full Convergence	30 (9.6%)	35 (11.3%)	38 (12.2%)	208 (66.9%)	311 (100.0%)

* note: 63.7% of the original grouped cases were correctly classified.

Subsequent to producing the prior analyses, it was also valuable to examine the 'Classification Function Coefficients' correlated with the discriminant analyses 'Classification Results' (pooled and unpooled coefficients are equivalent). These functions communicate the values associated by each variable used to predict group membership for convergent scoring classifications (number of screening instruments in concordance with the external criterion). In review of these findings, it becomes clear that in the current model the variables associated with 'primary drug of choice,' 'race,' and 'religious affiliation' were more valuable than the other variables, and groups of variables in the full model, with respect to discriminating across categorical findings of self-reported "need for treatment" (see Table 26 'Classification Function Coefficient for the – pooled and unpooled – Covariance Structure Classification Results for Extreme Cumulative Categorization of the Full Model').

Table 26

Classification Function Coefficient for the (Pooled & Unpooled) Covariance Structure Classification Results for Extreme Cumulative Categorization of the Full Model
(*n* = 424)

	Convergence/Divergence Level between Cumulative Diagnostic Screen Findings and Clinical Psychological Assessments			
	Full Divergence	Partial Divergence	Partial Convergence	Full Convergence
Caucasian	14.564	13.258	12.383	13.032
Black	13.195	13.989	14.800	13.800
Hispanic	12.897	12.473	13.461	13.440
Catholic	5.125	5.238	5.275	6.662
Baptist	6.225	6.630	7.449	8.342
Other-Christian	3.960	5.150	5.607	6.799
Part-Time	1.175	0.345	0.183	-0.736
Full-Time	1.546	0.914	1.699	1.292
Alcohol	33.916	33.905	30.060	30.837
Marijuana	26.971	33.696	28.686	30.143
Cocaine/Crack	22.824	30.525	28.094	30.173
Meth	26.583	32.453	28.772	31.473
Heroin	25.030	30.966	29.109	29.577
Daily User	2.458	-0.880	1.198	1.162
Weekly User	4.907	-0.089	1.173	1.104
Oral	-4.348	-0.503	-0.312	0.525
Smoke	2.675	0.433	0.360	0.412
Snort	5.168	0.474	-0.514	0.922
Substance Abuse Treatment	3.189	0.594	0.345	1.410
Community Based Treatment	1.828	-0.970	1.004	0.047
Current Offense	-0.757	-0.494	-0.042	-0.758
Institutional Misconduct	3.555	3.058	3.602	4.469
Under the Influence at Time of Offense	0.929	0.296	0.375	2.092
(Constant)	-29.591	-25.864	-24.605	-28.032

* Fisher's linear discriminant functions

Succeeding the analyses conducted on the full model where the dependent variable was made up of four possible cumulative screen scoring classifications (0, 1, 2, and 3), this model was analyzed another time employing a dichotomous dependent variable (a cumulative screen scoring classification of 0, 1 versus 2, 3). Here again, two analyses were conducted on the restructured full model, pooled and unpooled. However, because of the adjustments made to the full model (the dependent variable), a review of significance and measures of association were again conducted to ensure suitable variable inclusion.

Table 27

Tests of Equality of Group Means for the Full Model (majority) (*n* = 424)

	Wilks' Lambda	*F*	*df*1	*df*2	Significance
1) Current Age	.998	.796	1	422	.373
2) Caucasian	.999	.260	1	422	.610
3) Black	.996	1.537	1	422	.216
4) Hispanic	.995	2.318	1	422	.129
5) Education 8th -11th	1.000	.005	1	422	.945
6) Graduated	1.000	.005	1	422	.788
7) Some College	.999	.281	1	422	.596
8) Married	.999	.593	1	422	.741
9) No Longer-Married	.990	4.257	1	422	.040
10) Catholic	.999	.264	1	422	.608
11) Baptist	1.000	.000	1	422	.986
12) Other-Christian	.992	3.389	1	422	.066
13) Part-Time	.971	12.506	1	422	.000
14) Full-Time	.996	1.727	1	422	.190
15) Cognitive-Functioning	.999	.355	1	422	.552
16) Age of First Use	1.000	.072	1	422	.788
17) Alcohol	.996	1.788	1	422	.182
18) Marijuana	.950	22.005	1	422	.000
19) Cocaine/Crack	.982	7.580	1	422	.006
20) Meth	.980	8.831	1	422	.003
21) Heroin	.996	1.687	1	422	.195
22) Daily User	.967	14.188	1	422	.000
23) Weekly User	.983	7.285	1	422	.007
24) Oral	1.000	.197	1	422	.657
25) Smoke	.995	2.181	1	422	.140

Table 27 *continued...*

	Wilks' Lambda	*F*	*df*1	*df*2	Significance
26) Snort	.999	.370	1	422	.543
27) Inject	.979	8.947	1	422	.003
28) Substance Abuse Treatment	.997	1.088	1	422	.298
29) Mental Health Treatment	1.000	.127	1	422	.722
30) Community Based Treatment	.999	.594	1	422	.441
31) Lifetime Incarceration	1.000	.085	1	422	.771
32) Number of Adult Incarcerations	1.000	.000	1	422	.985
33) Current Offense	.987	5.648	1	422	.018
34) Sentence Minimum	.996	1.907	1	422	.168
35) Sentence Maximum	.991	3.643	1	422	.057
36) Institutional Misconduct	.990	4.215	1	422	.041
37) Under the Influence at Time of Offense	.941	26.281	1	422	.000

As was previously the case when analyzing the original full model, significance levels associated with variables to be included into the restructured full model were considered. After again conducting a "Tests of Equality of Group Means" for the restructured full model, it was held that several variables were not significant in their individual contributions to the model ($p > .100$). Again, as a number of the variables in the model were dummy coded, it was essential to consider variables within the context of their original groupings. As a result of this review it was determined that eleven variables, or sets of variables, from the model were not significant in their contributions, and therefore were removed prior to further analysis – 1) Current Age, 2) Race, 3) Education, 4) Cognitive Functioning, 5) Age of First Use, 6) Substance Abuse Treatment, 7) Mental Health Treatment, 8) Community Based Treatment, 9) Lifetime Incarceration, 10) Number of Adult Incarcerations, and 11) Sentence Minimum (see Table 27 'Tests of Equality of Group Means for the Full Model – majority').

Subsequent to the elimination of insignificant variables, it was found that nine residual variables also did not significantly contribute to the restructured full model individually; however, the collection of variables each was coupled with as a result of dummy coding did significantly contribute to the value of the model. Therefore, it was determined that these variables would be introduced into the restructured full model for analyses.

Measures of association for the remaining variables to be introduced into the full restructured model were next inspected. A "Within-Groups Matrices" evaluation found relatively few statistical results representing elevated correlations across variables ($x > .400$). In such cases, the variables were deemed theoretically suitable for introduction into restructured full model (see Table 28 'Within-Groups Matrices for the Full Model – majority'). Thus, it was held that the outstanding variables under deliberation would be incorporated into the pooled and unpooled analyses of the restructured full model.

Results from the pooled discriminant analysis evidenced that the restructured full model was capable of correctly classifying 75.7% of the original grouped cases (see Table 29 'Pooled Covariance Structure Classification Results for Majority Cumulative Categorization of the Full Model'). A subsequent unpooled discriminant analysis run on the full model produced a comparable finding of 75.2% (see Table 30 'Unpooled Covariance Structure Classification Results for Majority Cumulative Categorization of the Full Model').

Table 28

Within-Groups Matrices for the Full Model (majority)
($n = 424$)

	1	2	3	4	5	6	7	8	9	10	11	12	13	14	15	16	17	18	19	20	21	22
Married (1)	1.000	-.256	.019	.014	-.050	.003	.146	.049	-.021	-.088	-.023	-.040	-.160	.075	.084	-.092	-.070	-.008	-.014	.034	-.074	-.073
Not Married (2)		1.000	-.073	.031	.012	-.104	.153	.015	-.109	.025	.071	.034	.039	.033	-.005	-.030	.031	.052	.085	-.041	-.030	.121
Catholic (3)			1.000	-.344	-.547	-.019	.033	.045	-.095	-.016	.033	.076	-.086	.014	.065	-.075	.061	-.009	-.084	.099	-.016	-.144
Baptist (4)				1.000	-.321	-.039	.023	.018	.145	-.105	-.123	.014	.001	-.080	.003	-.019	-.039	-.013	.067	.023	-.083	-.112
Other-Christian (5)					1.000	.058	.026	-.014	.016	.094	-.033	-.051	.011	.070	-.018	.094	-.061	-.049	.061	-.081	-.011	.182
Part-Time (6)						1.000	-.374	-.012	.059	.018	-.005	-.049	.037	.041	-.048	.101	.013	-.051	-.052	-.015	.078	-.068
Full-Time (7)							1.000	.073	.032	-.126	.003	-.096	-.069	.003	.101	-.045	.040	-.108	.078	-.140	-.230	-.013
Alcohol (8)								1.000	-.332	-.197	-.473	-.093	-.214	.128	.944	-.524	-.186	-.270	-.196	-.023	-.055	-.004
Marijuana (9)									1.000	-.138	-.362	-.065	.101	-.067	-.333	.524	-.068	-.196	-.024	-.039	-.050	-.070
Cocaine/Crack (10)										1.000	-.275	-.060	-.060	.130	-.209	.049	.262	.029	-.075	.101	.185	-.011
Meth (11)											1.000	-.130	.221	-.079	-.408	.136	.103	.316	.290	-.093	.009	.154
Heroin (12)												1.000	.102	-.081	-.099	-.131	-.044	.345	-.073	.034	-.045	.034
Daily User (13)													1.000	-.791	-.262	.298	-.040	.080	.180	-.094	.117	.269
Weekly User (14)														1.000	.180	-.173	.071	.002	-.078	.042	-.080	-.071
Oral (15)															1.000	-.561	-.191	-.286	-.160	-.002	-.066	.009
Smoke (16)																1.000	-.259	-.380	.069	-.070	-.082	.013
Snort (17)																	1.000	-.128	.114	-.049	.006	-.033
Inject (18)																		1.000	.044	.036	.210	.122
Current Offense (19)																			1.000	-.111	-.069	.285
Sentence Maximum (20)																				1.000	.109	-.059
Institutional Misconduct (21)																					1.000	.028
Under the Influence at Time of Offense (22)																						1.000

* note: Column numbers correspond with row numbers and variable names.

Table 29

Pooled Covariance Structure Classification Results for Majority Cumulative Categorization of the Full Model ($n = 424$)

	Majority Divergence	Majority Convergence	Total
Original			
Majority Divergence	44 (73.3%)	16 (26.7%)	60 (100.0%)
Majority Convergence	87 (23.9%)	277 (76.1%)	364 (100.0%)
Cross-Validated			
Majority Divergence	42 (70.0%)	18 (30.0%)	60 (100.0%)
Majority Convergence	91 (25.0%)	273 (75.0%)	364 (100.0%)

* note: 75.7% of original grouped cases correctly classified.
* note: 74.3% of cross-validated grouped cases correctly classified.

Table 30

Unpooled Covariance Structure Classification Results for Majority Cumulative Categorization of the Full Model ($n = 424$)

	Majority Divergence	Majority Convergence	Total
Original			
Majority Divergence	44 (73.3%)	16 (26.7%)	60 (100.0%)
Majority Convergence	89 (24.5%)	275 (75.5%)	364 (100.0%)

* *note: 75.2% of the original grouped cases were correctly classified*

Next, it was again essential to review the 'Classification Function Coefficients' associated with the discriminant analyses 'Classification Results.' Here, results from the restructured full model supported previous findings of the original full model in that they indicated the variables associated with 'primary drug of choice,' and 'religious affiliation' were once again relatively more valuable than the other variables in discriminating across categorical findings (see Table 31 'Classification Function Coefficient for the – pooled and unpooled – Covariance Structure Classification Results for Majority Cumulative Categorization of the Full Model'). However, it should be noted that while the original full model held the variable of 'race' to be significant, the attributes associated with this variable were not introduced to the restructured full model for a lack of significant statistical contribution to the restructured full model (see Table 27 'Tests of Equality of Group Means for the Full Model – majority').

Table 31

Classification Function Coefficient for the (Pooled & Unpooled) Covariance Structure Classification Results for Majority Cumulative Categorization of the Full Model
(n = 424)

	Convergence/Divergence Level between Cumulative Diagnostic Screen Findings and Clinical Psychological Assessments	
	Majority Divergence	Majority Convergence
Married	4.144	4.146
No Longer Married	1.121	1.418
Catholic	7.081	9.018
Baptist	9.792	11.261
Other-Christian	8.225	9.539
Part-Time	1.772	.771
Full-Time	1.718	2.078
Alcohol	38.970	35.707
Marijuana	35.225	33.107
Cocaine/Crack	33.338	34.021
Meth	34.878	34.424
Heroin	33.932	33.599
Daily User	.078	1.342
Weekly User	.518	.593
Oral	-4.365	-2.260

Table 31 *continued...*

	Majority Divergence	Majority Convergence
Smoke	.433	.108
Snort	1.427	.567
Current Offense	.658	.667
Sentence Maximum	.012	.014
Institutional Misconduct	1.558	2.453
Under Influence at Time of Offense	-.885	.214
(Constant)	-22.677	-23.886

* Fisher's linear discriminant functions

Analysis of the Partial Models

As previously discussed, it was initially held that as a consequence of the full model involving 21 variables (prior to dummy coding) in combination with a limited number of sample cases available, that it would be improbable to produce statistically significant analytical findings. For that reason, the full model was next theoretically subdivided into three partial models for analyses. Because each model had access to a representative set of 424 cases, it was anticipated that analytical findings derived by means of discriminant analyses would have the capacity to produce statistically significant findings for all partial models. As was the case with previous analyses of the full model, each of the partial models were run both with pooled and unpooled covariance structures, and with both full categorical and dichotomous dependent variables.

The First Partial Model – Individual Level Attributes

Variables originally presented for analysis in the first partial model involve individual inmate demographics, to include stated age at the time of screening, institutionally recorded race (Caucasian, Black, Hispanic, and Native American/Other), documented education (no-formal/less than 8th grade, 8th thru 11th grade, high-school graduate, some college), official marital status (never married, currently married, no longer married), noted religious affiliation, and reported employment status immediately prior to incarceration (unemployed, part-time, or full-time). In addition, inmates' assessed intellectual cognitive functioning was included as a categorical variable (low-border line, average, high-average, and high-superior) for analysis in the first partial model (see Appendix H – Discriminant Analysis Modeling).

Significance levels associated with variables to be introduced into the model were reviewed. Subsequent to conducting a "Tests of Equality of Group Means" for the first partial model, it was determined that multiple variables were not significant in their individual contributions to the model ($p > .100$). As all variables in the first partial model, with the exception of 'current age' and 'cognitive functioning,' were dummy coded, it was next necessary to not only consider variables individually but also within the context of the collateral dummy coded variables derived from common original model variables. From this inspection it was determined that four variables, or sets of variables, from the model were not significant in their contributions, and therefore were removed prior to further analysis of the partial model – 1) Age, 2) Education (Education 8th – 11th, Graduated, and Some College), 3) Marital Status (Married, No Longer-Married), and 4) Cognitive Functioning (see Table 32 'Tests of Equality of Group Means for Individual Level Attributes – extreme').

Following the removal of previously identified variables from the original partial model, it was ascertained that three variables remained that did not significantly contribute to the model in isolation; however, the set of variables they were associated with as a consequence of dummy coding did significantly contribute to the value of the model. Therefore, it was held that these variables would be included in the analyses of the first partial model.

Table 32

Tests of Equality of Group Means
for Individual Level Attributes (extreme)
(*n* = 424)

	Wilks' Lambda	*F*	*df*1	*df*2	Significance
1) Age	.998	.335	3	420	.800
2) Caucasian	.929	10.694	3	420	.000
3) Blac	.932	10.294	3	420	.000
4) Hispanic	.989	1.555	3	420	.200
5) Education 8th-11th	.991	1.244	3	420	.293
6) Graduated	.998	.292	3	420	.831
7) Some College	.986	2.012	3	420	.112
8) Married	.997	.417	3	420	.741
9) No Longer-Married	.988	1.702	3	420	.166
10) Catholic	.998	.282	3	420	.838
11) Baptist	.980	2.795	3	420	.040
12) Other-Christian	.981	2.675	3	420	.047
13) Part-Time	.965	5.136	3	420	.002
14) Full-Time	.994	.862	3	420	.461
15) Cognitive-Functioning	.996	.526	3	420	.665

Next, measures of association for the remaining variables to be introduced into the first partial model were performed. As a consequence of conducting a "Within-Groups Matrices" review for the remaining variables introduced into the first partial model, it was determined that while there were a relatively small number of statistical scores indicating elevated correlations between variables ($x > .400$), none of these variables were theoretically inappropriate for inclusion in the current partial model (see Table 33 'Within-Groups Matrices for Individual Level Attributes – extreme'). Therefore, it was held that all the remaining variables under review would be included in the pooled and unpooled analyses of the first partial model, where the dependent variable was comprised of all four possible cumulative screen scoring classifications (0, 1, 2, and 3).

Table 33

Within-Groups Matrices for Individual Level Attributes (extreme) (n = 424)

	Caucasian	Black	Hispanic	Catholic	Baptist	Other Christian	Part-Time	Full-Time
Caucasian	1.000	-.600	-.451	-.049	-.152	.267	-.014	.020
Black		1.000	-.227	-.052	.317	-.215	.081	-.036
Hispanic			1.000	.239	-.145	-.064	-.031	.111
Catholic				1.000	-.343	-.554	-.016	.035
Baptist					1.000	-.312	-.049	.018
Other Christian						1.000	.066	.031
Part-Time							1.000	-.379
Full-Time								1.000

Findings from the pooled analysis indicated that the variables in first partial model were capable of correctly classifying 42.9% of the original grouped cases (see Table 34 'Pooled Covariance Structure Classification Results for Extreme Cumulative Categorization of Individual Level Attributes Partial Model). When a second unpooled analysis was run on this same partial model, there was an 8.8% increase in the ability of model variables to discriminate across categories, increasing the capacity for correct classification to 51.7% (Table 35 'Unpooled Covariance Structure Classification Results for Extreme Cumulative Categorization of Individual Attributes Partial Model').

Table 34

Pooled Covariance Structure Classification Results for Extreme Cumulative Categorization of Individual Level Attributes Partial Model (n = 424)

	Full Divergence	Partial Divergence	Partial Convergence	Full Convergence	Total
Original					
Full Divergence	7 (43.8%)	2 (12.5%)	0 (0.0%)	7 (43.8%)	16 (100.0%)
Partial Divergence	18 (40.9%)	4 (9.1%)	13 (29.5%)	9 (20.5%)	44 (100.0%)
Partial Convergence	6 (11.3%)	5 (9.4%)	28 (52.8%)	14 (26.4%)	53 (100.0%)
Full Convergence	82 (26.4%)	17 (5.5%)	69 (22.2%)	143 (46.0%)	311 (100.0%)
Cross-Validated					
Full Divergence	3 (18.8%)	4 (25.0%)	0 (0.0%)	9 (56.3%)	16 (100.0%)
Partial Divergence	18 (40.9%)	3 (6.8%)	14 (31.8%)	9 (20.5%)	44 (100.0%)
Partial Convergence	8 (15.1%)	7 (13.2%)	24 (45.3%)	14 (26.4%)	53 (100.0%)
Full Convergence	82 (26.4%)	17 (5.5%)	69 (22.2%)	143 (46.0%)	311 (100.0%)

* note: 42.9% of original grouped cases correctly classified.
* note: 40.8% of cross-validated grouped cases correctly classified.

Table 35

Unpooled Covariance Structure Classification Results for Extreme Cumulative Categorization of Individual Level Attributes Partial Model (n = 424)

Original	Full Divergence	Partial Divergence	Partial Convergence	Full Convergence	Total
Full Divergence	7 (43.8%)	2 (12.5%)	0 (0.0%)	7 (43.8%)	16 (100.0%)
Partial Divergence	7 (15.9%)	6 (13.6%)	11 (25.0%)	20 (45.5%)	44 (100.0%)
Partial Convergence	6 (11.3%)	7 (13.2%)	28 (52.8%)	12 (22.6%)	53 (100.0%)
Full Convergence	49 (15.8%)	17 (5.5%)	67 (21.5%)	178 (57.2%)	311 (100.0%)

* note: 51.7% of the original grouped cases were correctly classified.

In addition to generating the above analyses, it was also informative to produce 'Classification Function Coefficients' associated with the discriminant analyses 'Classification Results' (pooled and unpooled coefficients are equivalent). These functions communicate the values associated by each variable used to predict group membership for convergent scoring classifications (number of screening instruments in concordance with the external criterion). In review of these findings, it becomes clear that in the current partial model, the variables associated with 'race' were more valuable than 'religious affiliation' or 'employment status' with respect to discriminating across categorical findings of self-reported "need for treatment" (see Table 36 'Classification Function Coefficient for the – pooled and unpooled – Covariance Structure Classifcation Results for Extreme Cumulative Categorization of Individual Level Attributes Partial Model').

Following the discriminant analyses conducted on the first partial model where the dependent variable was comprised of all four possible cumulative screen scoring classifications (0, 1, 2, and 3), this model was run again utilizing a dichotomous dependent variable (a cumulative screen scoring classification of 0, 1 versus 2, 3). Again, two analyses were conducted on this restructured partial model, pooled and unpooled. However, because of the modification in the model (the dependent variable), an examination of significance and measures of association were again conducted to ensure appropriate variable inclusion.

Table 36

Classification Function Coefficient for the (Pooled & Unpooled) Covariance Structure Classification Results for Extreme Cumulative Categorization of Individual Level Attributes Partial Model (n = 424)

	Convergence/Divergence Level between Cumulative Diagnostic Screen Findings and Clinical Psychological Assessments			
	Full Divergence	Partial Divergence	Partial Convergence	Full Convergence
Caucasian	11.411	11.214	10.939	11.760
Black	10.502	12.028	12.746	11.653
Hispanic	9.688	10.791	11.811	11.394
Catholic	3.828	4.458	4.282	4.793
Baptist	3.926	4.499	5.221	4.973
Other-Christian	3.354	4.197	4.534	5.061
Part-Time	3.334	2.345	1.812	.843
Full-Time	1.666	1.221	1.652	1.094
(Constant)	-8.590	-8.944	-9.561	-9.373

* Fisher's linear discriminant functions

Subsequent to conducting a "Tests of Equality of Group Means" for the restructured (dichotomous dependent variable) first partial model, it was again determined that multiple variables were not found to be significant in their individual contributions to the model ($p > .100$). As many of the variables in the first partial model were dummy coded, it was yet again necessary to not only consider variables individually but also within the context of the collateral dummy coded variables derived from common original model variables. From this inspection, it was determined that four variables, or sets of variables, from the model were not significant in their contributions, and therefore were removed prior to further analysis of the restructured first partial model – 1) Age, 2) Race (Caucasian, Black, and Hispanic), 3) Education (Education 8th – 11th, Graduated, and Some College), 4) and, Cognitive Functioning (see Table 37 'Tests of Equality of Group Means for Individual Level Attributes – majority').

Table 37

Tests of Equality of Group Means for Individual Level Attributes (majority) ($n = 424$)

	Wilks' Lambda	*F*	*df*1	*df*2	Significance
1) Age	.998	.796	1	422	.373
2) Caucasian	.999	.260	1	422	.610
3) Black	.996	1.537	1	422	.216
4) Hispanic	.995	2.318	1	422	.129
5) Education 8th -11th	1.000	.005	1	422	.945
6) Graduated	1.000	.072	1	422	.788
7) Some College	.999	.281	1	422	.596
8) Married	.999	.593	1	422	.442
9) No Longer-Married	.990	4.257	1	422	.040
10) Catholic	.999	.264	1	422	.608
11) Baptist	1.000	.000	1	422	.986
12) Other-Christian	.992	3.389	1	422	.066
13) Part-Time	.971	12.506	1	422	.000
14) Full-Time	.996	1.727	1	422	.190
15) Cognitive-Functioning	.999	.355	1	422	.552

Following the removal of the identified non-significant variables it was ascertained that four variables remained that individually did not significantly contribute to the restructured partial model; nevertheless, the collection of variables each was associated with as a result of dummy coding did significantly contribute to the value of the model. Therefore, it was held that these variables would be included in the analyses of the restructured first partial model.

Next, measures of association for the remaining variables to be introduced into the restructured first partial model were performed. As a consequence of conducting a "Within-Groups Matrices" assessment of the remaining variables, it was observed that while there was only one statistical result demonstrating elevated correlations across variables ($x > .400$), these variables were theoretically appropriate for introduction into the restructured first partial model (see Table 38 'Within-Groups Matrices for Individual Level Attributes – majority'). Consequently, it was held that all the outstanding variables under examination would be incorporated in the pooled and unpooled analyses of the restructured first partial model.

Table 38

Within-Groups Matrices
for Individual Level Attributes (majority)
(n = 424)

	Married	No-Longer Married	Catholic	Baptist	Other Christian	Part-Time	Full-Time
Married	1.000	-.256	.019	.014	-.050	.003	.146
No-longer Married		1.000	-.073	.031	.012	-.104	.153
Catholic			1.000	-.344	-.547	-.019	.033
Baptist				1.000	-.321	-.039	.023
Other Christian					1.000	.058	.026
Part Time						1.000	-.374
Full-Time							1.000

Findings from the pooled analysis indicated that the variables in the restructured first partial model (where the dependent variable was dichotomous) were capable of correctly classifying 75.7% of the original grouped cases (see Table 39 'Pooled Covariance Structure Classification Results for Majority Cumulative Categorization of Individual Level Attributes'). When a second unpooled analysis was run on this same partial model, there was a 0.4% increase in the ability of model variables to discriminate across categories, increasing the capacity for correct classification to 75.9% (see Table 40 'Unpooled Covariance Structure Classification Results for Majority Cumulative Categorization of Individual Level Attributes').

Table 39

Pooled Covariance Structure Classification Results for Majority Cumulative Categorization of Individual Level Attributes ($n = 424$)

	Majority Divergence	Majority Convergence	Total
Original			
Majority Divergence	22 (36.7%)	38 (63.3%)	60 (100.0%)
Majority Convergence	65 (17.9%)	299 (82.1%)	364 (100.0%)
Cross-Validated			
Majority Divergence	22 (36.7%)	38 (63.3%)	60 (100.0%)
Majority Convergence	72 (19.8%)	292 (80.2%)	364 (100.0%)

* note: 75.7% of the original grouped cases correctly classified.
* note: 74.1% of cross-validated grouped cases correctly classified.

Table 40

Unpooled Covariance Structure Classification Results for Majority Cumulative Categorization of Individual Level Attributes ($n = 424$)

	Majority Divergence	Majority Convergence	Total
Original			
Majority Divergence	22 (36.7%)	38 (63.3%)	60 (100.0%)
Majority Convergence	64 (17.6%)	300 (82.4%)	364 (100.0%)

* note: 75.9% of the original grouped cases were correctly classified.

Subsequent to running the analyses above, it was also valuable to produce the associated 'Classification Function Coefficients.' These functions provide the values related to each variable employed in the first partial model to predict group membership for convergent scoring classifications. In review of these findings, it is evident that in the restructured model that the variables associated with 'religious affiliation' were more valuable than 'marital' or 'employment status' with respect to discriminating across categorical findings of self-reported "need for treatment" (see Table 41 'Classification Function Coefficient for the – pooled and unpooled – Covariance Structure Classifciaiton Results for Majority Cumulative Categorization of Individual Level Attributes Partial Model).

Table 41

Classification Function Coefficient for the (Pooled & Unpooled) Covariance Structure Classification Results for Majority Cumulative Categorization of Individual Level Attributes Partial Model
(n = 424)

	Convergence/Divergence Level between Cumulative Diagnostic Screen Findings and Clinical Psychological Assessments	
	Majority Divergence	Majority Convergence
Married	1.678	1.647
No-Longer Married	1.407	2.042
Catholic	7.375	8.073
Baptist	7.267	7.992
Other-Christian	6.907	8.086
Part-Time	3.507	1.958
Full-Time	1.622	1.469
(Constant)	-4.665	-5.135

* Fisher's linear discriminant functions

Null Hypothesis 9 – Demographics

Case variables (demographics – age, race, education, marital status, religious affiliation, and employment status) do not significantly influence the validity of diagnostic screen instrument findings (pooled screening scores) collected via the self-report methodology in criminal justice institutionalized venues.

The findings associated with the "Tests of Equality of Group Means" established that the demographic variables of 'age,' 'education,' and 'marital status' failed to produce significant contributions to the original first partial model (see Table 22 'Tests of

Equality of Group Means for Individual Level Attributes – extreme'), and moreover, this same analysis run on the restructured first partial model found that 'age,' 'race,' and 'education' were also not significant contributors to discriminant analyses (see Table 27 'Tests of Equality of Group Means for Individual Level Attributes – majority'). As these findings further resulted in the removal of such variables from their respective models, and the null hypothesis is stated such that all variables must demonstrate influence on validity, the researcher must accept the ninth null hypothesis.

However, it should be noted that while the ninth null hypothesis was accepted because some "demographic" variables were not found to be significant discriminators, other demographic variables did provide some significant insights across inspected models. To this end, the variable and associated attributed of 'religious affiliation' demonstrated a valuable predictive capacity to discriminate across classification categories of the dependent variable in all models examined thus far – the original and restructured full model, and the original and restructured first partial model. Moreover, 'prior employment status' was a significant discriminating variable in three of the first four models examined herein. Finally, the variable 'race' and 'marital status' also evidenced significant contributions across multiple models examined thus far (see Appendix I 'Variables demonstrating discriminant predictive validity by model).

Null Hypothesis 10 – Intellectual Functioning

Case variables (intellectual Functioning – cognitive functioning typology) do not significantly influence the validity of diagnostic screen instrument findings (pooled screening scores) collected via the self-report methodology in criminal justice institutionalized venues.

Because the findings associated with analyses (both the original and restructured first partial model) conducted on all the models to date determined that the 'cognitive-functioning' variable did not produce a significant contribution ($p > 1.000$), resulting in its removal from these models, the researcher accepts the tenth null hypothesis (see Table 22 'Tests of Equality of Group Means for Individual level Attributes – extreme' and Table 27 'Tests of Equality of Group Means for Individual level Attributes – majority').

The Second Partial Model – Drug-Related Experiences

Variables included for analysis in the second partial model involve drug-related experiences, to include self-reported age of onset (age of first alcohol/drug use), self-reported primary drug of choice (alcohol, marijuana, cocaine/crack, methamphetamine, heroin), and route of administration (oral/swallow, smoke, snort, inject). In addition, inmates' treatment histories were considered in this model by means of dichotomous variables (yes and no self-report responses) – previous substance abuse treatment, previous mental health treatment, and community-based support group involvement immediately prior to incarceration. The cumulative self-report-based screen scores across cases, and resulting four categories of convergent classification, were again used here as the dependent variable in the second partial model (see Appendix H – Discriminant Analysis Modeling).

To begin, significance levels related to variables to be introduced into the second partial model were reviewed. Subsequent to conducting a "Tests of Equality of Group Means," it was found that multiple variables were not individually significant in sustaining the model ($p >$ .100). As three of the seven variables in the second partial model were dummy coded, it was next appropriate to consider the significance of these variables within the context of other variables derived from common original model variables. From this review it was held that two variables from the model were not significant in their contributions, and therefore were removed prior to further consideration of the model – 1) Age of First Use, and 2) Mental Health Treatment (see Table 42 'Tests of Equality of Group Means for Drug-Related Experiences – extreme').

Table 42

Tests of Equality of Group Means for Drug-Related Experiences (extreme) (*n* = 424)

	Wilks' Lambda	*F*	*df*1	*df*2	Significance
1) Age of First Use	.989	1.615	3	420	.185
2) Alcohol	.988	1.750	3	420	.156
3) Marijuana	.929	10.712	3	420	.000
4) Cocaine/Crack	.973	3.891	3	420	.009
5) Meth	.941	8.850	3	420	.000
6) Heroin	.995	.654	3	420	.581
7) Daily User	.960	5.906	3	420	.001
8) Weekly User	.974	3.723	3	420	.012
9) Oral	.996	.554	3	420	.646
10) Smoke	.993	1.032	3	420	.378
11) Snort	.972	4.079	3	420	.007
12) Inject	.966	4.978	3	420	.002
13) Substance Abuse Treatment	.930	10.605	3	420	.000
14) Mental Health Treatment	.988	1.725	3	420	.161
15) Community Based Treatment	.939	9.045	3	420	.000

Following the elimination of the non-significant variables from the partial model, it was discovered that four variables remained that, individually, did not significantly contribute to the model; even so, the group of variables each was related to as a consequence of dummy coding did significantly promote the value of the model. Therefore, it was held that these variables would be included in the analyses of the second partial model.

Next, measures of association for the remaining variables to be included for analysis in the second partial model were conducted. As a result of generating a "Within-Groups Matrices" assessment for the residual variables introduced into the second partial model, it was found that while there were a number of statistical results indicative of elevated correlations between variables ($x > .400$), none of these variables were theoretically inappropriate for inclusion in the current partial model (see Table 43 'Within-Groups Matrices for Drug-Related

Experiences – extreme'). With this the case, all remaining variables under consideration would be included in the pooled and unpooled analyses of the second partial model, where the dependent variable was comprised of all four possible cumulative screen scoring classifications (0, 1, 2, and 3).

Table 43

Within-Groups Matrices for Drug-Related Experiences (extreme) (*n* = 424)

	1	2	3	4	5	6	7	8	9	10	11	12	13
Alcohol (1)	1.000	-.346	-.191	-.470	-.095	.945	-.528	-.186	-.263	-.208	.125	.021	.066
Marijuana (2)		1.000	-.126	-.344	-.069	-.346	.524	-.047	-.185	.115	-.063	-.040	.010
Cocaine/Crack (3)			1.000	-.302	-.058	-.205	.052	.257	.018	-.070	.131	.147	-.064
Meth (4)				1.000	-.127	-.405	.146	.081	.301	.208	-.083	-.039	-.027
Heroin (5)					1.000	-.101	-.132	-.042	.350	.105	-.082	.045	.104
Oral (6)						1.000	-.564	-.187	-.281	-.258	.188	-.025	.058
Smoke (7)							1.000	-.255	-.381	.302	-.171	-.025	-.112
Snort (8)								1.000	-.141	-.050	.060	-.075	.049
Inject (9)									1.000	.071	.004	.190	.092
Daily User (10)										1.000	-.797	.079	.009
Weekly User (11)											1.000	.020	.008
Substance Abuse (12) Treatment												1.000	.234
Community Based (13) Treatment													1.000

* note: Column numbers correspond with row numbers and variable names.

Results of the pooled analysis found that the variables in the first partial model were able to correctly classify 55.0% of the original grouped cases (see Table 44 'Pooled Covariance Structure Classification Results for Extreme Cumulative Categorization of Drug-Related Experiences Partial Model'). When a successive unpooled analysis was conducted on this unchanged partial model, there was a 0.5% decrease in the capacity of model variables to discriminate by convergent categories, decreasing the capacity for correct classification to 54.5% (Table 45 'Unpooled Covariance Structure Classification Results for Extreme Cumulative Categorization of Drug-Related Experiences Partial Model').

Table 44

Pooled Covariance Structure Classification Results for Extreme Cumulative Categorization of Drug-Related Experiences Partial Model ($n = 424$)

	Full Divergence	Partial Divergence	Partial Convergence	Full Convergence	Total
Original					
Full Divergence	13 (81.3%)	3 (18.8%)	0 (0.0%)	0 (0.0%)	16 (100.0%)
Partial Divergence	6 (13.6%)	27 (61.4%)	3 (6.8%)	8 (18.2%)	44 (100.0%)
Partial Convergence	7 (13.2%)	19 (35.8%)	16 (30.2%)	11 (20.8%)	53 (100.0%)
Full Convergence	40 (12.9%)	55 (17.7%)	39 (12.5%)	177 (56.9%)	311 (100.0%)
Cross-Validated					
Full Divergence	11 (68.8%)	3 (18.8%)	0 (0.0%)	2 (12.5%)	16 (100.0%)
Partial Divergence	6 (13.6%)	23 (52.3%)	7 (15.9%)	8 (18.2%)	44 (100.0%)
Partial Convergence	7 (13.2%)	21 (39.6%)	13 (24.5%)	12 (22.6%)	53 (100.0%)
Full Convergence	40 (12.9%)	57 (18.3%)	39 (12.5%)	175 (56.3%)	311 (100.0%)

* note: 55.0% of the original grouped cases correctly classified.
* note: 52.4% of cross-validated grouped cases correctly classified.

Table 45

Unpooled Covariance Structure Classification Results for Extreme Cumulative Categorization of Drug-Related Experiences Partial Model (n = 424)

Original	Full Divergence	Partial Divergence	Partial Convergence	Full Convergence	Total
Full Divergence	11 (68.8%)	3 (18.8%)	2 (12.5%)	0 (0.0%)	16 (100.0%)
Partial Divergence	6 (13.6%)	27 (61.4%)	3 (6.8%)	8 (18.2%)	44 (100.0%)
Partial Convergence	5 (9.4%)	21 (39.6%)	16 (30.2%)	11 (20.8%)	53 (100.0%)
Full Convergence	27 (8.7%)	55 (17.7%)	52 (16.7%)	177 (56.9%)	311 (100.0%)

* note: 54.5% of the original grouped cases were correctly classified.

In conjunction with the aforementioned analyses, a 'Classification Function Coefficients' was also produced for the discriminant analyses 'Classification Results.' Here, the values associated with each variable used to predict group membership for convergent scoring classifications are available for review. When inspected, it becomes evident that in the second partial model, variables associated with 'primary drug of choice' were more valuable than 'route of administration,' 'frequency of use,' 'substance abuse treatment,' or 'community based treatment' with respect to discriminating across categorical findings of self-reported "need for treatment" (see Table 46 'Classification Function Coefficient for the – pooled and unpooled – Covariance Structure Classification Results for Extreme Cumulative Categorization of Drug-Related Experiences Partial Model).

As was the case following the multiple analyses of the first partial model, the second partial model was also restructured for further exploratory analysis. Again, the dependent variable was collapsed to reflect the same dichotomous categories, and thereafter both pooled and unpooled analyses were conducted. However, given that the second partial model had been restructured, prior to these analyses an examination of significance and measures of association were conducted once more to guarantee appropriate variable inclusion.

Table 46

Classification Function Coefficient for the (Pooled & Unpooled) Covariance Structure Classification Results for Extreme Cumulative Categorization of Drug-Related Experiences Partial Model
(n = 424)

	Convergence/Divergence Level between Cumulative Diagnostic Screen Findings and Clinical Psychological Assessments			
	Full Divergence	Partial Divergence	Partial Convergence	Full Convergence
Alcohol	34.755	33.411	28.630	30.233
Marijuana	28.113	33.678	28.246	30.528
Cocaine/Crack	25.545	31.551	27.865	31.618
Meth	28.141	32.354	27.693	31.523
Heroin	27.650	31.964	28.524	30.821
Oral	-5.277	-1.079	-0.255	0.614
Smoke	1.594	-0.007	0.237	-0.235
Snort	4.615	0.238	-0.344	0.265
Daily-User	1.071	-2.074	0.270	0.421
Weekly-User	3.294	-1.247	0.309	0.107
Substance Abuse Treatment	1.974	-0.237	-0.417	0.496
Community-Based Treatment	1.846	-1.207	0.495	-0.092
(Constant)	-8.590	-8.944	-9.561	-9.373

* Fisher's linear discriminant functions

After carrying out a "Tests of Equality of Group Means" for the reorganized (dichotomous dependent variable) second partial model, it again was found that some variables were not significant in their sole contributions to the model ($p > .100$). As has previously been the case, because three of the variables in this model were dummy coded, it was necessary to consider variables within this context. From this, it was determined that four variables, or sets of variables were to be removed prior to further analysis – 1) Age of First Use, 2) Substance Abuse Treatment, 3) Mental Health Treatment, and 4) Community Based Treatment (see Table 47 'Tests of Equality of Group Means for Drug-Related Experiences – majority').

Table 47

Tests of Equality of Group Means for Drug-Related Experiences (majority) (*n* = 424)

	Wilks' Lambda	*F*	*df*1	*df*2	Significance
1) Age of First Use	1.000	.072	1	422	.788
2) Alcohol	.996	1.788	1	422	.182
3) Marijuana	.950	22.005	1	422	.000
4) Cocaine/Crack	.982	7.580	1	422	.006
5) Meth	.980	8.831	1	422	.003
6) Heroin	.996	1.687	1	422	.195
7) Daily User	.967	14.188	1	422	.000
8) Weekly User	.983	7.285	1	422	.007
9) Oral	1.000	.197	1	422	.657
10) Smoke	.995	2.181	1	422	.140
11) Snort	.999	.370	1	422	.543
12) Inject	.979	8.947	1	422	.003
13) Substance Abuse Treatment	.997	1.088	1	422	.298
14) Mental Health Treatment	1.000	.127	1	422	.722
15) Community Based Treatment	.999	.594	1	422	.441

Following the removal of identified variables from the restructured second partial model, it was held that five variables remained that individually did not significantly contribute to the model; however, the collection of variables each was linked with as a result of dummy coding did significantly contribute to the value of the model. Therefore, it was held that these variables would be included in the analyses of the restructured second partial model.

Measures of association for the remaining variables to be introduced into the restructured first partial model were next conducted. A "Within-Groups Matrices" evaluation of the remaining variables found that while there were relatively few statistical results demonstrating elevated correlations across variables ($x > .400$), these variables were theoretically acceptable for introduction into the first partial model (see Table 48 'Within-Groups Matrices for Individual Level Attributes – majority'). Consequently, it was held that all the remaining variables under consideration would be introduced into the pooled and unpooled analyses of the restructured second partial model.

Table 48

Within-Groups Matrices for Drug-Related Experiences (majority) (*n* = 424)

	1	2	3	4	5	6	7	8	9	10	11
Alcohol (1)	1.000	-.332	-.197	-.473	-.093	-.214	.128	.944	-.524	-.186	-.270
Marijuana (2)		1.000	-.138	-.362	-.065	.101	-.067	-.333	.524	-.068	-.196
Cocaine/Crack (3)			1.000	-.275	-.060	-.060	.130	-.209	.049	.262	.029
Meth (4)				1.000	-.130	.221	-.079	-.408	.136	.103	.316
Heroin (5)					1.000	.102	-.081	-.099	-.131	-.044	.345
Oral (6)						1.000	-.791	-.262	.298	-.040	.080
Daily (7)							1.000	.187	-.173	.071	.002
Weekly (8)								1.000	-.561	-.191	-.286
Smoke (9)									1.000	-.259	-.380
Snort (10)										1.000	-.128
Inject (11)											1.000

* note: Column numbers correspond with row numbers and variable names.

Results from the pooled analysis evidenced the variables in the restructured second partial model were able to correctly classify 71.2% of the original grouped cases (see Table 49 'Pooled Covariance Structure Classification Results for Majority Cumulative Categorization for Drug-Related Experiences Partial Model'). A follow-up unpooled analysis conducted on the same partial model and indicated a parallel finding of 71.2% (see Table 50 'Unpooled Covariance Structure Classification Results for Majority Cumulative Categorization of Drug-Related Experiences Partial Model').

Table 49

Pooled Covariance Structure Classification Results for Majority Cumulative Categorization of Drug-Related Experiences Partial Model (n = 424)

	Majority Divergence	Majority Convergence	Total
Original			
Majority Divergence	46 (76.7%)	14 (23.3%)	60 (100.0%)
Majority Convergence	108 (29.7%)	256 (70.3%)	364 (100.0%)
Cross-Validated			
Majority Divergence	46 (76.7%)	14 (23.3%)	60 (100.0%)
Majority Convergence	108 (29.7%)	256 (70.3%)	364 (100.0%)

* note: 71.2% of the original grouped cases correctly classified.
* note: 71.2% of cross-validated grouped cases correctly classified

Table 50

Unpooled Covariance Structure Classification Results for Majority Cumulative Categorization of Drug-Related Experiences Partial Model
(*n* = 424)

Original	Majority Divergence	Majority Convergence	Total
Majority Divergence	46 (76.7%)	14 (23.3%)	60 (100.0%)
Majority Convergence	108 (29.7%)	256 (70.3%)	364 (100.0%)

* note: 71.2% of the original grouped cases were correctly classified.

Table 51

Classification Function Coefficient for the (Pooled & Unpooled) Covariance Structure Classification Results for Majority Cumulative Categorization of Drug-Related Experiences Partial Model
(n = 424)

Convergence/Divergence Level between Cumulative Diagnostic Screen Findings and Clinical Psychological Assessments		
	Majority Divergence	Majority Convergence
Alcohol	33.331	29.611
Marijuana	31.903	29.849
Cocaine/Crack	29.370	30.272
Meth	30.517	30.081
Heroin	30.403	30.099
Daily User	-1.414	.236
Weekly User	-0.186	.031
Oral	-2.193	.365
Smoke	.514	-.086
Snort	1.036	-.173
(Constant)	-15.708	-15.281

* Fisher's linear discriminant functions

In consideration of these analyses, the 'Classification Function Coefficients' associated with the variables employed in the restructured second model were produced. This data evidenced that, relative to the 'frequency of use' and 'route of administration,' that the attributes grounded in the 'drug of choice' model variable, demonstrated a relatively significant capacity to discriminate across group membership for convergent scoring classifications (see Table 51 'Classification

Function Coefficient for the – pooled and unpooled – Covariance Structure Classification Results for Majority Cumulative Categorization of Drug-Related Experiences Partial Model').

Null Hypothesis 11 – Drug Use History

Case variables (drug use history – age of first drug use, current primary drug of choice, frequency of drug use, primary route of drug administration) do not significantly influence the validity of diagnostic screen instrument findings (pooled screening scores) collected via the self-report methodology in criminal justice institutionalized venues.

The findings associated with the "Tests of Equality of Group Means" established that the "drug use history" variable and the 'age of onset' variable failed to produce significant contributions to any of the models in which it was originally considered – the original and restructured full model, and the original and restructured second partial model. As such findings resulted in the deletion of this variable from the respective models, and the null hypothesis is stated such that all variables listed must demonstrate influence on validity, the researcher must accept the eleventh null hypothesis.

However, it should be noted that while the eleventh null hypothesis was accepted because "drug use history" variables in total were not found to be significant discriminators, one 'drug use history' variable did provide significant insights across inspected models. The variable and associated attributed of 'primary drug of choice' demonstrated a valuable predictive capacity to discriminate across classification categories of the dependent variable in all model examined thus far – the original and restructured full model, and the original and restructured second partial model (see Appendix I 'Variables demonstrating discriminant predictive validity by model).

Null Hypothesis 12 – Treatment History

Case variables (treatment history – previous substance abuse treatment, previous mental health treatment, current community-based support) do not significantly influence the validity of diagnostic screen instrument findings (pooled screening scores) collected via the self-report methodology in criminal justice institutionalized venues.

Results related to the "Tests of Equality of Group Means" held that the "treatment history" variable of 'prior mental health treatment' was consistently unsuccessful in producing a significant contribution to any of the models in which it was originally considered – the original and restructured full model, and the original and restructured second partial model. Moreover, the variables of 'prior substance abuse treatment,' and 'community-based treatment' were found to be non-significant contributors to two of the four models in which they were originally considered. As these findings resulted in the deletion of this variable from the respective models, and the null hypothesis is stated such that all variables listed must demonstrate influence on validity, the researcher accepts the twelfth null hypothesis.

The Third Partial Model – Developmental Attributes

Variables included for analysis in the third partial model involve inmates' prior criminal justice experiences, to include official records of prior lifetime incarceration (yes or no), documented number of prior adult incarcerations, recorded current offense (drug-related or non-drug related), current minimum and maximum sentence lengths (in months), and official incidents of drug-related institutional misconduct (yes or no). Moreover, inmates' self-reported "indexes of substance misuse" were included for analysis in the third partial model as it was dichotomously reported (yes or no) if the inmate had been under the influence of drugs or alcohol at the time they committed the offense for which they are currently serving time. The cumulative self-report-based screen scores across cases, and resulting four categories of convergent classification, were once again used as the dependent variable in the third partial model (see Appendix H – Discriminant Analysis Modeling).

Table 52

Tests of Equality of Group Means for Developmental Attributes (extreme) (*n* = 424)

	Wilks' Lambda	*F*	*df*1	*df*2	Significance
1) Lifetime Incarceration	.994	.870	3	420	.457
2) Number of Adult Incarcerations	.997	.369	3	420	.775
3) Current Offense	.985	2.112	3	420	.098
4) Sentence Minimum	.994	.815	3	420	.486
5) Sentence Maximum	.990	1.484	3	420	.218
6) Institutional Misconduct	.978	3.120	3	420	.026
7) Under the Influence at Time of Offense	.871	20.692	3	420	.000

To begin, variables to be introduced into the third partial model were reviewed for significance. After running a "Tests of Equality of Group Means," it was determined that multiple variables were not individually significant in sustaining the model ($p > .100$). From this review, it was held that four variables from the model were not significant in their contributions, and therefore were removed prior to further consideration of the model – 1) Lifetime Incarceration, 2) Number of Adult Incarcerations, 3) Sentence Minimums, and 4) Sentence Maximums (see Table 52 'Tests of Equality of Group Means for Developmental Attributes – extreme').

Table 53

Within-Groups Matrices for Developmental Attributes (extreme) (n = 424)

	Current Offense	Institutional Misconduct	Under the Influence at Time of Offense
Current Offense	1.000	-.074	.286
Institutional Misconduct		1.000	-.001
Under the Influence at Time of Offense			1.000

Next, measures of association for the remaining variables to be included for analysis in the third partial model were conducted. As a result of generating a "Within-Groups Matrices" assessment for the remaining variables introduced into the third partial model, it was found that no statistical results indicated elevated correlations between variables ($x > .400$) (see Table 53 'Within-Groups Matrices for Developmental Attributes – extreme'). With this the case, all remaining variables under consideration would be included in the pooled and unpooled analyses of the third partial model.

Table 54

Pooled Covariance Structure Classification Results for Extreme Cumulative Categorization of Developmental Attributes Partial Model (n = 424)

	Full Divergence	Partial Divergence	Partial Convergence	Full Convergence	Total
Original					
Full Divergence	0 (0.0%)	8 (50.0%)	0 (0.0%)	8 (50.0%)	16 (100.0%)
Partial Divergence	0 (0.0%)	26 (59.1%)	4 (9.1%)	14 (31.8%)	44 (100.0%)
Partial Convergence	0 (0.0%)	22 (41.5%)	11 (20.8%)	20 (37.7%)	53 (100.0%)
Full Convergence	0 (0.0%)	58 (18.6%)	13 (4.2%)	240 (77.2%)	311 (100.0%)
Cross-Validated					
Full Divergence	0 (0.0%)	8 (50.0%)	0 (0.0%)	8 (50.0%)	16 (100.0%)
Partial Divergence	0 (0.0%)	26 (59.1%)	4 (9.1%)	14 (31.8%)	44 (100.0%)
Partial Convergence	0 (0.0%)	22 (41.5%)	11 (20.8%)	20 (37.7%)	53 (100.0%)
Full Convergence	0 (0.0%)	58 (18.6%)	13 (4.2%)	240 (77.2%)	311 (100.0%)

* note: 65.3% of the original grouped cases correctly classified.
* note: 65.3% of cross-validated grouped cases correctly classified.

Table 55

Unpooled Covariance Structure Classification Results for Extreme Cumulative Categorization of Developmental Attributes Partial Model (n = 424)

Original	Full Divergence	Partial Divergence	Partial Convergence	Full Convergence	Total
Full Divergence	0 (0.0%)	8 (50.0%)	0 (0.0%)	8 (50.0%)	16 (100.0%)
Partial Divergence	0 (0.0%)	26 (59.1%)	4 (9.1%)	14 (31.8%)	44 (100.0%)
Partial Convergence	0 (0.0%)	22 (41.5%)	11 (20.8%)	20 (37.7%)	53 (100.0%)
Full Convergence	22 (7.1%)	58 (18.6%)	15 (4.8%)	216 (69.5%)	311 (100.0%)

* note: 59.7% of the original grouped cases were correctly classified.

Results of the pooled discriminant analysis evidenced that the variables incorporated in the third partial model were capable of correctly classifying 65.3% of the original grouped cases (see Table 54 'Pooled Covariance Structure Classification Results for Extreme Cumulative Categorization of Developmental Attributes Partial Model'). A subsequent unpooled analysis was conducted on this same partial model resulting in a 5.6% decrease in the capacity for correct classification to 59.7% (see Table 55 'Unpooled Covariance Structure Classification Results for Extreme Cumulative Categorization of Developmental Attributes Partial Model').

Table 56

Classification Function Coefficient for the (Pooled & Unpooled) Covariance Structure Classification Results for Extreme Cumulative Categorization of Developmental Attributes Partial Model
(n = 424)

	Convergence/Divergence Level between Cumulative Diagnostic Screen Findings and Clinical Psychological Assessments			
	Full Divergence	Partial Divergence	Partial Convergence	Full Convergence
Current Offense	.427	.791	1.184	.976
Institutional Misconduct	.073	.128	.191	1.627
Under the Influence at Time of Offense	2.368	1.344	1.517	3.460
(Constant)	-2.032	-1.708	-1.896	-2.964

* Fisher's linear discriminant functions

As a follow-up to the analysis of the third partial model, the 'Classification Function Coefficients' correlated with the discriminant analyses 'Classification Results' were generated for review. A review of these findings demonstrated that the variable 'under the influence at time of offense' was relatively valuable in discriminating across dependent variable categories (see Table 56 'Classification Function Coefficient for the – pooled and unpooled – Covariance Structure Classification Results for Extreme Cumulative Categorization of Developmental Attributes Partial Model').

Following the discriminant analyses conducted on the third partial model where the dependent variable was comprised of all four possible cumulative screen scoring classifications (0, 1, 2, and 3), this model was run again using a dichotomous dependent variable (a cumulative screen scoring classification of 0, 1 versus 2, 3). Again, two analyses were conducted on this restructured partial model, pooled and unpooled. However, because of the modification in the model, an examination of significance and measures of association were again conducted to ensure appropriate variable inclusion.

Table 57

Tests of Equality of Group Means for Developmental Attributes (majority) (n = 424)

	Wilks' Lambda	*F*	*df*1	*df*2	Significance
1) Lifetime Incarceration	1.000	.085	1	422	.771
2) Number of Adult Incarcerations	1.000	.000	1	422	.985
3) Current Offense	.987	5.648	1	422	.018
4) Sentence Minimum	.996	1.907	1	422	.168
5) Sentence Maximum	.991	4.643	1	422	.057
6) Institutional Misconduct	.990	4.215	1	422	.041
7) Under the Influence at Time of Offense	.941	26.281	1	422	.000

Subsequent to conducting a "Tests of Equality of Group Means" for the restructured third partial model, it was again found that a number of variables did not significantly contribute to the value of the model ($p > .100$). From this inspection, it was determined that three variables were not significant in their contributions, and therefore were removed prior to further analysis – 1) Lifetime Incarceration, 2) Number of Adult Incarcerations, and 3) Sentence Minimum (see Table 57 'Tests of Equality of Group Means for Developmental Attributes – majority').

Table 58

Within-Groups Matrices for Developmental Attributes (majority) ($n = 424$)

	Current Offense	Maximum Sentence	Institutional Misconduct	Under the Influence at Time of Offense
Current Offense	1.000	-.111	-.069	.285
Maximum Sentence		1.000	.109	-.059
Institutional Misconduct			1.000	.028
Under the Influence at Time of Offense				1.000

Measures of association for the remaining variables to be introduced into the restructured third partial model were performed. As a consequence of conducting a "Within-Groups Matrices" assessment of the remaining variables, it was observed that there were no statistical results demonstrating elevated correlations across variables ($x > .400$). Therefore, it was held that all the remaining variables under consideration would be incorporated in the pooled and unpooled analyses of the restructured third partial model (see Table 58 'Within-Groups Matrices for Developmental Attributes – majority').

Table 59

Pooled Covariance Structure Classification Results for Majority Cumulative Categorization of Developmental Attributes Partial Model ($n = 424$)

	Majority Divergence	Majority Convergence	Total
Original			
Majority Divergence	38 (63.3%)	22 (36.7%)	60 (100.0%)
Majority Convergence	102 (28.0%)	262 (72.0%)	364 (100.0%)
Cross-Validated			
Majority Divergence	38 (63.3%)	22 (36.7%)	60 (100.0%)
Majority Convergence	102 (28.0%)	262 (72.0%)	364 (100.0%)

* note: 70.8% of the original grouped cases correctly classified.
* note: 70.8% of cross-validated grouped cases correctly classified.

Findings from the pooled analysis indicated that the variables in the restructured third partial model were capable of correctly classifying 70.8% of the original grouped cases (see Table 59 'Pooled Covariance Structure Classification Results for Majority Cumulative Categorization of Developmental Attributes'). When a second unpooled analysis was run on this same partial model, there was an identical result of 70.8% (see Table 60 'Unpooled Covariance Structure Classification Results for Majority Cumulative Categorization of Developmental Attributes').

Table 60

Unpooled Covariance Structure Classification Results for Majority Cumulative Categorization of Developmental Attributes Partial Model ($n = 424$)

	Majority Divergence	Majority Convergence	Total
Original			
Majority Divergence	38 (63.3%)	22 (36.7%)	60 (100.0%)
Majority Convergence	102 (28.0%)	262 (72.0%)	364 (100.0%)

* note: 70.8% of the original grouped cases were correctly classified.

In conjunction with running the analyses above, the associated 'Classification Function Coefficients' were also produced. An examination of these results found that in the restructured model the variables associated with 'under the influence at time of offense' and 'current offense' demonstrated some capacity in discriminating across categorical findings of self-reported "need for treatment" (see Table 61 'Classification Function Coefficient for the – pooled and unpooled – Covariance Structure Classification Results for Majority Cumulative Categorization of Developmental Attributes Partial Model).

Table 61

Classification Function Coefficient for the (Pooled & Unpooled) Covariance Structure Classification Results for Majority Cumulative Categorization of Developmental Attributes Partial Model
(n = 424)

	Convergence/Divergence Level between Cumulative Diagnostic Screen Findings and Clinical Psychological Assessments	
	Majority Divergence	Majority Convergence
Current Offense	.793	1.182
Maximum Sentence	.003	.005
Institutional Misconduct	-.167	.909
Under Influence at Time of Offense	1.523	2.970
(Constant)	-1.147	-2.226

* Fisher's linear discriminant functions

Null Hypothesis 13 – Criminal Justice Experience

Case variables (criminal justice experiences – prior lifetime incarceration, number of prior adult incarcerations, current offense, current sentence length, institutional misconduct) do not significantly influence the validity of diagnostic screen instrument findings (pooled screening scores) collected via the self-report methodology in criminal justice institutionalized venues.

The research results associated with the "Tests of Equality of Group Means" established that the "criminal justice experience" variables of 'lifetime incarceration,' 'number of adult incarcerations,' and 'sentence minimum' failed to produce significant contributions to all of the models in which they were originally considered – the original and restructured full model, and the original and restructured third partial model. As such findings resulted in the elimination of these variables from their respective models, and the null hypothesis is stated such that all variables listed must demonstrate influence on validity, the researcher must accept the thirteenth null hypothesis.

However, it should be noted that while the thirteenth null hypothesis was accepted because "criminal justice experience" variables in total were not found to be significant discriminators, two 'criminal justice experience' variables did provide some insight across inspected models. The variables and associated attributes of 'current offense' and 'institutional misconduct' demonstrated marginal predictive capacity to discriminate across classification categories of the dependent variable.

Null Hypothesis 14 – Indexes of Substance Misuse

Case variables (indexes of substance misuse – under the influence at time of current offense) do not significantly influence the validity of diagnostic screen instrument findings (pooled screening scores) collected via the self-report methodology in criminal justice institutionalized venues.

The findings associated with the "Tests of Equality of Group Means" established that the "indexes of substance misuse" variable of 'under the influence at time of offense,' was found to produce significant contributions to all of the models in which it was originally considered – the original and restructured full model, and the original and restructured third partial model. In addition, in the analyses of the third partial model, this variable demonstrated the largest classification function coefficient scores across both the original and restructured models. With this the case, the researcher rejects the fourteenth null hypothesis.

CHAPTER 6

Advancing the Self-Report Methodology

The purpose of the current study was to examine the effectiveness of the self-report screening methodology in generating valid data regarding drug and alcohol disorders within institutionalized criminal justice venues. Questions addressed in this research included (1) Do screening instrument findings derived via self-report methodologies generate high levels of confidence (i.e., convergent/criterion validity, efficacy, and construct validity) when compared to forensic clinical psychological assessments, and (2) Does the value of the self-report screening methodology vary based on case attributes (i.e., demographics, cognitive functioning, drug use history, treatment history, criminal justice experiences)?

This study used various data drawn from prison populations in order to address these questions. Specifically, self-report-based screen results (pooled cumulative screening scores) were compared with forensic psychological assessment findings in terms of their classification accuracies for substance use "need for treatment." A variety of statistical analyses provided insights to issues of criterion validity, efficacy, construct validity, and case variable influences with respect to the self-report screening methodology, as employed within an institutionalized criminal population. Having informed the above research questions, this study has served to improve the understanding and inform policies and practices related to self-report-based screening protocols designed to triage "need for treatment" in criminal justice institutionalized populations.

Chapter Organization

The current chapter is divided into five primary sections in order to facilitate a discussion of the current research effort. The first section discusses overall study findings, as this information informs the principal research questions herein. Section two of this chapter provides a discussion of research cautions and limitations to be aware of regarding this study's empirical findings. The third primary section of this chapter provides a consideration of the strengths of this research. This is followed in section four by an inspection of prospective policy implications derived from study results. Finally, section five of this chapter deals with implications for future research generated by the current study.

CONSIDERING THE VALIDITY AND EFFICACY OF THE SELF-REPORT SCREENING METHODOLOGY

Findings from this research have advanced the understanding of the self-report screening methodology in the context of institutionalized criminal populations by employing a "meta-methodology" resulting in findings that have yet to be reported or similarly examined in earlier studies. Some of the findings in this research are consistent with earlier research conducted on self-report screening protocols (Peters, et. al., 2000; Miller & Lazowski, 1999; Lazowski, et. al., 1998). Other findings in this research, however, refute or extend much of the earlier research conducted (Wentland and Smith, 1993; Miller & Lazowski, 1999; Lazowski, et. al., 1998).

In the course of this research, a recently adjudicated prison sample (n = 424), drawn from the State of Nebraska Department of Corrections (DOC) Diagnostic Evaluation Center (DEC) (N = 1,518), was analyzed to assess the utility of self-report screening instrumentation as an effective methodological tool for producing valid data regarding drug and alcohol disorders within institutionalized criminal justice settings – specifically, incoming prison populations. In order to inform this study's research questions, a variety of statistical analyses were conducted and reported in Chapter 5 – Research Questions and Results. This section discusses these findings in light of current study objectives.

Aggregate Criterion Validity

This research has provided a unique contribution to the self-report screening literature by employing a "meta-methodology," whereby a battery of self-report screening tools (a "model" screening package) were used in order to more readily focus on the self-report methodology itself, rather than the examination of any one particular instrument. This process provided the means to produce a cumulative screen score (an index score derived from the number of positive screens per inmate case) for each sample respondent for purposes of detailed investigations. Results of these analyses, grounded in self-report-based screen findings, demonstrated a 72.2% population prevalence rate for the highest cumulative screen score classification, with an amplified score to 87.8% when a cut-off of "two or more" positive screens was employed. Analysis of the level of "need for treatment" for this same research population based on forensic clinical psychological assessments, resulted in an 83% prevalence rate.

A series of chi-square analyses demonstrated that screen results derived by means of self-report were highly correlated and statistically significant with forensic assessment findings produced across the same population by clinical psychologists. Moreover, a parallel finding of significance was demonstrated for each possible cumulative screen scoring classification examined. In other words, in the search for a potential cut-off score where self-report screen findings would no longer be valuable, none was found where self-report screen data were not significantly related to clinical assessment findings. Therefore, significant results were obtained in assessing the relationship between screening outcomes and an 'optimal' external criterion in this study's setting, as findings supported the criterion validity of the self-report screening methodology at the aggregate level of analysis.

. In addition, it should be noted that prior research suggested validity problems potentially associated with the collection of self-report-based diagnostic data from within a criminal justice institutionalized setting (Wentland & Smith, 1993; Reynolds, 1993; Bradburn, 1983; Del Boca & Noll, 2000; Cottler, Zipp, Robins, & Spitznagel, 1987). Here, it was assumed that various institutional and cultural norms and task demands may influence the accuracy and value of self-report-based screening data. However, it would appear that concerns associated with the use of self-report in a criminal justice institutionalized evaluation setting did not, on the face of the findings herein, seem to be sustained. With this the case, the current findings support much prior research valuing the self-report screening methodology (Miller & Lazowski, 1999; Lazowski, et. al., 1998), especially results derived in the context of criminal populations (Peters, et. al., 2000).

Of course, it is important to acknowledge potential cautions with respect to the results of these analyses. For example, while comparisons across aggregated data will certainly provide important insights into issues of criterion validity, such analyses are not capable of providing insights with respect to the accuracy of an individual's response. This limitation is a result of aggregated data potentially reflecting compensating errors that balance out. Such a cancellation effect across error types would certainly be problematic; therefore, it is essential to the broader understanding of the validity of self-report screen findings that additional analyses be conducted.

Self-Report Screening Efficacy

In addition to an examination of criterion validity at the aggregate level of analysis, self-report screen results were also explored in terms of efficacy. In the current study, two scoring classifications were used to disaggregate sample cases for analysis, essentially producing information for a 2-by-4 (*extreme*) and a 2-by-2 (*majority*) concordance table. Subsequent to this, five epidemiological criteria were explored by means of these analyses – sensitivity, specificity, positive predictive power, negative predictive power, and accuracy.

In an examination of the first of the above-listed epidemiological criteria, both extreme and majority sensitivity were found to be relatively high (83.0% and 94.3% respectively). Counter to these findings for sensitivity, both extreme and majority specificity were found to be relatively low (25.0% and 44.4% respectively). Next, positive predictive power demonstrated relatively high values across both extreme and majority models (95.4% and 89.2% respectively). Negative predictive power findings were mixed with the extreme model resulting in 90.0%, and the majority model resulting in 61.5%. Finally, accuracy also presented somewhat mixed findings with extreme accuracy analysis demonstrating findings of 73.1% and majority accuracy at 85.8 %.

Overall, the self-report screening methodology was found to demonstrate mixed levels of epidemiological efficacy. Specifically, statistical evidence described a methodology highly accurate in identifying those in "need of treatment," yet, also demonstrating a tendency to produce overly conservative findings with respect to those individuals clinically found not to be in "need of treatment." In other words, the self-report screening process used in its strictest objective form, without access to, or benefit of, the interpretation of contextual variables, demonstrated results that were "overly cautious," or more likely to "excessively classify" individuals in this population as demonstrating an elevated probability of "need for treatment."

While such an inclination toward conservative classification practices may actually be desirable when dealing with general populations, where the literature has identified a 22% prevalence rate for lifetime substance abuse disorders (Kessler et. al, 1994), it becomes less effective when employed in institutionalized criminal populations where such diagnoses have often been evidenced in the preponderance of individuals (National Institute of Justice, 1998, 1999, 2000, 2001, 2002). In other words, with the goal of self-report-based screening instrumentation providing an expedited and efficient means by which to appropriately allocate organizational treatment resources (Broner, Borum, Whitmire, & Gawley, 2002; Winters & Zenilman, 2000), the practice of "over classification" of individuals to "need for treatment" may be relatively less valuable than in other populations (e.g., general, vocational rehabilitation, and general psychiatric populations). Nevertheless, because there is evidence realized in the current study regarding a relatively high probability of respondents clinically identified as having a substance use disorder also having been correctly screened positive (sensitivity), it would appear that the self-report screening methodology is nevertheless useful even in a population where an elevated prevalence of individuals in "need for treatment" may be expected.

However, as was the case in the examination of aggregate criterion validity, here again, various limitations must be directly considered. For example, while a battery of screening instruments was used to generate index scores across inmate cases, with each screening instrument sharing the same statistical weight in the resulting cumulative case scores, it is possible that screening instruments were not equal in their capacity to identify "need for treatment." Moreover, screening instruments may have also not been equal in their capacity to distinguish individuals not in "need of treatment." In other words, the scoring methodology employed in the current study was based on the assumption of normality and equality across the instrumentation employed. Should this assumption have been false, then it is reasonable to assume that research findings would have been skewed, and perhaps less meaningful in their examination of the self-report screening methodology with respect to estimates of efficacy.

Another limitation to the current set of research inquires concerning the efficacy of the self-report screening methodology rests in the lack of a contrasting population for analytical comparisons. While it was possible to adequately explore issues of efficacy through an examination of the criminal population in this study, it may have been additionally insightful to have been able to conduct analyses across differing populations using the same methodological techniques of investigation. However, because the methodological procedures used in the current study are unique in their application, no such comparable data set was available, and therefore further relationships related to this research topic could not be presently examined via statistical analyses.

Construct Validity

To add to the current exploration of validity with respect to the self-report screening methodology, it was next important to extend this research beyond the investigation of aggregate criterion validity and efficacy, to also consider validity from a more theoretically grounded perspective. Therefore, this study once again used the comparison of self-report-based screen findings and clinical assessment outcomes in order to explore issues of construct validity. Here, outcomes across a series of variables were examined in order to understand their levels of support for theoretically expected results.

Variables under analysis with respect to the exploration of construct validity in this study included 1) age of first drug use, 2) frequency of drug use, 3) primary route of drug administration, 4) previous substance abuse treatment, 5) under the influence at time of current offense, 6) current offense dynamics, and 7) institutional misconduct specific to the use of drugs. Data linked to these variables was theoretically assessed and statistically analyzed (via analysis of variance and chi-square analyses) against pooled self-report screening score results for applicable inmate cases. Results of such analyses held that five of the seven relationships under review with respect to the construct validity of self-report screening results were found to support, both theoretically and statistically, the use of the self-report screening methodology. In other words, the self-report-based screen findings associated with forensic assessments resulted in relationships across variables that traveled in the direction anticipated. Only the first (age of first drug use) and seventh (institutional misconduct specific to the use of drugs) set of variable relationships presented some disagreement between theoretical expectations and statistical findings. However, ultimately six out of the seven relationships explored were found to produce significant results. Therefore, general research support was established for the construct validity of the self-report screening methodology as used in this study population.

As is the case with all methodological and analytical strategies involved in such research endeavors, there are innate limitations and cautions that must be considered. In the current set of analyses examining issues of construct validity, cautions must include an understanding of the limitation of the research variables selected, and moreover, how such variables were analyzed in relationship to the external standard. Specifically, it is feasible that the general findings of support for the construct validity of self-report-based screen results were, in part, an artificial construct derived as a by-product of the research variables available, selected, and introduced into the current study's analyses. In addition, research findings herein were dependent not only on the independent variables selected for theoretical examination, but also on the correctness of the actual external criterion itself. Therefore, the confidence in this external standard must also be taken into consideration when interpreting the value of research findings.

Influences on Criterion Validity

In addition to exploring criterion validity at the aggregate level of analysis, the current research also afforded an opportunity to examine the effects of multiple independent variables on convergent screen score classifications (based on concordance levels associated with psychological assessment findings). As a result of this research approach, a more precise understanding of how the interactions of variables in the self-reporting process impact the validity of screen findings was achieved. Specifically, potential influences of case and individual-level variables on the criterion validity of self-report-based screen findings were examined by means of a series of discriminant analyses. Here, one full model and three partial models were analyzed to estimate independent and collective variable influences on categorically arranged criterion validity (categories of convergence between multiple self-report screen findings and the external standard). In other words, an examination of a statistical model's ability to discriminate (to correctly classify cases) across dependent variable categories was estimated, resulting in the percentage of originally grouped cases correctly classified.

Following the analysis of a full research model (containing all research variables), variables were grouped into partial models in order to provide the necessary analytical "power" to arrive at statistically significant analyses, and moreover, to provide for a more theoretically bounded review of research findings. The construction of partial models included three groupings of variables based on related characteristics: 1) individual level attributes (demographics and intellectual functioning), 2) drug-related experiences (drug use history and treatment histories), and 3) developmental attributes (criminal justice experiences and other indexes of substance misuse). Statistical analyses revealed that several independent variables failed to produce any significant discriminant capacity across dependent variable categories (i.e., age of onset, prior mental health treatment, and sentence minimums), while other independent variables demonstrated a recurring ability to produce correct classifications of grouped cases (i.e., primary drug of choice, religious affiliation, institutional misconduct, employment status, race, under the influence at time of offense, and current offense). Based on these results, evidence was established for a number of the case and individual-level research variables examined throughout the current study to demonstrate moderate to strong capacities to discriminate across categorical convergent "need for treatment" findings.

The First Partial Model – Individual Level Attributes

The first partial model examined inmates' demographics and assessed intellectual cognitive functioning variables associated with concordance levels (between self-report screen results and psychological assessment findings) of respondent cases. Predictive classification statistics for the first partial model ranged from 42.9% to 75.9% (depending on the covariance structure employed and how the model's dependent variable was constructed). To this end, an individual's current age and education were not found to be significant contributions to the partial model, nor surprisingly was their cognitive function classification. As was considered in the previous review of the literature in this study (Richter & Johnson, 2001; Del Boca & Noll, 2000; Reynolds, 1993; Wilson, 1985; Groves, 1989), many of the concerns surrounding questions of validity with respect to self-report-based screen findings are specific to whether individuals adjudicated into criminal justice populations are readily competent reporters of their feelings, behaviors, attitudes and mental orientations. Moreover, it was reported that criminal populations tend to suffer from various shortcomings and deficiencies in competency and intellectual functioning at much higher rates than the general population (Broner et. al., 2002; Regier et. al., 1984; Tonry & Wilson, 1990). As such, an individual's chronological and emotional age, intellectual-educational capacity, and cognitive functioning plays a central role in delivering valid response data via self-report methodology. However, analyses conducted by means of the current research found no empirical support for these contentions. In fact, in none of the four models (2 full and 2 partial) in which the above mentioned variables (age, education, and cognitive-function) were considered, were any of them found to be significant.

On the other hand, there were independent variables explored in the first partial model that did provide some capacity to discriminate across categorical convergent "need for treatment" scoring categories. Specifically, 'marital status' and 'race' were found to be moderately predictive variables, whereas 'employment status' was more so.

Finally, 'religious affiliation' was found to be a variable that demonstrated recurring significance across all statistical models where it was incorporated. Because these variables are characteristic of, and would seem to contribute to, an individual's "identity formation," their demonstrated capacity to predicatively discriminate across convergent scoring categories may be informed by discussions on the phenomena of "social desirability" and "self-disclosure" provided at earlier points in this research (Chapter 3 "Self Report Screening and Issues of Validity). In particular, a variety of research to date has suggested that because of the unique venue in which criminal justice is couched, the issue of social desirability and lack of self-disclosure produced additional threats to validity that were of concern when employing self-report methodology. However, the expression of significance on the part of the above mentioned independent variables would suggest that this was not the case in the current research population. In other words, the self-report screening methodology seemed to overcome, at least in part (42.9% to 75.9% predictive model values), such threats to criterion validity. Nevertheless, without research information beyond that provided by the current study, it is not possible to meaningfully speculate as to why this cluster of variables proved significantly insightful into the criterion values in this study (e.g., identity formation, social learning, bonding).

The Second Partial Model – Drug-Related Experiences

The second partial model examined inmates' prior drug-related experiences and treatment history variables associated with concordance levels of respondent cases. Predictive classification statistics for the second partial model ranged from 55.0% to 71.2% (depending on the covariance structure employed and how the model's dependent variable was constructed). Results of these analyses found that several variables anticipated to have been capable of providing discriminant insights actually did not. In particular, 'age of onset' and 'prior mental health treatment' did not demonstrate significance across any of the four statistical models in which they were involved. In a similar manner, the variables 'prior substance abuse treatment' and 'community-based treatment' provided only modest support to this model's capacity to correctly classify cases along categories of the dependent variable. As the selection of these variables for analysis, to a great extent, rested in the culmination of various insights from the literature (Burke, Burke, Rae & Regier, 1991) previously reviewed as part of this study, the lack of significant contribution to the current partial model is noteworthy.

In contrast to such findings, the single variable included in the second partial model, which established a significant capacity to provide insight to the dependent variable across all analyses where it was incorporated, was 'primary drug of choice.' As this was the sole variable that emerged as predictive in the current model, with a marked absence of other theoretically-related variables, such as 'frequency of use' and 'route of administration,' it is likely that it is not the relationship to an individual's general 'drug use history' that is theoretically explanatory here. Moreover, in review of the relative classification function coefficient statistics, this independent variable's influence in the current model was not driven by one drug, or even a select set of drugs. Rather, all attributes (all drugs) associated with the variable 'primary drug of choice' demonstrated relatively similar statistical contributions and insights (statistical values) into issues of criterion validity. In other words, while the overall range of predictive values for the second partial model was nearly equivalent to the first partial model (55.0% to 71.2%), it was different in that this predictive capacity was grounded in the single variable 'primary drug of choice.' While the development of this information by means of the current exploratory study is not capable of assigning a meaningful theoretical explanation to this single predictive variable, it is nevertheless a valuable contribution to the groundwork required to develop a meaningful understanding of the self-report screening methodology and its potential value and limitations.

The Third Partial Model – Developmental Attributes

The third partial model examined inmates' prior criminal justice experiences and indexes of substance misuse associated with concordance levels of respondent cases. Predictive classification statistics for the first partial model ranged from 59.7% to 70.8% (depending on the covariance structure employed and how the model's dependent variable was constructed). Findings produced by this collection of analyses indicated that several of these variables demonstrated a lack of significant contribution to the model. Specifically, 'lifetime incarceration,' 'number of adult incarcerations,' and 'sentence minimum' did not provide discriminant insights. Moreover, the variable 'sentence maximum' also provided limited support in understanding issues of self-report-based screen validity. As was previously the case, the selection of such variables for analysis, to a large extent, had been the end result of a variety of information grounded in the research literature regarding social desirability (Richter & Johnson, 2001; Wilson, 2003; Bauman & Ennett, 1994; Presser & Stinson, 1998; Dads, Perrin, & Yule, 1998) and self-disclosure (Borchers, 2005; Mieczkowski, Barzelay, Gropper, & Wish, 1991; Feucht, Stephens, & Walker, 1994; Broner, Borum, Whitmire, & Gawley, 2002; Wentland & Smith, 1993). Therefore, the lack of significant contributions to the current partial model on the part of these independent variables is important.

On the other hand, the variables of 'institutional misconduct specific to the use of drugs,' 'current offense type,' and 'under the influence at the time of offense' did provide some capacity to discriminate across categorical concordance levels of the dependent variable. Specifically, in combination with each other by means of the third partial model, the overall range of predictive values was 59.7% to 70.8%. The first two of these variables were based on an inmate's prior criminal justice experiences, whereas the third variable expressing a significant predictive value was used as a proxy indicator of substance misuse. However, while these variables were drawn from different theoretical underpinnings, they do appear to express some characteristic commonalities. Specifically, they are all grounded in drug using behaviors resulting in, or highly associated with, the inmates' current incarceration. While the rational for why this grouping of like variables has demonstrated a distinct capacity to discriminate across convergent categories is not readily apparent, this cluster nevertheless has emerged and would seem to warrant further consideration. However, while this information in itself is a unique contribution to the literature regarding self-report screening methodology, it is important to note that the current research effort is exploratory in nature, and therefore a grounded theoretical examination is beyond its scope.

The Full Model

While the partial models provided an understanding of how individual attributes, drug-related experiences, and developmental attributes selected for discriminant analysis contribute to the validity of the self-report screening methodology, the full model provides an explanation of how the combination of all variables used herein influence criterion validity. Predictive classification statistics for the first partial model ranged from 63.7% to 75.7% (depending on the covariance structure employed and how the model's dependent variable was constructed). In this model, variables found to affect criterion validity included 'primary drug of choice,' 'race,' 'religious affiliation,' and 'institutional misconduct specific to the use of drugs.' As anticipated, there were no variables that presented themselves as significant discriminators in the full model that did not also present themselves as such within their respective partial models. However, as is realized in the discussion above, there were significant variables evidenced in the partial models that did not present themselves as such in the full model. Therefore, it might be understood that the methodological choice to use partial models so that analytical findings and individual variables might have the capacity to produce statistically significant results was well founded. With such insights realized, it became clear that further model building and empirical research is vitally needed in determining the extent to which respondent characteristics, experiences, motivational constructs and cognitive processes contribute to the accuracy of information provided by the verbal report method – as it applies to "need for treatment" and other areas of criminological applications. Once sufficient exploratory research, like that produced by the current study, has been generated with respect to employment of the self-report screening methodology in criminal populations, it will thereafter be possible to establish grounded theories for empirical examination.

SUMMARY

Following a series of statistical exercises and theoretical observations, this research has been able to provide significant insights into the two primary research questions posed at the outset of this study. The first of these research questions was expressed as, "Do screening instrument findings derived via self-report methodologies generate high levels of confidence (i.e., criterion validity, construct validity, and efficacy) when compared to forensic clinical psychological assessments?" Here, the data suggested that a high level of criterion validity has been evidenced, especially at the aggregate level of analyses, to support the deployment of self-report screening within this population. In addition, while data demonstrated some mixed support for the efficacy of self-report-based screen findings, as they were critically compared to psychological assessment findings along a variety of epidemiological criterion, it nevertheless became clear that with the exception of some limited "overclassification" of individuals to "need for treatment," that this methodology has the capacity to meaningfully inform institutional decision making processes. Finally, with respect to the first research question, significant supporting evidence was also garnered through various examinations of construct validity regarding self-report screen results. These findings suggest that this methodology not only seems to arrive at similar outcomes as clinical assessments, but that it is theoretically tied to many of the variables understood to associate with the phenomena of substance abuse.

Next, following a review of the full statistical model and the multiple partial models, this research has additionally been capable of providing data to inform the second primary research question posed at the outset of this study. This question was stated as, "Does the value of the self-report screening methodology vary based on case attributes (i.e., demographics, cognitive functioning, drug use history, treatment history, criminal justice experiences)?" Again, data collected and analyzed as part of the current study demonstrated that a number of variables did not demonstrate a significant capacity to discriminant across convergent screen score classifications. However, a series of other variables established a frequent capacity to generate a correct sorting of grouped cases. Moreover, a good deal of the information was provided in the current study to potentially inform the development of grounded theory in this research subfield, as significant support was realized for a number of the case and individual-level research variables explored as part of this study to express moderate to strong discrimination power across categorical convergent "need for treatment" findings.

LIMITATIONS OF THE RESEARCH

The research herein has provided some insight into the validity and efficacy of the self-report screening methodology, as employed in institutionalized criminal populations; however, as with all research, findings should be interpreted with caution. While some of the limitations of the current research have previously been discussed in this chapter, additional and more specific issues related to the research design and other related topics will be presented in this section.

A limitation central to all findings derived from the current research deals with problems inherent in the design. In the current study, it was necessary to assume that the external criterion used (forensic psychological assessment findings) was indeed actually accurate. This assumption was imperative to this research effort as the most practical and valuable means for establishing the validity of individual and cumulative screening instrument data collected by means of self-report methodology was to generate comparisons between findings from screening instrument outcomes and the corresponding clinical psychological assessments for these same inmate cases. Because psychologists operated under the generally accepted criteria of the Diagnostic and Statistical Manual, 4th Edition (DSM-IV) of the American Psychiatric Association (1994), and because of the professionalism, care, and diligence exercised by the psychologists producing each inmate's psychological review, combined with the careful scrutiny of each record on the part of the Principal Investigator (PI), the use of clinically-based assessments in this study was considered acceptable as a sufficient amount of confidence has been established in their accuracy. This procedure for assessing the clinical value of screening inventories has previously been used throughout the literature as a criterion measure to identify participants with substance abuse and dependence disorders (Torrens et al., 2004; Lazowski et al., 1998; Millon et al., 1997; Gastfriend, Najavits, & Reif, 1994; Bohn, Babor, & Kranzler, 1995).

In addition to the assumption regarding external criteria, it is also noteworthy to acknowledge that while this study sought to generate research findings representative of the respondent population drawn upon for the purposes of data collection – adult male inmates adjudicated in the state of Nebraska – generalizability beyond this population must be done with caution. Specifically, while analyses of the current research sample was found to be representative of the population from which it was drawn (across designated census variables), it is nevertheless limited in its ability to fully estimate the value of the self-report screening methodology as it might be administered throughout other criminal justice system venues (e.g., parole, probation, court settings, community corrections). Furthermore, because of the cross-sectional nature of this study, the findings are also limited to the time period from which the data were collected (the year 2001). Moreover, this study is bound by its use of secondary data collections and analysis. Specifically, as is traditionally the case when pre-existing data is employed, there existed an innate inability to select potential research variables beyond those available in the case files.

Finally, it is important to note that originally this research was to incorporate data from across multiple criminal justice institutional settings (e.g., prisons, jails, detention centers) – throughout the state of Nebraska and Iowa. However, while self-report screening inventories are readily used in a variety of such organizations and settings, there was rarely an appropriate external criterion also available for comparison to screen findings (e.g., clinical psychological assessment findings). Admittedly, it may have been possible to evaluate a specific screening instrument (e.g., one not already assessed in the literature) by comparing findings across other empirically grounded instruments. However, the current study opted for a more stringent and accepted external criterion for comparative analyses (clinical assessments), thereby making data from venues where this criterion was not available impractical for the current study.

STRENGTHS OF THE RESEARCH

While there are some limitations or weaknesses in this research, there are also several strengths. These general strengths include: the creativity of the research effort, the utilization of advanced statistical procedures to examine the validity of self-report screen findings, and its contribution to the existing knowledge base regarding the scientific measurement of substance abuse in special populations.

To this point, the research literature has identified a variety of insights and limitations regarding the use of self-report-based information as it has developed with respect to each new application and venue in which it was used. However, as self-report-based information has begun to be used in a very critical mode – to screen individuals housed in institutional criminal justice settings for "need for treatment" – it has become essential that a more in-depth understanding of potential threats to validity be developed. Because of this, the current research effort proved significant in that it produced an examination of a specific and unique sub-population, which is beginning to heavily employ the use of the self-report screening methodology for variables of potential influence on self-report-based diagnostic screen outcomes.

Previous evaluations of self-report-based screening instruments have typically involved the testing of individual screens, rather than the underlying methodology itself. However, the testing of individual screening instruments has not demonstrated a capacity to readily evaluate the aggregate validity of self-report-based screen findings, nor have such evaluations been able to address the common institutional practice of using and consulting multiple screening instruments. When such evaluations have been presented throughout the literature, they have typically employed relatively "weak" criterion measures, typically other DSM-IV-based self-report instruments. Finally, most studies in this area were not designed to test directly hypotheses (atheoretical) regarding the utility of different assessment approaches. Rather, they have involved secondary analyses of data originally collected for different purposes.

The strengths of the current study have therefore involved addressing several of these gaps in the literature. First, the current study employed a "meta-method" examination to assess issues of aggregate convergent validity between self-report screen findings and an optimal independent external criterion – forensic clinical psychological findings. Specifically, the culmination of three self-report-based screening instruments logistically available and serendipitously designed for different audiences, and used within the Nebraska state prison system (Diagnostic Evaluation Center) to provide insights toward institutional decisions were used. Moreover, as a result of aggregating a battery of self-report screen findings for criterion comparison, this research provided insight into the value of the self-report screening methodology overall. This is the first time a "meta-methodological" examination of self-report screen findings has been generated to explore issues of validity and efficacy. As a result, insights into the value of the emerging practice of self-report screening have been presented.

Employing this methodology, this study additionally examined theoretical relationships (construct validity) between screen outcomes and various indexes of substance misuse. Finally, individual and case-level variables were analyzed against cumulative screen scores and concordance findings in order to ascertain potential variables influencing the validity of such findings. As a result, this research has provided a new understanding of variables that promote or inhibit the value of self-report screening in criminal populations.

The research design employed in the current study is also an important strength of the research. Here, the use of secondary data allowed for a systematic collection and examination of relevant research variables. In addition, this protocol made it possible to obtain a large enough sample size within the logistical constraints of the researcher. Finally, this research design allowed for data to be collected by means of a random sampling process, resulting in a representative sample population. With this the case, a greater confidence in the research findings might be held when extrapolating the findings to the represented population and timeframe (Nebraska Department of Correction's Diagnostic Evaluation Center for the year 2001).

POLICY IMPLICATIONS

As was discussed early on in this study, clinically valid instruments for use in drug abuse and dependency screening are becoming increasingly essential to clinicians and other public agency workers (Inciardi, 2000). While various screening methodologies have become extensively employed by medical institutions throughout the United States as tools to collect diagnostic information in place of clinicians in recent years (Atkinson, Zibin, & Chuang, 1997; Reynolds, 1993), recently American criminal justice system policies and practices have begun to reflect this same practice of using self-report-based screening methodologies to inform a variety of institutional decisions (Winters & Zenilman, 2000; Andrews & Bonta, 1994). This innovation has come about as criminal justice policies have begun to focus more on the benefits of treatment for offender populations rather than the traditional strict use of incarceration.

While it has been realized through a review of the literature and as a result of some of the analytical findings in the current study, a variety of limitations and cautions must be understood as associated with the self-report-based screening methodology. However, despite such limitations, the self-report screening methodology would appear to provide some utility as deployed throughout institutionalized criminal populations. Given the interest in reducing criminal recidivism associated with substance abuse, policies supporting the use of screening would seem to be one potential strategy to seriously take into account. To this end, individuals expressing substance abuse disorders and related behaviors which are seemingly interconnected with their offenses (like some of the finding in this study suggest – significant variables of 'institutional misconduct specific to the use of drugs,' 'current offense type,' and 'under the influence at the time of offense') are principal candidates to target in an effort to address recidivism.

When considering behaviors associated with addiction, especially as they may be exacerbated within institutionalized populations like that under review in the current study (correctional populations), there are certainly unique health and management considerations presented. Substance abuse treatment programming of adequate duration and intensity have been found to be effective in realizing recovery from drug dependence (Zywiak, Hoffmann, & Floyd, 1999). Moreover, such recovery has often demonstrated a significant influence on successive arrests (Belenko, 1998). With this the case, self-report-based screen practices in the context of appropriate treatment resources, advocates for a potentially valuable policy in dealing with substance abusing offenders. To this end, the current research has also held that the practice of employing self-report-based screening methodologies has become more commonplace in criminal justice settings throughout the early part of this century; therefore, the findings of this research would support the continued implementation of such institutional policies.

IMPLICATIONS FOR FUTURE RESEARCH

While reporting many new findings that contribute to the existing literature in self-report, substance abuse screening, and scientific measurement, these findings have also provided more unanswered questions even while providing ideas for future avenues of exploration in self-report screening methodologies. In addition to what has already been discussed in the context of future research, other avenues of study include an extensive analysis of additional variables that might be expected to be theoretically linked to, or demonstrate influence on, the validity and efficacy of general self-report dynamics; self-report by special populations (e.g. criminals, social deviants, diagnostically positive individuals), self-report of sensitive topics (e.g., drug addiction, behavior related to substance misuse), and self-report by various screening protocols. As reported in the discriminant analysis models, some capacity was demonstrated to correctly predict classification outcomes based on selected research variables. While these findings did provide additional insight into the self-report screening methodology, additional research in the dynamics of gender, attitudes, and other associated personal attributes and processes should also be conducted before the full value of the self-report methodology can be comprehensively understood.

One effective method to capture the dynamics of the self-report screening process is through qualitative analysis. By taking a qualitative case study approach, a great deal of additional information may be obtained regarding issues of respondent reactivity, dramaturgical and symbolic interactions, and emerging concepts of interest. As indicated by various qualitative researchers (Berg, 2004; Yin, 2003; Neuman, 2000), this immersion into the topic will provide the researcher with an intimate familiarity into their area of investigation. The use of qualitative analysis will also compliment the existing quantitative analysis related to self-report methodologies employed in criminal populations, providing a greater understanding of factors that affect the self-report screening process for this special population of respondents.

Another avenue of research could be the examination of respondents from other institutionalized criminal justice settings (e.g. jails, detention centers, drug courts, day reporting centers) where self-report screening methodologies are employed. By using the same variables as used in this research but applied to other settings, similarities related to environmental and screening specific issues could be discovered, further validating findings from the current study. Differences across settings in terms of the context in which self-report screen data are collected from respondents may also highlight how different dynamics may affect the validity and efficacy of this methodology.

CONCLUSION

This research began by considering the need to address a contemporary mandate to develop and employ mechanisms to triage incoming inmates for purposes of efficient allocation of institutional criminal justice resources. Through a review of the literature it was found that the use of this methodology within criminal justice venues has, in recent years, exponentially increased. Moreover, it was held that although various self-report screening instruments based on diagnostic criteria have indeed experienced scientific support as applied within the general population, there exists a vacuum and need for empirically-based support for this enhanced self-report screening methodology as used within criminal justice populations. With these insights recognized, a compelling paradox seemed to present itself. Specifically, why has the practice of triaging institutionalized criminal justice populations using the self-report-based screening methodology exponentially increased in the absence of ample empirically grounded support for the validity of this practice? It was therefore the goal of this research to examine the effectiveness of the self-report screening methodology in generating valid data regarding drug and alcohol disorders within institutionalized criminal justice venues.

To begin to address this issue, the practice of using self-report-based screening instruments to establish the probability of "need for treatment" in criminal justice settings was considered in terms of the history and development of the self-report methodology, to include associated empirical values and issues of validity. More specifically, the self-report screening methodology was assessed for issues of criterion validity, efficacy, and construct validity. Here, strong support was established for the aggregate criterion validity and construct validity of this methodology. In addition, while some cautions regarding a bias for "overclassification" were realized, this methodology also produced relatively valuable findings with respect to efficacy. Finally, the examination of individual and collective case variables developed some basic insights into relationships associated with levels of criterion validity.

As previously suggested, recent research has held that the validity of report measures are matters of degree rather than absolute properties of a measuring device (Barbor, Brown & Del Boca, 1990) and that "evaluation of these psychometric qualities depends upon the researchers' purpose and the context within which data are collected" (Del Boca & Noll, 2000, p. 348). Therefore, "the objective of attaining a perfectly valid indicator – one that represents the intended, and only the intended, concept – is unachievable. Instead, validity is a matter of degree, not an all-or-none property" (Carmines & Zeller, 1979, p. 13). With this the case, it is essential that norming information specific to a criminal justice setting be established and further used in the development and deployment of self-report-based screening instruments.

Having informed the research questions posed herein, this study has served to improve the understanding and inform policies and practices related to self-report-based screening protocols designed to triage "need for treatment" in criminal justice institutionalized populations. Coupled with this approach to gaining a better understanding of self-report screening, this research builds upon the limited research that exists on institutionalized criminal populations. The review of the literature illustrates the need for a contemporary understanding of the self-report methodology as it has begun to be employed in screening protocols within special populations. With this the case, research findings herein may be used to inform evidence-based-policy for researchers and institutions involved in the designing, interpretation, and deployment of self-report-based screening instruments.

Appendix A

Threats to Research Validity

Internal Validity = without which any experiment is uninterpretable: Did in fact the experimental treatments make a difference in this specific experimental instance?

History: the specific events occurring between the first and second measurement in addition to the experimental variable.

- Because the administration to respondents of the instrumentation collected for purposes of the current study was done so within a relatively short period of time (typically 1 to 30 days) and in no systematic order (random order), it was anticipated that any 'history' effect, even if applicable to a small number of respondents would not demonstrate a significant influence upon findings derived from analysis of such data.

Maturation: processes within the respondents operating as a function of the passage of time and not specific to the particular events (e.g. growing older).

- Because the administration to respondents of the instrumentation collected for purposes of the current study was done so within a relatively short period of time (typically 1 to 30 days), it was anticipated that any 'maturation' effect would be minimal in consequence to research findings

Testing: the effects of taking a test upon the scores of a second testing.

- Instrumentation collected for purposes of the current study (i.e., clinical psychological assessment, the SSI, the SATOP, the SASSI) were administered to respondents utilizing no systematic method (random order), therefore, it is anticipated that subsequent data analysis of such information would not demonstrate a significant 'testing' influence upon research findings.

Instrumentation: changes in the calibration of a measuring instrument or changes in the observers/scorers used may produce changes in the obtained measurements.

- Because screening instruments (i.e., the SSI, SATOP and SASSI screens) used to collect data for the current study were administered to each respondent only once and subsequently scored used a standard scoring methodology, there was no opportunity to introduce the threat of 'instrumentation' into subsequent research findings involving such measures. In addition, the clinical psychological assessment findings applicable to the research respondents under consideration here were produced by the small number (2 to 4 psychologists) of institutional psychologist practicing within the prison venue in which the data was collected. Therefore, as there are only a small number of practitioners and a clinical standard followed (DSM-IV criterion), it was anticipated that the threat of 'instrumentation' would not present a significant influence upon research findings.

Statistical Regression: operating where groups have been selected on the basis of their extreme scores.

- Cases for inclusion in the current research study were randomly selected from an inventory of all available cases meeting research parameters, therefore, it was anticipated that subsequent data analysis of such information would not demonstrate a 'statistical regression' influence upon research findings.

Selection Biases: resulting in differential selection of respondents for the comparison groups.

- Cases for inclusion in the current research study were randomly selected from an inventory of all available cases meeting research parameters, therefore, it was anticipated that subsequent data analysis of such information would not demonstrate a 'selection bias' influence upon research findings.

Experimental Mortality: differential loss of respondents from the comparison groups.

- Because the current study employed secondary analysis of pre-existing data, it there was therefore no evidence of 'experimental mortality' that may have influenced research findings.

Selection-Maturation Interaction: which in certain of the multiple-group quasi-experimental designs is confounded with the effect of the experimental variable.

- Cases for inclusion in the current research study were randomly selected from an inventory of all available cases meeting research parameters. Moreover, because the administration to respondents of the instrumentation collected for purposes of the current study was done so within a relatively short period of time (typically 1 to 30 days), it was anticipated that any 'selection-maturation' effect would be minimal in consequence to research findings

External Validity = asks the question of generalizability: To what populations, settings, treatment variables, and measurement variables can this effect be generalized?

Reactive or Interaction Effect of Testing: a pretest might increase or decrease the respondent's sensitivity or responsiveness to the experimental variable and thus make the results obtained for a pretested population unrepresentative of the effects of the experimental variable for the unpretested universe from which the experimental respondents were selected.

- Because no pretest was involved in the current study, there was no evidence of a 'reactive or interaction effect of testing' upon research findings.

Interaction Effects: of selection bias and the experimental variable.

- Because cases for inclusion in the current research study were randomly selected from an inventory of all available cases meeting research parameters and there was no 'experimental variable exposure,' it was therefore anticipated that subsequent data analysis would not demonstrate the influence of a 'interaction effect' upon research findings.

Reactive Effects of Experimental Arrangements: which would preclude generalization about the effect of the experimental variable upon persons being exposed to it in non-experimental settings.

- Because the current research effort did not employ a non-experimental study group, it was anticipated that there would be no 'reactive effects of experimental arrangements' upon research findings.

Multiple-Treatment Interference: likely to occur whenever multiple treatments are applied to the same respondents, because the effects of prior treatments are not usually erasable. This is a particular problem for many one-group designs.

- Because the order of the instrumentation collected for purposes of the current study (i.e., clinical psychological assessment, the SSI, the SATOP, the SASSI) were administered to respondents utilizing no systematic method (random order), subsequent data analysis of such information would therefore not demonstrate a significant 'testing' influence upon research findings.

(Campbell and Stanley, 1963)

Appendix B

Substance Abuse Treatment Offender Program (SATOP) Screening Instrument

1) Have you ever had to drink or use other drugs more than you did in the past to get the same high?

2) Have you ever experienced loss of memory (black-outs) while using alcohol and/or other drugs?

3) Have you ever sneaked around to have a drink or use other drugs?

4) Have you ever thought a lot about using alcohol and/or other drugs?

5) Have you ever hurried to do that first hit or gulp that first drink?

6) Have you ever avoided talking about your personal alcohol or other drug use?

7) Has loss of memory while drinking or using other drugs gotten worse or more often?

8) Have you ever lost control of your alcohol and/or other drug use?

9) Have you ever used excuses for your alcohol and/or other drug use?

10) Have you ever been put down or argued with family and/or friends because of your alcohol and/or other drug use?

11) Have you ever "shown off" with your money, time or advice regarding your alcohol and/or other drug use?

12) Have you ever gotten into a physical fight while/about your drinking and/or other drug use?

13) Have you ever felt guilty about your alcohol and/or other drug use?

14) Have you ever stopped drinking and/or using for short periods of time?

15) Have you ever changed your alcohol and/or other drug use patterns?

16) Have you experienced loss of friends due to your alcohol and/or other drug use?

17) Have you ever lost a job or client because of your alcohol and/or other drug addiction before this program?

18) Have you ever been in treatment for alcoholism and/or other drug addiction before this program?

19) Have others ever stopped or changed their habits because of your alcohol and/or other drug use?

20) Have you ever held grudges related to your alcohol and/or other drug use?

21) Have you ever changed friends or moved to try to stop or cut down on your alcohol and/or other drug use?

22) Have you ever hidden or lied about your alcohol and/or other drug supply?

23) Have you ever used alcohol and/or other drugs shortly after waking up?

24) Have you ever used alcohol and/or other drugs about 18 hours straight?

25) Have you ever done anything against your morals and/or values due to alcohol and/or other drugs?

26) Have you ever experienced "crazy thoughts" when drinking and/or using other drugs?

27) Does it take less alcohol and/or other drugs to get high than before?

28) Have you ever been afraid and did not know why?

29) Have you ever had the shakes?

30) Have you ever stumbled and staggered around when you got drunk or high?

31) Have you ever felt you needed to improve your life (change your ways) regarding your alcohol and/or other drug use?

Substance Abuse Treatment Offender Program (SATOP)

Instrument Key

Question #	Diagnostic Criterion Correlate
1. (one)	Increased tolerance
2. (two)	Blackouts
4. (four)	Preoccupation
8. (eight)	Loss of control
14. (fourteen)	Unsuccessful attempt to stop using
16. (sixteen)	Loss of friends
17. (seventeen)	Loss of employment
18. (eighteen)	Previous treatment
27. (twenty-seven)	Decreased tolerance
28. (twenty-eight)	Unexplained anxiety
29. (twenty-nine)	Withdrawal symptoms
30. (thirty)	Excessive use

1 point is added to the overall score for each of the above questions answered 'Yes.' If the total score is 3 or more, then the instruments suggest a high probability of 'Need for Treatment.'

Appendix C

The Diagnostic and Statistical Manual of Mental Disorders, 4th Edition's (DSM IV) Definitions and Criteria for Substance Abuse and Substance Dependence

The DSM IV breaks the "disease" of alcoholism down into two separate "disorders," *alcohol abuse* and *alcohol dependence*. These definitions are listed under the topic of substance disorders in the DSM IV. The DSM IV defines *substance abuse* as the maladaptive pattern of substance (e.g. alcohol) use leading to clinically significant impairment or distress, as manifested by one (or more) of the following, occurring within a 12-month period:

1. Recurrent substance use resulting in a failure to fulfill major role obligations at work, school or home (e.g. repeated absences or poor work performance related to substance use; substance-related absences, suspensions, or expulsions from school; neglect of children or household)

2. Recurrent substance use in situations in which it is physically hazardous (e.g. driving a car or operating a machine when impaired by substance use)

3. Recurrent substance-related legal problems (e.g. arrests for substance-related disorderly conduct)

4. Continued substance use despite having persistent or recurrent social or interpersonal problems caused or exacerbated by the effects of the substance (e.g. arguments with spouse about consequences of intoxication, physical fights)

The symptoms of *substance abuse* have never met the criteria for *substance dependence* for this class of substance.

When defining *substance dependence*, the DSM IV states that *substance dependence* is a maladaptive pattern of substance use, leading to clinically significant impairment or distress, as manifested by three (or more) of the following, occurring at any time in the same 12-month period:

1. Tolerance, as defined by either of the following:

    a. A need for markedly increased amounts of substance to achieve intoxication or desired effect

    b. Markedly diminished effect with continued use of the same amount of the substance

2. Withdrawal, as manifested by either of the following:

    a. The characteristic withdrawal syndrome for the substance…
    b. The same (or closely related) substance is taken to relieve or avoid withdrawal symptoms

3. The substance is often taken in larger amounts or over a longer period than was intended (*loss of control*).

4. There is a persistent desire or unsuccessful efforts to cut down or control substance use.

5. A great deal of time is spent in activities necessary to obtain the substance, use the substance or recover from its effects.

6. Important social, occupational or recreational activities are given up or reduced because of substance use.

7. The substance use is continued despite the knowledge of having a persistent or recurrent physical or psychological problem that is likely to have been caused or exacerbated by the substance (e.g. continued drinking despite recognition that an ulcer was made worse by alcohol consumption).

When using these criteria to diagnose alcohol *abuse* or alcohol *dependence*, we must specify whether *substance dependence* is with physiologic dependence (evidence of tolerance or withdrawal) or without physiologic dependence (no evidence of tolerance or withdrawal).

Source: Association, A. P. (1994). Diagnostic and Statistical Manual of Mental Disorders (4th ed.). Washington, D.C.

Appendix D

Sources for Items Included in the 'Alcohol and Other Drug' (AOD) Simple Screening Instrument (SSI)

SSI Question Number	Source Instrument
1	Revised Health Screening Survey (RHSS)
2	Michigan Alcohol Screening Test (MAST)
3	CAGE
4	MAST, CAGE
5	History of Trauma Scale, MAST, CAGE
6	MAST, Drug Abuse Screening Test (DAST)
7	MAST, Problem-Oriented Screening Instrument for Teenagers (POSIT)
8	MAST, DAST
9	MAST, DSM-II-R
10	POSIT, DSM-II-R
11	POSIT
12	POSIT
13	MAST, POSIT, CAGE, RHSS, Alcohol Use Disorders Identification Test (AUDIT), Addiction Severity Index (ASI)

Winters, K. C. and J. M. Zenilman (2000). Simple Screening Instruments for Outreach for Alcohol and Other Drug Abuse and Infectious Diseases. Rockville, MD, U.S. Department of Health and Human Services, Public Health Services, Substance Abuse and Mental Health Services Administration, Center for Substance Abuse Treatment.

* Note that primary references for these sources appear in the bibliography.

Appendix E

Examples of Concordance Table Analyses

<u>A 2-by-2 Table</u>

		Clinical Psychological Diagnoses		
		Criterion Positive	**Criterion Negative**	Total
Self-Report Diagnostic Screen Findings	**Screened Positive** ("in need of treatment")	187 (a)	23 (b)	210 (c)
	Screened Negative (not in "need of treatment")	80 (d)	110 (e)	190 (f)
	Total	267 (g)	133 (h)	400 (i)

Analytical Terms and Formulas:

Prevalence = a / i = 187 / 400 = **46.8%**

Sensitivity = a / a + d = 187 / 187 + 80 = **70.0%**

Specificity = e / e + b = 110 / 110 + 23 = **82.7%**

Positive Predictive Power (PPP) = a / a + b = 187 / 187 + 23 = **89.0%**

Negative Predictive Power (NPP) = e / e + d = 110 / 110 + 80 = **57.9%**

Accuracy = a + e / i = 187 + 110 / 400 = **74.3%**

A 2-by-4 Table

		Self-Report Diagnostic Screen-Findings				
		Screened Positive ("in need of treatment")		**Screened Negative** (not "in need of treatment")		Total
		3	**2**	**1**	**0**	
Clinical Psychological Diagnoses	**Criterion Positive**	80 (a)	15 (b)	10 (c)	5 (d)	110 (e)
	Criterion Negative	20 (f)	30 (g)	50 (h)	290 (i)	390 (j)
	Total	100 (l)	45 (m)	60 (n)	295 (o)	500 (p)

Analytical Terms and Formulas:

Prevalence = e / p = 110 / 500 = **22.0%** (lifetime prevalence rate of adult substance dependence in U.S. – Kessler et. al., 1994)

Extreme Sensitivity = a / a + b + c + d = 80 / 80 + 15 + 10 + 5 = **72.7%**

Majority Sensitivity = a + b / a + b + c + d =
80 + 15 / 80 + 15 + 10 + 5 = **86.4%**

Extreme Specificity = i / f + g + h + i = 290 / 20 + 30 + 50 + 290 = **74.4%**

Majority Specificity = i + h / f + g + h + i =
290 + 50 / 20 + 30 + 50 + 290 = **87.2%**

Extreme Positive Predictive Power (PPP) = a / a + f = 80 / 80 + 20 = **80.0%**

Majority PPP = a + b / a + b + f + g =
80 + 15 / 80 + 15 + 20 +30 = **67.6%**

Extreme Negative Predictive Power (NPP) = i / d + i = 290 / 290 + 5 = **98.3%**

Majority NPP = h + i / c + d + h + i =
290 + 50 / 10 + 15 + 50 + 290 = **95.8%**

Extreme Accuracy = a + i / p = 80 + 290 / 500 = **74.0%**

Majority Accuracy = a + b + h + i / p =
80 + 15 + 50 + 290 / 500 = **87.0%**

Appendix F – METHODOLOGY VISUAL

Nebraska DEC Population (2001)
(N = 1,518) .... (N = 424 = 27.9%)
Nebraska DEC Sample (2001)

Chi-Square 'Goodness of Fit Test'

31 Q. SATOP (n=424)
SSI (n=424)
SASSI (n=424)

(Self-Report Cumulative Scoring Index) (n=424)

Concordance Tables to Examine Criterion Validity between Self-Report Screen Scores and Psych Evals.

DEC Clinical Psych. Evaluations (n=424)

Prevalence Rate of Clinically Diagnosed Substance Abuse for DEC Sample Pop. = Standard Criterion= (83%)

Efficacy
a) Sensitivity
b) Specificity
c) Positive Predictive Power (PPP)
d) Negative Predictive Power (NPP)
e) Accuracy

1. Score inmate cases by 'number of positive' (high probability of 'need for treatment') screens evidenced per case = each positive finding indexed at 1 point.

2. Examine Construct Validity = compare 'Substance Misuse Indexes' to instrument findings generated via self-report methodology (cumulatively indexed into a continuum score of 0, 1, 2, & 3).

   (e.g., age of first drug use, frequency of use, primary route of administration, prior treatment history, under the influence at time of arrest, current offense dynamics)

   ANOVA and Chi-Square calculations to assess differences across groupings

3. Group individual inmate cases by 'convergent/divergent scoring schemata' (self-report screen findings compared to clinical psychological assessment findings).

   Classify cases (e.g., 0, 1, 2 or 3) via three scoring methodologies
   - Categorical = 0, 1, 2 or 3
   - Dichotomous = 0 & 1 vs. 2 & 3 or 0, 1 & 2 vs. 3
   - Extreme Dichotomy = 0 vs. 3

   Power analysis conducted to assure sample sizes necessary for various statistical analyses

4. Test of variables theoretically expected, and logistically available, for possible influences on convergent screen findings derived via the self-report methodology.

   (demographics, cognitive functioning, treatment histories, criminal justice experiences, 'substance misuse index' variables)

   Discriminate Analysis of selected case models/variables upon convergent/divergent scoring classifications (= dependent variable)

Appendix G – ASSUMPTIONS OF NORMALITY

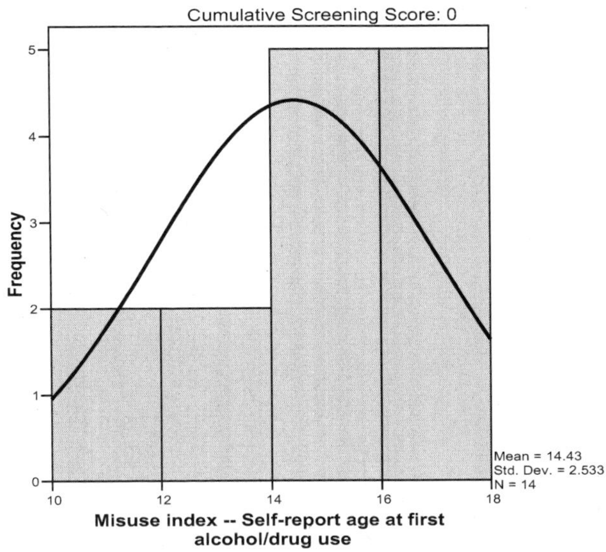

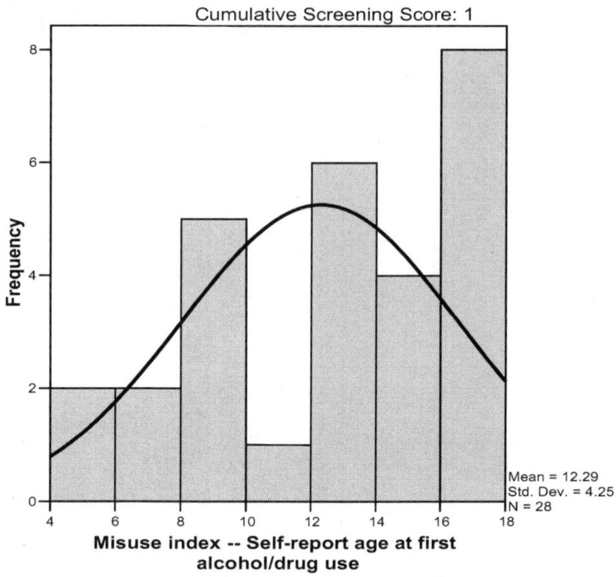
Cumulative Screening Score: 1
Frequency
8
6
4
2
0
4
6
8
10
12
14
16
18
Mean = 12.29
Std. Dev. = 4.25
N = 28
Misuse index -- Self-report age at first alcohol/drug use

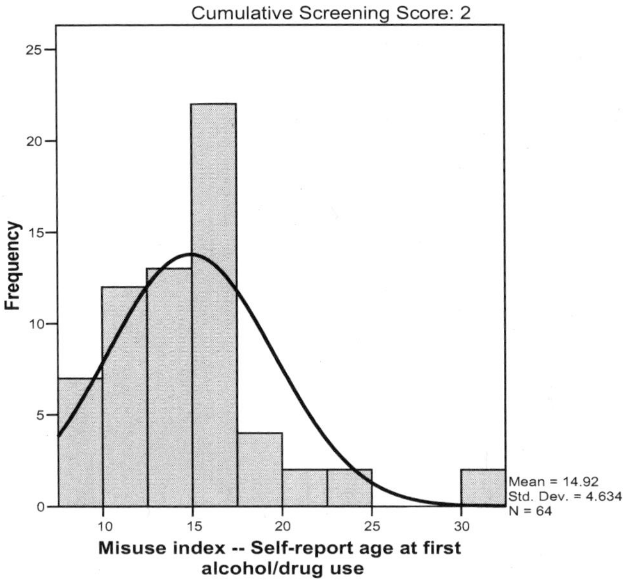
Cumulative Screening Score: 2
Frequency
25
20
15
10
5
0
10
15
20
25
30
Mean = 14.92
Std. Dev. = 4.634
N = 64
Misuse index -- Self-report age at first alcohol/drug use

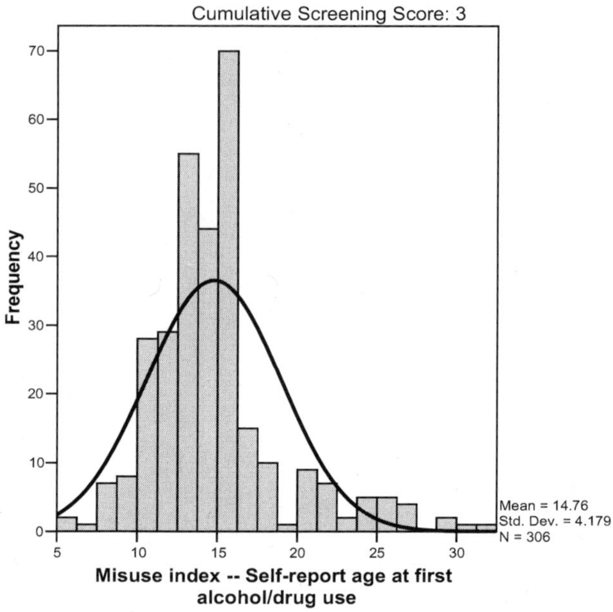
Cumulative Screening Score: 3
Frequency
0
10
20
30
40
50
60
70
5
10
15
20
25
30
Mean = 14.76
Std. Dev. = 4.179
N = 306
Misuse index -- Self-report age at first alcohol/drug use

Appendix H – DISCRIMINANT ANALYSIS MODELING

The following models were constructed for purposes of discriminant analyses.

Partial Model – Individual Level Attributes

Demographics						Intellectual Functioning
Current Age	Race	Education	Marital Status	Religious Affiliation	Employment	Cognitive Functioning
1) Metric Measure	Native Amer.	No Formal Education	Never-Married	Non-Christ	Unemployed	Metric Measure
2)	Caucasian	$8^{th} - 11^{th}$	No Longer	Catholic	Part-Time	
3)	Black	Graduated	Married	Baptist	Full-Time	
4)	Hispanic	Some College		Other-Christian		

Partial Model – Drug-Related Experiences

Drug Use History				Treatment History		
Age of Onset	Primary Drug	Frequency of Use	Route of Admin.	Sub-Abuse Treatment	Mental-H Treatment	Community Based-Treat
1) Metric Measure	None	Monthly and Don't Use	Not User	No	No	No
2)	Alcohol	Daily	Oral	Yes	Yes	Yes
3)	Marijuana	Weekly	Smoke			
4)	Cocaine-Crack		Snort			
5)	Meth		Inject			
6)	Heroin					

Partial Model – Developmental Attributes

Criminal Justice Experience						Index of Substance Misuse
Lifetime Incarceration	Number of Adult Incarc.	Current Offense	Sentence Minimum	Sentence Maximum	Institutional Misconduct	Under Influ.
1) Metric Measure	Metric Measure	Non-Drug Related	Metric Measure	Metric Measure	No Yes	No Yes
		Drug-Related				

Appendix I –VARIABLES DEMONSTATING DISCRIMINANT PREDICTIVE VALIDITY BY MODEL

	Full Model	R-Full Model	1st Partial Model	R-1st Partial Model	2nd Partial Model	R-2nd Partial Model	3rd Partial Model	R-3rd Partial Model
First Partial Model Individual Level Attributes								
Race	2		1					
Marital Status				3				
Religious Affiliation	3	2	2	1				
Employment Status		4	3	2				
Second Partial Model Drug-Related Experiences								
Primary Drug of Choice	1	1			1	1		
Third Partial Model Developmental Attributes								
Current Offense							2	2
Institutional Misconduct	4	3					3	
Under the Influence at Time of Offense							1	1

* note: variables are ranked based on their position by model from the highest to the lowest classification function coefficient scores.
* note: for a full operationalization of the partial models listed above, see Appendix H.
* R = restructured

Appendix J – DISCRIMINANT PREDICTIVE VALIDITY VALUES BY MODEL

Full Model		Restructured Full Model	
Pooled CSCR	Unpooled CSCR	Pooled CSCR	Unpooled CSCR
63.7% (57.1%)	63.7%	75.7% (74.3%)	75.2%

First Partial Model		Restructured First Partial Model	
Pooled CSCR	Unpooled CSCR	Pooled CSCR	Unpooled CSCR
42.9% (40.8%)	51.7%	75.7% (74.1%)	75.9%

Second Partial Model		Restructured Second Partial Model	
Pooled CSCR	Unpooled CSCR	Pooled CSCR	Unpooled CSCR
55.0% (52.4%)	54.5%	71.2% (71.2%)	71.2%

Third Partial Model		Restructured Third Partial Model	
Pooled CSCR	Unpooled CSCR	Pooled CSCR	Unpooled CSCR
65.3% (65.3%)	59.7%	70.8% (70.8%)	70.8%

* note: Cross-Validated % of grouped cases correctly classified = (x%)
* note: Pooled Covariance Structure Classification Results = "Pooled CSCR"
* note: Unpooled Covariance Structure Classifcation Results = "Unpooled CSCR"

REFERENCES

Abram, K. M., & Teplin, L. A. (1991). Co-occurring disorders among mentally ill jail detainees: Implications for public policy. *American Psychologist, 46*(10), 1036 –1045.

Akers, R. L., Krohn, M. D, Lanza-Kaduce, L. & Radoscevich, M. (1979). Social learning and deviant behavior: A specific test of a general theory. *American Sociological Review, 44,* 636-655.

American Psychiatric Association. (1994). *Diagnostic and Statistical Manual* (4th ed.). Washington, D.C.

American Psychological Association. (1999). Behaviorism: The rise and fall of a discipline. *APA Monitor*, 30(11), American Psychological Association.

Anderson, L. S., Chiricos, T. G., & Waldo, G. P. (1977). Formal and informal sanctions: A comparison of deterrent effects. *Social Problems, 25*, 103-112.

Andrews, D. A., & Bonta, J. (1994). COMPAS User's Case Management Guide. In Brennan, T. & Fretz, R., & Wells, D. (Eds.) (2000). *Northpointe Institute for Public Management*, Traverse City, MI.

Angleitner A. & Wiggins, J. S. (1986). Introduction. *Personality assessment via questionnaires: Current issues in theory and measurement*, Berlin: Springer-Verlag, 1-3.

APA Monitor Online. (1999, December). Behaviorism: the rise and fall of a discipline. 30(11). Retrieved October 6, 2008, from http://www.apa.org/monitor/dec99/toc.html

Arrestee Drug Abuse Monitoring Program (ADAM). (2000). ADAM Interview Instrument. National Institute of Justice. Department of Justice. Washington, D.C.

Atkinson, M., Zibin, S. and Chuang, H. (1997). Characterizing quality of life among patients with chronic mental illness: A critical examination of the self-report methodology. *American Journal of Psychiatry, 154*, 99-105.

Babbie, E. (1992). *The practice of social research* (6th ed.). Belmont, CA: Wadsworth Publishing Company.

Babor, T. F., Stephens, R. S. & Marlatt, G. A. (1987). Verbal report methods in clinical research on alcoholism: Response bias and its minimization. *Journal of Studies on Alcohol, 48,* 410- 424.

Babor, T. F. & Del Boca, F. K. (1992). Just the facts: Enhancing measurement of alcohol consumption using self-reports methods. In R. Z. Litten and J. P. Allen (Eds.), *Measuring Alcohol Consumption: Psychosocial and chemical methods* (pp. 3-19). Totowa, NJ, Humana Press.

Babor, T. F., Steinberg, K., Anton, R., & Del Boca, F. K. (2000). Talk is cheap: Measuring drinking outcomes in clinical trials. *Journal of Studies in Alcohol, 61*, 55-63.

Ball, J. C., Schaffer, J. W., & Nurco, D. N. (1983). The day to day criminality of heroin addicts in Baltimore - A study in the continuity of offence rates. *Drug and Alcohol Dependence, 12*, 119-142.

Barbor, T. F., Brown, J. and Del Boca, F. K. (1990). Validity of self-reports in applied research on addictive behaviors: Fact or fiction? *Behavioral Assessment*, *12*, 5-31.

Bauman, K. E. & Ennett, S. T. (1994). Tobacco use by black and white adolescents: The validity of self reports. *American Journal of Public Health*, *84,* 394-398.

Baumer, T. L. (1998). Assessing the need for treatment in the arrestee population. *Journal of Crime and Justice, 21*(2), 173-189.

Bayley, D. H. (1985). *Patterns of policing: A comparative international analysis*. New Brunswick: Rutgers University Press.

Begin, G. & Boivin, M. (1980). Comparison of data gathered on sensitive questions via direct questionnaire, randomized response technique, and a projective method. *Psychological Reports*, *47*(3), 743-750.

Belenko, S. (2006). Assessing released inmates for substance-abuse-related service needs. *Crime & Delinquency, 52*(1), 94-113.

Belenko, S. (1998). Research on drug courts: A critical review. *National Drug Court Institute Review*, *1*, 1-42.

Belli, R. R. (1998). The structure of autobiographical memory and event history calendar: Potential improvements in the quality of retrospective reports in surveys. *Memory*, *6,* 383-406.

Berg, B. L. (2004). *Qualitative research methods for the social sciences* (5th ed.), Boston, MA: Allyn and Bacon.

Berman, A. H., Bergman, H., Palmstierna, T., Schlyter, F. (2005). Evaluation of the Drug Use Disorders Identification Test (DUDIT) in criminal justice and detoxification settings and in a Swedish population sample. *European Addiction Research, 11*(1), 1-10.

Blackmore, J. (1974). The relationship between self-reported delinquency and official convictions amongst adolescent boys. *British Journal of Criminology*, *14*, 172-176.

Blanchard, K. A., Morgenstern, J., Morgan, T. J., Labouvie, E., and Bux, D. (2003). Motivational subtypes and continuous measures of readiness for change: Concurrent and predictive validity. *Psychology of Addictive Behavior, 45*(1), 56-65.

Bohn, M. S., Babor, T. F., & Kranzler, H. R. (1995). The alcohol use disorders identification test (AUDIT): Validation of a screening instrument for use in medical settings. Journal of Studies on Alcohol*, 56(4), 423-432.*

Borchers, Tim (2005). Moorhead State University. [Online]. Retrieved on October 6, 2008, from http://www.abacon.com/commstudies/interpersonal/indisclosure.html

Borum, R., Dean, M., Steadman, H., & Morrissey, J. (1998). *Law enforcement responses to people with mental illness: A community policing perspective.* (unpublished manuscript). In Landsberg, G., Rock, M., Berg, L., & Smiley, A. (Eds.) *Serving Mentally Ill Offenders* (pp. 289-337). New York, NY, Springer Publishing Company.

Bradburn, N. M. & Sudman, S. (Eds.). (1981). *Improving interview method and questionnaire design*, San Francisco, CA, Jossey-Bass.

Bradburn, N. M. (1983). Response effects. In P. E. Rossi and J. D. Wright (Eds.), *Handbook of Survey Research* (pp. 289-328). New York, NY, Academic Press.

Braithwaite, J. (1981). The myth of social class and rime reconsidered. *American Sociological Review*, *46*, 36-57.

Brennan, T. (1987). Classification for control in jails and prisons. In D. M. Gottfredson & M. Tonry (Eds.), *Prediction and classification: Criminal justice decision making* (pp. 323-366). Chicago: University of Chicago Press.

Brennan, T. (1993). Risk assessment: An evaluation of statistical classification methods. In *Classification: A tool for managing today's offenders.* Laurel, MD: American Correctional Association.

Brennan, T., Fretz, R. & Wells, D. (2000). *COMPAS User's Case Management Guide*. Northpointe Institute for Public Management, Traverse City, MI.

Broner, N., Borum, R., Whitmire, L., & Gawley, K. (2002). A review of screening instruments for co-occurring mental illness and substance use in criminal justice programs. In G. Landsberg, M. Rock, L. K. W. Berg, and A. Smiley (Eds.) *Serving Mentally Ill Offenders: Challenges and Opportunities for Mental Health Professionals.* (pp. 289-337). New York, NY: Springer Publishing Company.

Brown, J., Kranzler, H. R. & Del Boca, F. K. (1992). Self-reports of alcohol and drug abuse inpatients: Factors affecting reliability and validity. *British Journal of Addiction*, *87*, 1013-1024.

Brownson, R. C., Baker, E. A., Leet, B. L., & Gillespie, K. N. (Eds.). (2003). *Evidence-Based Public Health*. New York, Oxford University Press.

Bureau of Justice Statistics. (1995). *Drug and Crime Facts, 1994.* U.S. Department of Justice, Washington, D.C.

Bureau of Labor Statistics (2004). *National Longitudinal Survey of Youth [NLSY]. Washington DC, U.S. Department of Labor.*

Burke, K. C., Burke, J. D., Rae, D. S., & Regier, D. A. (1991). Comparing age at onset of major depression and other psychiatric disorders by birth cohorts in five U.S. community populations. *Archives of General Psychiatry*, *48*, 789-795.

Cahalan, D. (1968). Correlates of respondent accuracy in the Denver validity survey. *Public Opinion Quarterly*, *32*, 607-621.

Campbell, D. T. & Stanley, J. C. (1963). *Experimental and Quasi-Experimental Designs for Research.* Houghton Mifflin Company: Boston.

Cannell, C. F., Miller, P. V. and Oksenberg, L. (1981). Research on interviewing techniques, In J. Leinhardt (Ed.), *Sociological Methodology* (pp. 389-437). San Francisco, CA, Jossey-Bass.

Cantor, D. and Lynch, J. P. (2000). Self-report surveys as measures of crime and criminal victimization. In *Measurement and analysis of crime and justice*. U.S. Department of Justice, Office of Justice Programs, National Institute of Justice.

Carmines, E. G. & Zeller, R.A. (1979). *Reliability and validity assessment:*

Quantitative applications in the social sciences. Sage Publications, Thousand Oaks, CA.

Caulkins, J. P. (2000). Measurement and Analysis of Crime and Justice: Measurement and Analysis of Drug Problems and Crime Control Efforts. *Criminal Justice 2000, 4*. Washington DC: National Institute of Justice.

Center for Adolescent Health (2004). *Youth Risk Behavior Survey (YRBS).* Atlanta, GA, Center for Disease Control.

Chaiken, M. R. (1986). Crime rates and substance abuse among types of offenders. In B.D. Johnson and E. Wish (eds.). *Crime rates among drug-abusing offenders.* Final report to the National Institute of Justice. New York: Narcotic and Drug Research, Inc.

Clark, J. P. & Tifft, L. L. (1966). Polygraph and interview validation of self-reported delinquent behavior. *American Sociological Review, 31,* 516-523.

Coalition for Evidene-Based Policy [CEBP]. (2003, December). Bringing evidence-driven progress to crime and substance-abuse policy: A recommended federal strategy. United States Justice Department, Washington, D.C.

Cohen, J. and Cohen, P. (1983). *Applied multiple regression/correlational analysis for the behavioral sciences* (2nd ed.). Hillsdale, NJ: Erlbaum.

Cohen, J. (1988). *Statistical power analysis for the behavioral sciences* (2nd ed.). Hillsdale, NJ: Erlbaum.

Collins, J. J., Hubbard, R. L., Rachal, J. V., Cavanaugh, E. R., Craddock, S. G., & Kristiansen, P. L. (1982). Criminality in a drug treatment sample: Measurement issues and initial findings. *Report to the National Institute on Drug Abuse.* Research Triangle Park, N.C:: Research Triangle Institute.

Conrad, F. G., Brown, N. R. & Cashman, E. R. (1998). Strategies for estimating behavioral frequency in survey interviews. *Memory, 6,* 339-366.

Cottler, L. B., Zipp, J. F., Robins, L. N. & Spitznagel, E. L. (1987). Difficult-to-recruit respondents and their effect on prevalence estimates in an epidemiological survey. *American Journal of Epidemiology.* The Johns Hopkins University School of Hygiene and Public Health.

Crawley, W. & Wakefield, W. (2002). Fourth judicial district research initiative examining drug prevalence in the recent arrestee population. Research monograph prepared for the Pottawattamie County Attorney's Office, Fourth Judicial District, Council Bluffs, IA.

Crawley, W. (2003). *It's the same difference? A comparative examination of criminal population drug dynamics in bordering counties of adjacent states.* Research report prepared for the National Institute of Justice, U.S. Department of Justice.

Creager, C. (1989). SASSI Test breaks through denial. Professional Counselor: July/Aug. *Criminology, 64,* 464-470.

Crowne, D. P. & Marlowe, D. (1964). *The approval motive: Studies in evaluative dependence.* New York: Wiley.

Crowne, D. P. (1979). *The experimental study of personality.* Hillsdale, NJ: Lawrence Erlbaum Associates.

Dadds, M. R., Perrin, S., & Yule, W. (1998). Social desirability and self-reported anxiety in children: An analysis of the RCMAS Lie scale. *Journal of Abnormal Child Psychology, 26*(4), 311.

Deane, M., Steadman, H., Borum, R., Veysey, B., & Morrissey, J. (1998). Police/mental health system interactions: Program types and needed research. *Psychiatric Services, 50*, 99-101.

Del Boca, F. K. & Noll, J. A. (2000). Collecting valid data from community sources – Truth or consequences: The validity of self-report data in health services research on addiction. *Addiction, 95*(3), S347-S360.

Dentler, R. A., & Monroe, L. J. (1961). Social correlates of early adolescent theft. *American Sociological Review, 26,* 733-743.

Duncan, S., Rosenberg, M. J., & Finkelstein, J. (1969). The paralanguage of experimenter bias. *Sociometry, 32,* 207-219.

Eaton, W. W., Regier, D. A., Locke, B. Z., & Taube, C. A. (1981). The Epidemiological Catchment Area Program of the National Institute of Mental Health. *Public Health Report, 96*(4), 319-335.

Elliot, D. S. (1966). Delinquency, school attendance, and dropout. *Social Problems, 13*, 306-318.

Elliot, D. S. & Voss, H. L. (1974). *Delinquency and dropout.* Lexington, Massachusetts: D.C. Health.

Elliott, D. S., & Ageton, S. S. (1980). Reconciling race and class differences in self-reported and official estimates of delinquency. *American Sociological Review, 45*(1) 95-110.

Elliott, D. S., Huizinga, D. & Morse, B. (1987). Self-reported violent offending. *Journal of Interpersonal Violence*, *1*, 472-514.

Epstein, S. (1979). The stability of behavior: I. On predicting most of the people much of the time. *Journal of Personality and Social Psychology, 37,* 674-685.

Erickson, M. L. & Empey, L. T. (1963). Court records, undetected delinquency, and decision-making. *Journal of Criminal Law, Criminology, and Police Science, 54,* 456-469.

Exner, J. E. & Weiner, I. B. (1982). The Rorschach: A comprehensive system, *Vol. 3: Assessment of children and adolescents*. New York: John Wiley and Sons.

Farrington, David P. (1977). The effects of public labeling. *British Journal of Criminology, 17,* 112-125.

Farrington, David P. (1977). The effects of public labeling. *British Journal of Criminology, 17,* 112-125.

Farrington, D. P., Loeber, R., Stouthamer-Loeber, M., van Kammen, W. B., & Schmidt, L. (1996). Self-reported delinquency and a combined delinquency seriousness scale based on boys, mothers, and teachers: Concurrent and predictive validity for African Americans and Caucasians. *Criminology, 34*, 501-525.

Feucht, T. E., Stephens, R. C., & Walker, M. L. (1994). Drug use among juvenile arrestees: A comparison of urinalysis, and hair assay. *Journal of*

Drug Issues, 3, 345-358.

Fishbein, D. H. & Reuland, M. (1994). Psychological correlates of frequency and type of drug use among jail inmates. *Addiction Bevhavior, 19,* 583-598.

Fisher, K. W. (1980). A theory of cognitive development: The control and construction of hierarchies of skills. *Psychological Review, 87,* 477-531.

Gastfriend, D. R., Najavits, L. M. & Reif, S. (1994). Chapter 4 – Assessment Instruments. *American Society of Addiction Medicine: Principles of Addiction Medicine.* American Society of Addiction Medicine, Chevy Chase, Maryland.

Gibbons, D. C. (1979). *The criminological enterprise: Theories and perspectives.* Upper Saddle River, New Jersey: Prentice Hall.

Gold, M. (1966). *Delinquent behavior in an American city.* Belmont, California: Brooks-Cole Publishing Company.

Gottfredson, M. R. & Hindelang, M. J. (1977). A consideration of memory decay and telescoping biases in victimization surveys. *Journal of Criminal Justice, 5,* 202-216.

Gottfredson, S. D. (1987). Prediction: An overview of selected methodological issues. In D. M. Gottfredson and M. Tonry (Eds.). *Prediction and Classification: Criminal Justice Decision Making.* The University of Chicago Press, Chicago.

Gove, W. R., Hughes, M., & Geerken, M. (1985). Are uniform crime reports a valid indicator of the index crimes? *Criminology, 23*(3), 451-501.

Gray, P. G. (1955). The memory factor in survey. *Journal of the American Statistical Association, 50,* 344-363.

Grove, W. M., Zald, D. H., Lebow, B. S., Snitz, B. E., Nelson, C. (2000). Clinical versus mechanical prediction: A meta-analysis. *Psychological Assessment, 12*(1), 19-30.

Grove, W. M., and Meehl, P. E. (1996). Comparative efficiency of informal (subjective, impressionistic) and formal (mechanical, algorithmic) Prediction procedures: The clinical-statistical controversy. *Psychology, Public Policy,and Law, 2,* 293-323.

Groves, R. M. (1989). *Survey errors and survey costs.* New York: Wiley.

Hagan, F. E. (1993). *Research methods in criminal justice and criminology* (3rd ed.). New York: Macmillan.

Hagan, F. E. (1997). Research methods in criminal justice and criminology. Allyn and Bacon: Boston.

Haigler, K., Harlow, C., O'Connor, P., & Campbell, A. (1994). Literacy behind prison walls. *National Center for Education Statistics.* Publication No.: NCES 94102.

Hair, J. F., Anderson, R. E., Tatham, R. L., and Black, W. C. (1998). *Multivariate data analysis* (5th ed.). Upper Saddle, NJ: Prentice Hall.

Hammond. (1996). COMPAS User's Case Management Guide. In T. Brennan, R. Fretz, & D. Wells (2000). *Northpointe Institute for Public Management.* Traverse City, MI.

Hardt, R. H. & Petersen-Hardt, S. (1977). On determining the quality of the delinquency self-report method. *Journal of Research in Crime and Delinquency, 14,* 247-261.

Hasin, D., Li, Q., McCloud, S., & Endicott, J. (1996). Agreement between DSM-III, DSM-III-R, DSM-IV and ICD-10 alcohol diagnoses in US community-sample heavy drinkers. *Addiction, 91*(10), 1517-1527.

Hasin, D.,Van Rossem, R., McCloud, S., & Endicott, J. (1997). Alcohol dependence and abuse diagnoses: Validity in community sample heavy drinkers. *Alcoholism: Clinical and Experimental Research, 21,* 213-219.

Hathaway, R. S., Monachesi, E. D., & Young, L. A. (1960). Delinquency rates and personality. *Journal of Criminal Law, Criminology, and Police Science, 50,* 433-440.

Hilgard, E. R. (1989). *Psychology in America: A historical survey.* New York: Harcourt Brace Jovanovich.

Hindelang, M. J., Hirschi, T., & Weis, J. G. (1979). Correlates of delinquency: The illusion of discrepancy between self-report and official measures. *American Sociological Review, 44,* 995-1014.

Hindelang, M. J., Hirschi, T., & Weis, J. G. (1981). *Measuring delinquency.* Beverly Hills: Sage Publication.

Hippler, H. J., Schwarz, N., & Sudman, S. (1987). *Social information processing survey and methodology.* Springer Verlag: New York.

Hirschi, T. (1969). UCauses of delinquencyU. Berkeley: University of California Press.

Hirschi, T., Hindelang, M., & Weis, J. (1980). The status of self-report measures. In M.Klein and K. Teilman (Eds.), *Handbook of criminal justice.* Sage, USA.

Holtgraves, T. M. (2004). Social desirability and self-reports: Testing models of socially desirable responding. *Personality and Social Psychology Bulletin, 30*, 161-172.

Howard, G. S. (1994). Why do people say nasty things about self-reports? *Journal of Organizational Behavior, 15*(5), 399-404.

Huizinga, D., & Elliott, D.S. (1986). Reassessing the reliability and validity of self-report delinquent measures. *Journal of Quantitative Criminology, 2*(4), 293-327.

Hurtado, A. (1994). Does similarity breed respect? Interviewer evaluations of Mexican descent respondents in a bilingual survey. *Public Opinion Quarterly, 58,* 77-95.

Inciardi, J. A. (1979). Heroin use and street crime. *Crime and Delinquency, 25,* 335-346.

Inciardi, J. A. (1995). The therapeutic community: An effective model for corrections based drug abuse treatment. In K. C. Haas and G. P. Alpert (Eds.), *The dilemmas of punishment* (pp. 406-417). Waveland Press, Prospect Heights, Illinois.

Inciardi, J. A. (2000). *Screening and assessment for alcohol and other drug abuse among adults in the criminal justice system.* U.S. Department of Health and Human Services, Public Health Services, Substance Abuse and

Mental Health Services Administration and Center for Substance Abuse Treatment. Rockville, MD.

Institute of Medicine. (1990). *Broadening the base of treatment for alcohol problems: A report of a study by a committee of the Institute of Medicine, Division of Mental Health and Behavioral Medicine.* Washington, D.C., National Academy Press.

Jensen, G. F. (1973). Inner containment and delinquency. *Journal of Criminal Law and Criminology, 64,* 464-470.

Jensen, G. F., Erickson, M. L., & Gibbs, J. P. (1978). Perceived risk of punishment and self-reported delinquency. *Social Forces, 57,* 57-78.

Johnson, P. B. & Glassman, M. (1999). The moderating effects of gender and ethnicity on the relationship between effect expectancies and alcohol problems. *Journal of Studies on Alcohol, 60*(1), 64-69.

Johnson, T. P., Fendrich, M., Shaligram, C., Garcy, A., & Gillespie, S. (2000). An evaluation of the effects of the interviewer characteristics in an RDD telephone survey of drug use. *Journal of Drug Issues, 30*(1), 77-102.

Johnson, T. P. & Fendrich, M. (2002). *A Validation of the Crowne-Marlowe Social Desirability Scale.* Conference paper presentation at the American Association for Public Opinion Research, St. Petersburg, FL.

Jones, P. R. (1994). Risk prediction in criminal justice. In A. T. Harland (Ed.), *Choosing correctional options that work: Defining the demand and evaluating the supply.* Thousand Oaks, CA: Sage Publications.

Jones, R. & Cooper, J. (1971). Mediation of experimenter effects. *Journal of Personality and Social Psychology, 20,* 70-74.

Junger-Tas, J., & Marshall, H. (1999). The self-report methodology in crime research. In Tonry, M. (1999). *Crime and Justice: An Annual Review of Research. Vol. 25.* The University of Chicago.

Kaplan, H. B. (1972). Toward a general theory of psychosocial deviance: The case of aggressive behavior. *Social Science and Medicine, 6,* 593-617.

Kachigan, S. K. (1991). *Multivariate statistical analysis: A conceptual introduction.* New York: Radius Press.

Kessler, R. C., McGonagel, K. A., Zhao, S., Nelson, C. B., Hughes, M., Eshleman, S., Wittchen, H., & Kendler, K. S. (1994). Lifetime and 12-month prevalence of DSM-III-R psychiatric disorders in the United States. *Archives of General Psychiatry, 51,* 8-19.

Kinsey, A. (1948). *Sexual behavior in the human male.* Bloomington, IN: Indiana University Press.

Kinsey, A. (1953). *Sexual behavior in the human female.* Bloomington, IN: Indiana University Press.

Klein, M. W. (1984). *Western systems of juvenile justice.* Beverly Hills: Sage Publications.

Klein, M. W. (1986). Labeling theory and delinquency policy: An experimental test. *Criminal Justice and Behavior, 13,* 47-79.

Klein, M. W. (1989). *Cross-national research in self-reported crime and delinquency.* Kluwer Academic Publishers, NATO Scientific Affairs

Division. London.

Knight, J. R., Sherritt, L., Harris, S. K., Gates, E. C. & Chang, G. (2003). Validity of brief alcohol screening tests among adolescents: A comparison of the AUDIT, POSIT, CAGE, and CRAFFT. *Alcoholism: Clinical & Experimental Research, 27*(1), 67-73.

Knight, J. R., Sherritt, L., Shrier, L. A., Harris, S. K., Chang, G. (2002). Validity of the CRAFFT substance abuse screening test among adolescent clinic patients. *Archives of Pediatrics & Adolescent Medicine, 156*, 607-614.

Knight, J. R., Wechsler, H., Kuo, M., Seibring, M., Weitzman, B. R., & Schuckit, M. A. (2002). Alcohol abuse and dependence among U.S. college students. *Journal of Studies on Alcohol, 63*(3), 263-270.

Knight, K., Hiller, M. L., Simpson, D. D., & Broome, K. M. (1998). The validity of self-reported cocaine use in a criminal justice treatment sample. *American Journal of Drug and Alcohol Abuse. 24*(4), 647.

Kouri, E. M., Pope, Jr., H. G., Poweell, K. F., & Oliva, P. S. (1997). Drug use history and criminal behavior among 133 incarcerated men. *American Journal of Drug and Alcohol Abuse, 23*(3), 413-419.

Kubiak, S. P., Boyd, C., Slayden, J., Young, A. (2005). The substance abuse treatment needs of prisoners: Implementation of an integrated statewide approach. *Journal of Offender Rehabilitation, 41*(2), 1-19.

La Greca, A. M. (1990). Issues and perspective of the child assessment process. In A. M. La Greca (Ed.), *Through the eyes of the child: Obtaining self-reports from children and adolescents* (pp. 3-17). Boston: Allyn and Bacon.

Lamb, H. R., & Weinberger, L. E. (1998). Persons with severe mental illness in jails and prisons: A review. *Psychiatric Services, 49*(4), 483-492.

Lazowski, L., Miller, F. G., Boye, M. W. & Miller, G.A. (1998). Efficacy of the Substance Abuse Subtle Screening Inventory-3 (SASSI-3) in Identifying substance dependence disorders in clinical settings. *Journal of Personality Assessment, 1*, 114-128.

Letteri D., Nelson, J. & Sayers, M. (1985). *Alcoholism treatment assessment research instruments*. Washington DC, National Institute on Alcohol Abuse and Alcoholism.

Locander, W. B., Sudman, S., & Bradburn, N. (1976). An investigation of interview method, threat, and response distortion. *Journal of the American Statistical Association, 71*, 269-275.

Lynch, M. J. & Grove, W. B. (1986). *A Primer in Radical Criminology.* Albany, NY: Harrow and Heston.

Mabe, P. A. & Treiber, F. A. (1989). Social desirability response tendencies in psychiatric inpatient children. *Journal of Clinical Psychology, 45*, 194-201.

Magura, S., Goldsmith, D., Casriel, C., Goldstein, R. J., & Lipton, D. S. (1987). The validity of methadone clients' self-reported drug use. *International Journal of the Addictions, 22*, 727-749.

Malbin, J. H. and Moskowitz, J. M. (1983). Anonymous versus identifiable self-reports of adolescent drug attitudes, intention, and use. *Public Opinion*

Quarterly, 47(4), 557-566.
Manly, B. (1994). *Multivariate statistical methods: A primer.* London: Chapman & Hall.
Mateyoke-Scrivner, A., Webster, J. M., Hiller, M. L., Staton, M. & Leukefeld, C. L. (2003). Criminal history, physical and mental health, substance abuse, and services use among incarcerated substance abusers. *Journal of Contemporary Criminal Justice, 19*(1), 82-97.
Matthews, V. M. (1968). Differential identification: An empirical note. *Social Problems, 14,* 376-383.
Mauldin, W. P. & Marks, E. S. (1950). Problems of response in enumerative surveys. *American Sociological Review, 15*, 649-657.
Maxfield, M. G. & Babbie, E. (1995). *Research methods for criminal justice and criminology*. Wadsworth Publishing Company: Albany.
McFarland, S. G. (1981). Effects of question order on survey responses. *Public Opinion Quarterly, 45*(2), 208-215.
Meehl, P. (1954). *Clinical versus statistical prediction: A theoretical analysis and a review of the evidence.* Minneapolis: University of Minnesota Press.
Meehl, P. (1965). Seer over sign: The first good example. *Journal of Experimental Research in Psychology, 1*, 27-32.
Meier, R. F. (1988). Discovering Delinquency. Sociological Inquiry, 58(3), 231-239.
Meyers, K., Haga, T. A., Zanis, D., Webb, A., Frantz, J., Ring-Kurtz, S., Rutherford, M., & McLellan, T. (1999). Critical issues in adolescent substance use assessment. *Drug and Alcohol Dependence, 55,* 235-246.
Mieczkowski, T., Barzelay, D., Gropper, D., & Wish, E. (1991). Concordance of three measures of cocaine in an arrestee population: Hair, urine, and self-report. *Journal of Psychoactive Drugs. 23*, 241-249.
Miller, F. (1995). Assessment for criminal justice: Accurate therapeutic assessment is the key to reducing recidivism in the criminal justice system. *Professional Counselor*, 33 & 49.
Miller, F. G. & Lazowski, L. E. (1999). *The SASSI Manual: Substance Abuse Measures* (2nd ed.). The SASSI Institute: Springville, IN.
Miller, G. A. (1985). *The Substance Abuse Subtle Screening Inventory (SASSI) Manual.* The SASSI Institute, Springville, IN.
Miller, H. P. (1953). An appraisal of the 1950s census income data. *Journal of the American Statistical Association, 48,* 28-43.
Millon, T. (1997). COMPAS User's Case Management Guide. *Northpointe Institute for Public Management.* Traverse City, MI.
Mills, J. A. (1999). *Control: A history of behavioral psychology.* New York: New York University Press.
Motiuk, M. S., Motiuk. L. L. & Bonta, J. (1992). Comparison between self-report and interview-based inventories in offender classification. *Criminal Justice and Behavior, 19*(2), 143–159.
National Institute of Alcohol Abuse and Alcoholism (1987). *Alcohol and Health.* Rockville, MD.

National Institute of Alcohol Abuse and Alcoholism (1994). *Alcohol Alert* (No. 25). Washington, DC: National Institutes of Health.

National Institutes of Health (NIH) (2004). *Monitoring the Future (MTF).* Washington, DC, National Institutes of Health (NIH), U.S. Department of Health and Human.

National Institute of Justice (1998). *Arrestee Drug Abuse Monitoring Program 1997 Annualized Site Reports.* Washington, DC, U.S. Department of Justice, Office of Justice Programs.

National Institute of Justice (1999). *Arrestee Drug Abuse Monitoring Program 1998 Annualized Site Reports.* Washington, DC, U.S. Department of Justice, Office of Justice Programs.

National Institute of Justice (2000). *Arrestee Drug Abuse Monitoring Program 1999 Annualized Site Reports.* Washington, DC, U.S. Department of Justice, Office of Justice Programs.

National Institute of Justice (2001). *Arrestee Drug Abuse Monitoring Program 2000 Annualized Site Reports.* Washington, DC, U.S. Department of Justice, Office of Justice Programs.

National Institute of Justice (2001a). *ADAM preliminary 2000 findings on drug use & drug markets.* Washington, DC, U.S. Department of Justice, Office of Justice Programs.

National Institute of Justice (2001b). *Arrestee Drug Abuse Monitoring program 2000: Annualized site reports.* Washington, DC, U.S. Department of Justice, Office of Justice Programs.

National Institute of Justice (2002). *Arrestee Drug Abuse Monitoring program 2001 Annualized Site Reports.* Washington, DC, U.S. Department of Justice, Office of Justice Programs.

National Institute of Justice (2002a). *Preliminary data on drug use & related matters among adult male arrestees: January-September 2001.* Washington, DC, U.S. Department of Justice, Office of Justice Programs.

Neuman, W. L. (2000). *Social research methods: Qualitative and quantitative approaches.* Allyn and Bacon: Boston.

Orne, M. T. (1962). On the social psychology of the psychological experiment: With particular reference to demand characteristics and their implications. *American Psychologist, 17,* 776-783.

Palys, T. (1997). *Research decisions: Quantitative and qualitative perspectives* (2nd ed.). Harcourt Canada: Toronto.

Panzer, P.G., Broner, N., & McQuistion, H. L. (2001). Mentally ill populations in jails and prisons: A misuse of resources. *Psychiatric Quarterly, 72*(1), 41-43.

Paschall, M. J., Ornstein, M. L., & Flewelling, R. L. (2001). African American male adolescents' involvement in the criminal justice system: The criterion validity of self-report measures in a prospective study. *Journal of Research in Crime and Delinquency, 38*(2), 174-187.

Patrick, D. L., Cheadle, A., Thompson, D. C., Diehr, P., Koepsell, T., & Kinne, S. (1994). The validity of self-reported smoking: A review and meta-analysis. *American Journal of Public Health, 84*(7), 1086-1093.

Paulus, D. L. (1991). Measurement and control of response bias. In J. P. Robinson and P. R. Shaver (Eds.), *Measures of personality and social psychological attitudes* (pp. 17-59). San Diego: Academic Press.

Peters, R. H. & Kearns, W. D. (1992). Drug abuse history and treatment needs of jail inmates. *American Journal of Drug Alcohol Abuse, 18*(3), 355-366.

Peters, R. H. & Greenbaum, P. E. (1996). *Texas Department of Criminal Justice/Center for Substance Abuse Treatment: Prison Substance Abuse Screening Project.* Millford, MA: Civigenics, Inc.

Peters, R. H., Greenbaum, P. E., Edens, J. F., Carter, C. R. & Ortiz, M. M. (1998). Prevalence of DSM-IV substance abuse and dependence disorders among prison inmates. *American Journal of Drug and Alcohol Abuse*, *24*(4), 573-587.

Peters, R. H., & Hills, H. A. (1999). Community treatment and supervision strategies for offenders with co-occurring disorders: What works? In E. Latessa (Ed.), *Strategic solutions: The International community corrections association examines substance abuse,* (pp. 81-137). Lanham, MD: American Correctional Association.

Peters, R. H., Greenbaum, P. E., Steinberg, M. L., Carter, C. R., Ortiz, M. M., Fry, B. C., & Valle, S. K. (2000). Effectiveness of screening instruments in detecting substance use disorders among prisoners. *Journal of Substance Abuse Treatment, 8*, 349-358.

Polk, K. (1969). Class strain and rebellion among adolescents. *Social Problems, 17,* 214-224.

Porterfield, A. L. (1943). Delinquency and outcome in court and college. *American Journal of Sociology, 49,* 199-208.

Porterfield, Austin L. (1946). *Youth in trouble.* Fort Worth: Leo Potishman Foundation.

Presser, S. & Stinson, L. (1998). Data collection mode and social desirability bias in self reported religious attendance. *American Sociological Review*, *63*(1), 137.

Rapp, L. A., Dulmus, C. N., Wodarski, J. S., & Feit, M. D. (1999). Screening of substance abuse in public welfare and child protective service clients: A comparative study of rapid assessment instruments vs. the SASSI. *Journal of Addict Dis, 8*(2), 83-88.

Regier, D. A., Myers, J. K., Kramer, M., Robins, L. N., Blazer, D. G., Hough, R. L., Eaton, W. W., & Locke, B. Z. (1984). The NIMH Epidemiological Catchment Area program. Historical context, major objectives, and study population characteristics. *Arch Gen Psychiatry, 41*(10), 934-941.

Regier, D., Farmer, M., Rae, D., Locke, B., Keither, S., Judd, L., & Goodwin, F. (1990). Comorbidity of mental disorders with alcohol and other drug abuse: Results from the Epidemiological Catchment Area (ECA) Study. *JAMA, 264* (19), 2511-2518.

Reiss Jr., A. J. & Rhodes, A. L. (1964). An empirical test of differential association theory. *Journal of Research in Crime and Delinquency, 1,* 5-18.

Reynolds, W. M., and Stark, K. D. (1983). Cognitive behavior modification: The clinical application of cognitive strategies. In M. Pressley and J. R. Levin (Eds.), *Cognitive strategy research: Psychological foundations* (pp. 221-266). New York: Springer-Verlag.

Reynolds, W. M. (1993). Self-report methodology. In T.H. Ollendick and M. Hersen (Eds.), *Handbook of child and adolescent assessment* (pp. 98-123). New York: Pergamon.

Richter, L. & Johnson, P. (2001). Current methods of assessing substance use: A review of strengths, problems, and developments. *Journal of Drug Issues, 21*(4), 809-832.

Rogers, R. (1997). *Clinical assessment of malingering and deception* (2nd ed.). New York, NY: Thee Guilford Press.

Rojek, D. G. (1983). Social status and delinquency: Do self-reports and official reports match? In G. P. Waldo (Ed.), *Measurement issues in criminal justice.* Beverly Hills: Sage Publications.

Rosenthal, R. (1966). *Experimenter effects in behavioral research.* New York: Appleton-Century-Crofts.

Sandra, L. (2004). Screening and brief intervention in the criminal justice system. *Alcohol, Research & Health,* 28(2), 85-93.

Schwarz, N. (1996). *Cognition and communication: Judgmental biases, research methods, and the logic of conversation.* Mahwah, NJ: Lawrence Erlbaum Associates.

Schwarz, Norbert (1999). Self-report: How the questions shape the answer. *American Psychologist, 54,* 93-105.

Sedlmeier, P. & Gigerenzer, G. (1989). Do studies of statistical power have an effect on the power of studies? *Psychological Bulletin, 105*, 309-316.

See, S. T. K. & Ryan, E.B. (1998). Intergenerational communication: The survey interview as a social exchange. In N. Schwartz, D. C. Park, B. Knauper, & S. Sudman(Eds.), *Cognition, aging, and self-reports* (pp. 245-262). Philadelphia, PA: Psychology Press.

Sellin, T. (1931). The basis of a crime index. *Journal of Criminal Law and Criminology, 22*, 335-356.

Seltzer, R. (1983). Sponsorship effects in an attitudinal survey. *Political Methodology*, *9*(4), 447-452.

Selzer, M. L. (1971). The Michigan Alcohol Screening Test: The quest for a new diagnostic instrument. *American Journal of Psychiatry, 127*, 1653-658.

Short, J. F. (1957). Differential association and delinquency. *Social Problems, 4,* 233-239.

Short, J. F., Jr. & Nye, F. I. (1958). Extent of unrecorded juvenile delinquency: Tentative conclusions. *Journal of Criminal Law and Criminology*, *49,* 296-302.

Silberman, M. (1976). Toward a theory of criminal deterrence. *American Sociological Review, 41,* 442-461.

Singer, E., Frankel, M. R., & Glassman, M. B. (1983). The effect of interviewer characteristics and expectations on response. *Public Opinion Quarterly, 47*(1), 68-83.

Singleton, R., Straits, B., Straits, M., & McAllister, R. (1988). *Approaches to Social Research.* New York: Oxford University Press.

Sloan, J. J., III, Bodapati, M. R., & Tucker, T. A. (2004). Respondent misreporting of drug use in self-reports: Social desirability and other correlates. *Journal of Drug Issues, 34*(2) 269.

Sobell, L. C. & Sobell, M. B. (1990). Self-report issues in alcohol abuse: State of the art and future directions. *Behavioral Assessment, 12,* 77-90.

Spanier, G. B. (1976). Use of recall data in survey research on human sexual behavior. *Social Biology, 23*(3), 244-253.

Spector, P. E. (1994). Using self-report questionnaires in OB research: A comment on the use of a controversial method. *Journal of Organizational Behavior, 15,* 385-392.

Spitzer, R. L. (1983). Psychiatric diagnosis: Are clinicians still necessary? *Comprehensive Psychiatry, 24*(5), 399-411.

Stanfield, R. (1966). The interaction of family variables and gang variables in the etiology of delinquency. *Social Problems, 13,* 411-417.

Steadman, J. J., Morris, S. M., & Dennis, D. L. (1995). The diversion of mentally ill persons from jails to community-based services: A profile of programs. *American Journal of Public Health, 85*(12), 1630-1635.

Stino, Z. H., & Palmer, B. C. (1999). Motivating women offenders through process-based writing in a literacy learning circle. *Journal of Adolescent & Adult Literacy. 43*(3), 282.

Substance Abuse and Mental Health Services Administration (2004). The 12-month prevalence and trends in DSM-IV alcohol abuse and dependence: United States, 1991-1992 and 2001-2002. *Drug and Alcohol Dependence, 74*(3), 223-234.

Substance Abuse and Mental Health Services Administration (SAMHSA). (1995). *Annual Medical Examiner Data 1993,* Series I, No. 13-B, pp. 7-8, Washington, DC: U.S. Department of Health and Human Services.

Substance Abuse and Mental Health Services Administration (SAMHSA) (1996). *Advance Report No. 18. Preliminary estimates from the 1995 National Household Survey on Drug Abuse.* Rockville, MD: Office of Applied Studies.

Substance Abuse and Mental Health Services Administration (SAMHSA) (2003). *Drug Abuse Warning Network (DAWN).* Washington, DC, Office of Applied Studies, U.S. Department of Health and Human Services.

Substance Abuse and Mental Health Services Administration (SAMHSA) (2004). *National Household Survey on Drug Abuse (NHSDA).* Washington, DC, Office of Applied Studies, U.S. Department of Health and Human Services.

Sudman, S. & N. Bradburn (1974). *Response effects in survey.* Chicago: Aldine.

Sudman, S., Bradburn, N. M., & Schwarz, N. (1996). *Thinking about answers:*

The application of cognitive processes to survey methodology. San Francisco: Jossey-Bass.

Sundberg, N. D. (1977). *Assessment of persons* (2nd ed.). Englewood Cliffs, NJ: Prentice Hall.

Swets, J. A., Dawes, R. M., & Monahan, J. (2000). Psychological science can improve diagnostic decisions. *Psychological Science in the Public Interest, 1,* 1-26.

Teplin, L. A. (1994). Psychiatric and substance abuse disorders among male urban jail detainees. *American Journal of Public Health, 84,* 292-293.

Thornberry, T. & Farnworth, M. (1982). Social correlates of criminal involvement: Further evidence on the relationship between social status and criminal behavior. *American Sociological Review, 47*, 505-518.

Thornberry, T. (1989). Panel effects and the use of self-reported measures of delinquency in longitudinal studies. In M. W. Klein. (Ed.), *Cross-national research in self-reported crime and delinquency.* Los Angeles: Kluwer Academic Publishers.

Thornberry, T. P. & Krohn, M. D. (2000). *The Self-Report Method for Measuring Delinquency and Crime. In Criminal Justice 2000: Measurement and Analysis of Crime and Justice*, 4. U.S. Department of Justice, Office of Justice Programs, National Institute of Justice.

Tilley, N. & Laycock, G. (2002). *Working out what to do: Evidence-based crime reduction.* London: Home Office.

Tonry, M., & Wilson, J. Q. (eds.) (1990). *Drugs and Crime.* Chicago: University of Chicago Press.

Torrens, M., Serrano, D., Astals, M., Perez-Dominguez, G., & Martin-Santos, R. (2004). Diagnosing Comorbid Psychiatric Disorders in Substance Abusers: Validity of the Spanish Versions of the Psychiatric Research Interview for Substance and Mental Disorders and the Structured Clinical Interview for DSM-IV. *The American Journal of Psychiatry. 161*(7), 1231-1239.

Torrey, E. F., Steiber, J., Ezekiel, J., Wolfe, S. M., Sharfstein, J., & Flynn, L. M. (1993). Criminalizing the mentally ill: The abuse of jails as mental hospitals. *Innovations & Research, 2,* 11-14. Washington, DC: Public Citizen's Health Research Group.

Tourangeau, R. & Smith, T. W. (1996). Asking sensitive questions: The impact of data collection mode, questions format, and question context. *Public Opinion Quarterly, 60,* 275-304.

Turner , C. F., Ku, L. S., Rogers, S. M., Lindberg, L. D., Pleck, J. H., & Sonenstein, F. L. (1998). Adolescent sexual behavior, drug use, and violence: Increased reporting with computer survey technology. *Science, 280,* 867-873.

Tyon, L. P. (1988). *Final report: Baseline management and assessment data project.* Portland, OR: National TASC Programs and the Bureau of Justice Assistance.

U.S. Department of Justice, National Institute of Justice (1990). *1988 Drug Use*

Forecasting annual report: Drugs and crime in America. Research in Action, NCJ 122225. Washington, D.C.

U.S. Department of Justice, National Institute of Justice. (1998). *ADAM: 1997 Annual Report on Adult and Juvenile Arrestees*, Washington, D.C.

U.S. Department of Justice, National Institute of Justice. (2001). *ADAM: 1997 Annual report on Adult and Juvenile Arrestees*, Washington, D.C.

Vacca, J. (2004). Educated prisoners are less likely to return to prison. *Journal of Correctional Education, 55*(4). 297-305.

Victorin, K., Haag-Gronlund, M., Y Skerfving, S. (1998). Methods for health risk assessment of chemicals: Are they relevant for alcohol? *Alcoholism: Clinical and Experimental Research*, *22*(7), 270S-276S.

Vold, G. B. (1958). *Theoretical Criminology.* New York, Oxford University Press.

Voss, H. L. (1964). Differential association and reported delinquent behavior: A replication. *Social Problems, 12,* 78-85.

Walker, S. (2006). *Sense and Non-Sense about Crime and Drugs: A Policy Guide.* Belmont, CA, Thomson Wadsworth.

Waldo, G. P., and Chiricos, T. G. (1972). Perceived penal sanction and self-reported criminality: A neglected approach to deterrence research. *Social Problems, 19,* 522-540.

Wallerstein, J. S. and Wyle, C. J. (1947). Our law-abiding law-breakers. *Probation, 25,* 107-112.

Watson, R. I. & Evans, R. B. (1990). *The Great Psychologists: An Intellectual History* (5th ed.). New York: Harper Collins.

Wentland, E. J. & Smith, K. W. (1993). *Survey Responses: An Evaluation of Their Validity.* Academic Press, Inc. San Diego, CA.

Welsh, W. N. (2007). A multisite evaluation of prison-based therapeutic community drug treatment. *Criminal Justice and Behavior,* 34(11), 1481-1498.

White, H. R. & Gorman, D. M. (2000). The nature of crime: Continuity and change – dynamics of the drug-crime relationship. *Criminal Justice 2000, 1*, 151-218.

Willis, G.B. (1997). The use of psychological laboratory to study sensitive survey topics. In L. Harrison and A. Hughes (Eds.), *Validity of self-reported drug use: Improving the accuracy of survey estimates,* Research Monograph 167, NIH Publication No. 97-4147 (pp. 416-438). Rockville, MD: National Institute on Drug Abuse.

Wilson, H. W. (2003). Age-related social desirability responding among Australian women. *The Journal of Social Psychology, 143*(5), 669.

Wilson, T. D. (1985). Strangers to ourselves: The origins and accuracy of beliefs about one's own mental states. In J. H. Harvey and G. Weary (Eds.), *Attributions: Basic Issues and Applications.* (pp. 9-36). Orlando, FL: Academic Press.

Winters, K.C. (1995). Clinician's guide to self-evaluation workbook for alcohol and drug abuse: Screening for alcohol and drug abuse (SADA). Center City,

MN: Hazelden Press.

Winters, K. C. & Zenilman, J. M. (2000). *Simple Screening Instruments for Outreach for Alcohol and other Drug Abuse and Infectious Diseases.* U.S. Department of Health and Human Services, Public Health Service, Substance Abuse and Mental Health Services Administration, and Center for Substance Abuse Treatment. Rockville, MD.

Yin, R. K. (2003). *Case study research: Design and methods* (3rd ed.), Thousand Oaks, CA: Sage Publications.

Zywiak, W. H., Hoffmann, N. G., and Floyd, A. S. (1999). Enhancing alcohol treatment outcomes through aftercare and self-help groups. *Medicine and Health – Rhode Island, 82*(3), 87-90.

INDEX

competency .... See cognitive functioning
construct validity.......*x*, *11*, *22*, *54*, *55*, *57*, *72*, *73*, *75*, *77*, *78*, *88*, *97*, *100*, *106*, *108*, *113*, *114*, *115*, *129*, *135*, *136*, *137*, *138*, *139*, *140*, *141*, *142*, *143*, *201*, *206*, *207*, *213*, *217*, *221*
convergent validity....*vii*, *73*, *125*, *217*
criminal justice...*x*, *1*, *2*, *4*, *5*, *7*, *8*, *9*, *10*, *11*, *13*, *15*, *16*, *19*, *21*, *22*, *23*, *32*, *34*, *35*, *36*, *37*, *40*, *41*, *42*, *44*, *45*, *46*, *52*, *53*, *54*, *59*, *60*, *61*, *62*, *63*, *64*, *65*, *66*, *68*, *69*, *70*, *71*, *72*, *74*, *75*, *76*, *77*, *78*, *80*, *81*, *88*, *95*, *100*, *103*, *113*, *116*, *121*, *125*, *127*, *128*, *129*, *135*, *137*, *138*, *139*, *140*, *141*, *143*, *174*, *175*, *187*, *188*, *198*, *199*, *201*, *202*, *203*, *208*, *209*, *210*, *211*, *212*, *214*, *215*, *216*, *218*, *219*, *220*, *221*, *222*, *252*, *257*, *259*, *260*, *261*, *263*, *265*, *268*
criterion validity...... *vii*, *x*, *11*, *54*, *55*, *58*, *69*, *72*, *75*, *77*, *88*, *95*, *102*, *103*, *106*, *109*, *110*, *113*, *114*, *115*, *122*, *124*, *147*, *201*, *203*, *204*, *205*, *206*, *208*, *210*, *211*, *213*, *221*, *265*
diagnostic screening ...*x*, *8*, *10*, *11*, *15*, *16*, *19*, *22*, *23*, *50*, *51*, *52*, *53*, *70*, *76*, *90*, *91*, *99*, *102*, *104*
discriminant analysis *109*, *110*, *146*, *147*, *152*, *157*, *192*, *212*, *219*
drug abuse *1*, *2*, *39*, *41*, *46*, *50*, *51*, *61*, *65*, *85*, *95*, *218*, *252*, *259*, *267*, *273*
drug misuse 46, 58
efficacy.... *vii*, *x*, *2*, *11*, *12*, *22*, *23*, *43*, *48*, *72*, *75*, *77*, *88*, *91*, *96*, *100*, *103*, *104*, *106*, *108*, *113*, *114*, *115*, *125*, *127*, *128*, *129*, *201*, *204*, *205*, *206*, *213*, *214*, *217*, *219*, *220*, *221*
Evidence-Based Policy........*15*, *20*
Institutional Review Board...*vi*, *80*
meta-methodology...........*202*, *203*
need for treatment......*x*, *4*, *5*, *7*, *9*, *10*, *11*, *12*, *14*, *15*, *21*, *40*, *44*, *46*, *47*, *51*, *54*, *68*, *70*, *71*, *74*, *91*, *96*, *97*, *101*, *102*, *103*, *104*, *105*, *107*, *108*, *116*, *121*, *124*, *125*, *127*, *128*, *129*, *135*, *137*, *139*, *142*, *143*, *153*, *167*, *173*, *180*, *197*, *201*, *203*, *205*, *206*, *209*, *213*, *214*, *216*, *221*, *222*, *250*
norming.................*45*, *61*, *62*, *221*
psychological assessment...*81*, *88*, *89*, *90*, *93*, *96*, *102*, *105*, *106*, *114*, *201*, *208*, *209*, *214*, *215*, *216*, *224*, *225*, *228*
sampling..............*35*, *81*, *100*, *218*
self-disclosure .. *9*, *23*, *68*, *70*, *210*, *212*
self-report..........*x*, *1*, *2*, *3*, *4*, *5*, *6*, *7*, *8*, *9*, *10*, *11*, *12*, *13*, *15*, *16*, *19*, *20*, *21*, *22*, *23*, *24*, *25*, *26*, *27*, *28*, *29*, *30*, *31*, *32*, *33*, *34*, *35*, *36*, *37*, *38*, *39*, *40*, *41*, *42*, *43*, *44*, *45*, *46*, *47*, *48*, *49*, *50*, *51*, *52*, *53*, *54*, *55*, *56*, *57*, *58*, *59*, *60*, *61*, *62*, *63*, *64*, *65*, *66*, *67*, *68*, *69*, *70*, *71*, *72*, *73*, *75*, *76*, *77*, *78*, *81*, *82*, *88*, *89*, *90*, *91*, *92*, *93*, *94*, *95*, *96*, *97*, *99*, *100*, *101*, *102*, *103*, *104*, *105*, *106*, *107*, *108*, *109*, *110*, *113*, *114*, *115*, *121*, *124*, *125*, *127*, *128*, *129*, *132*, *133*, *134*, *135*,

136, *137*, *138*, *139*, *140*, *141*, *142*, *143*, *147*, *148*, *174*, *175*, *187*, *188*, *198*, *199*, *201*, *202*, *203*, *204*, *205*, *206*, *207*, *208*, *209*, *210*, *211*, *212*, *213*, *214*, *215*, *216*, *217*, *218*, *219*, *220*, *221*, *222*, *249*, *258*, *259*, *260*, *263*, *264*, *265*, *269*

Simple Screening Instrument (SSI)..... *10*, *76*, *77*, *91*, *95*, *236*

social desirability ... *23*, *25*, *66*, *67*, *68*, *210*, *212*, *273*

Substance Abuse Subtle Screening Instrument (SASSI) *20*

Substance Abuse Treatment Oriented Program (SATOP) *10*, *20*, *76*, *91*, *93*